GUIDE TO
MAGAZINE AND SERIAL AGENTS

GUIDE TO MAGAZINE AND SERIAL AGENTS

BILL KATZ
and
PETER GELLATLY

R. R. Bowker Company
A Xerox Education Company
New York & London, 1975

Published by R. R. Bowker Co. (A Xerox Education Company)
1180 Avenue of the Americas, New York, N.Y. 10036
Copyright © 1975 by Xerox Corporation
All rights reserved
Printed and bound in the United States of America

Library of Congress Cataloging in Publication Data

Katz, Bill, 1924–
　Guide to magazine and serial agents.

　1. Acquisition of serial publications.　2. Libraries—Special collections—Periodicals.　I. Gellatly, Peter, joint author.　II. Title.
Z689.K33　　025.2′1　　75-26616
ISBN 0-8352-0789-7

For Lou and Harriet

CONTENTS

Preface xi

I. SERIALS, PERIODICALS, AND THE LIBRARY

1. INTRODUCTION: LIBRARIES AND PERIODICALS ... 3
   Serials and Periodicals............................... 4
   Sources of Serials 7
   Patterns of Library Serials Organization.............. 8
   Selection of Serials 11

2. THE PERIODICALS PUBLISHER 19
   Ordering from the Publisher 19
   Publisher-Agency Relationships 21
   The Publisher's Viewpoint............................ 21
   The Agent and the Publisher.......................... 26

II. SUBSCRIPTION AGENTS AND WHAT THEY DO

3. SUBSCRIPTION AGENTS 33
   Legal Responsibilities of the Agent 34
   Types of Agencies.................................... 35
   Agency-Library Relationships 42

4. AGENCY SERVICES 48
   Serials Catalogs..................................... 48
   Missing and Back Issues 49
   Blanket and Consolidated Orders 52
   Miscellaneous Services and Procedures 55

5. SELECTING AN AGENT 62
   Selection Factors.................................... 63
   To Employ or Not to Employ an Agent 67

III. MANAGING A SERIALS COLLECTION

6. LIBRARY SERIALS RECORDS AND ROUTINES 75
Basic Serials Records 76
Check-in Records 81
Public Access to Serials 83

7. THE PERIODICALS COLLECTION: SIZE AND COST .. 85
Periodicals Costs..................................... 86
Library Costs for Processing Serials 90
Agency Charges....................................... 93
Estimating Charges 96

8. BIDS AND QUOTES 103
Bids 103
Quotes... 105

9. LIBRARY ORDERS 108
The Library Order 108
Agency Processing of an Order 112
Agency Order Plans 115
Annual Review Lists 120

10. AGENCY INVOICES 123
Special Invoicing 124
Library Payment to the Agent 126
Canceled and Discontinued Titles 126

11. CLAIMS AND CLAIMING 130
Library Responsibility for Claiming 131
Disposition of Claims 135
Agency Acknowledgment of Claims...................... 139
Evaluating Agency Claims Service 142

IV. DIRECTORIES FOR ANALYZING AND LOCATING SERIAL AGENTS AND SERVICES

12. CHECKLIST OF AGENCY SERVICES AND PROCEDURES 149
I. Agency-Library Relationships..................... 151
II. Agency Processing of Library Orders 154
III. Agency Order Plans and Review Lists 161
IV. Agency Invoices 163

	V. Library Payment to the Agent	*168*
	VI. Claims and Related Services	*170*
	VII. Canceled and Discontinued Titles	*176*
	VIII. Added Agency Services	*177*
	IX. Library Orders	*179*
13.	AGENCY SURVEY SUMMARY	*182*
	Number of Libraries and Agents Surveyed	*182*
	Most Often Employed Domestic Agents	*183*
	Most Often Employed International Agents	*184*
	Ratings of Agents by Librarians	*185*
14.	LIBRARY SURVEY SUMMARY	*187*
	Number of Periodical Titles Held by American Libraries	*187*
	Sources of Periodical Titles for 850 American Libraries	*188*
	Agency Rating by 850 American Libraries	*189*
15.	SUBSCRIPTION AGENTS DIRECTORY	*199*
	Domestic Agents	*200*
	Canadian Agents	*223*
	International Agents	*225*
	Geographical Index	*236*

PREFACE

Who is the best periodicals or serials subscription agent for my library? This is a question asked perennially by librarians everywhere, regardless of the type and size of library in which they find themselves. The primary purpose of *Guide to Magazine and Serial Agents* is to answer that question by giving enough background information concerning serials and their management to provide an understanding of the agent-library relationship and by providing facts, details, and descriptions of the services and procedures of the major and selected smaller domestic and foreign serials subscription agents. In order to keep within manageable bounds, this book concentrates primarily on the periodical agent (who may or may not handle other kinds of serials) and no effort is made to describe in detail operations and procedures that are applicable only in large libraries. Emphasis is placed upon the "fundamentals" in order to make this guide as useful as possible. *Guide to Magazine and Serial Agents* is intended for the librarian in any kind of library—school, academic, public, or special—from the smallest to the largest. Directing a guide to such a wide audience may seem overly ambitious, but it is not unrealistic. The school librarian with 100 periodicals faces the same basic problem as the university librarian with 15,000 to 40,000 serials: both, at one time or another, must select and evaluate a subscription agent or agents.

Each agency has its own particular specialty and method of operation. A librarian has to select the agent best suited to the library's particular needs. Beyond that, the librarian ought to be able to expect the agent to do whatever is necessary to insure the prompt delivery and continuous flow of serials to the library. There are always questions, of course: What services does X agent render that Y does not? Is X a better agent for the purpose of this library than Y? Is one of two agents likely to prove more reliable than the other? In what respects? And there are countless other questions of a considerably more specialized nature that the librarian must ask before employing an agent. An effort is made here to try to answer these questions in a specific way.

xii Preface

This guide is an extension of a study made by Bill Katz in 1973 for the U.S. National Libraries Task Force on Cooperative Activities. The study was primarily designed to describe the agency relationship with the Library of Congress, the National Agricultural Library, and the National Library of Medicine. After the study was completed, it became apparent that it would be of value to expand and modify the findings for use by a larger audience. This required interviewing more agents, both domestic and foreign, than had been interviewed in the original study, as well as much consultation with serials librarians in libraries of all sorts and sizes.

Essentially, the information given about agents has been gathered from questionnaires sent to all major domestic and foreign agents. The majority of them replied. These replies were often supported by discussions and follow-up correspondence when needed for purposes of clarification and for double-checking of fact and procedure. However, what the agent says about services and what the agent actually does may be two different things. Therefore, a random sampling of 1,245 libraries was constructed and questionnaires were mailed to them. Eight hundred and fifty replies were received from librarians in various parts of the country. The librarians were asked to rank agents in order of preference. In a number of cases, once the ranking was compiled, correspondence followed to determine specific complaints or points of praise. The data were then evaluated, often with the help of librarians and agents. The results, as far as is possible, is a comprehensive and, the authors believe, a clear analysis of the agents' work and the agent-library relationship. Obviously, no questionnaire, no number of follow-up interviews, no amount of correspondence is going to elevate a guide like this from the subjective to the objective. Each library and each agency has its own particular practices. A continual striving for objectivity is highly desirable, but it is not easily attained. There is always room for interpretation, for misunderstanding, even for mistakes and misstatements of facts. Still, the present effort should at least clear the grounds for a report of the Ralph Nader kind, if one should ever transpire. Until then, and with no apology, the guide stands on its own as a factual analysis of the agent-library relationship.

The *Guide to Magazine and Serial Agents* has been divided into four parts: Part I gives background information on the fundamentals of periodicals acquisition and the library and discusses the periodicals publisher. Part II covers these fundamentals in relation to agent operations. Part III analyzes procedures used by libraries in handling periodicals and serials and how these procedures affect the agent-library relationship. Part IV presents the data from the agent/library survey in three different formats. The first is a checklist of agency services and procedures for the librarian to use when selecting an agent. It lists questions a librarian might ask a prospective agent and provides representative answers actually reported to the authors (cross-references are given throughout the earlier chapters to the corresponding parts of the checklist). The second is a summary of the raw data in tabular form and the third is a directory, arranged alphabetically by name, of all agencies with their addresses and a description of their services.

Reference is made throughout this guide to the American Library Association *Guidelines*. This report, whose full title is *Guidelines for Publishers, Agents, and Librarians in Handling Library Orders for Serials and Periodicals*, was issued in 1973 by the American Library Association Resources and Technical Services Division. As the title indicates, it provides guidelines to be used by librarians, publishers, and agents in the work they do together. Thanks is offered the American Library Association Resources and Technical Services Division for allowing us to quote liberally from this source.

The authors wish to thank the hundreds of librarians who took the time and effort to reply to the questionnaire on subscription agents. Many of their remarks and suggestions appear in this guide.

Thanks go also to the scores of subscription agents who answered a much longer questionnaire, and who were helpful in clarifying questions that arose during the preparation of the guide. Special thanks to Frank Clasquin of the F. W. Faxon Company, who read the complete manuscript and provided much information regarding technical and business aspects of agency operation. Mr. Clasquin is, of course, a partisan for his company, but his evaluation of the manuscript was admirably objective.

And finally, thanks to two of Bill Katz's students, Sherry Gaherty and Diane Davis. Ms. Gaherty assisted in the collecting and assembling of bibliographic data and Ms. Davis compiled the statistical data that make up Chapters 13 and 14. Ms. Davis's contribution is particularly impressive, in that it consisted of many hours of work spent not only in gathering material but also in deciphering and interpreting it.

Bill Katz
Professor, School of Library Science
State University of New York, Albany

Peter Gellatly
Head, Serials Division
University of Washington Libraries
Seattle, Washington

I.
SERIALS, PERIODICALS, AND THE LIBRARY

1.
INTRODUCTION: LIBRARIES AND PERIODICALS

This guide is an effort to indicate the best type of subscription agent for a particular library. Librarians accepting two premises—that most agents are reliable and that most librarians should employ agents—need not withhold criticism of the individual agent or agents. Too many articles about agents, or so it appears, are either rhapsodic (usually written by agents) or highly critical (usually written by less than happy librarians). There is an obvious need for a middle ground, and that's what this guide is all about.

At one time it was thought that a "consumer report" type of approach might be used in answering the question: Who is the best subscription agent for my library? Ideally, one should be able to list types and sizes of libraries, and after each give the most appropriate agent, the next best, and so on. It does not work out that way. However, there is enough objective and subjective evidence in this book at least to indicate the better and best agents plus those with lower ratings. The librarian is shown objective tests whereby prospective agents are asked specific questions regarding procedures and services.

For a library with more than one hundred periodical titles on order, it is generally a good idea to employ an agent. This is so even in the case of an agent whose service charge is from 5 to 20 percent. A section is given over to charges, but from the beginning one point should be made clear to all readers: agents are not in business for their health; they have to charge the library for services. Sometimes, as when the total list shows a discount, the charge is not apparent. Even with a discount, the agent is charging in the sense that he is not giving the library the periodical at cost. However, with a discount, the library usually receives the title for less than the cost when ordered directly from the publisher.

Given the charges, hidden or apparent, it still is more economic and efficient to employ a subscription agent for periodicals and other types of serials. Not all librarians agree, and their arguments are summarized later on.

SERIALS AND PERIODICALS

Beginners have a difficult time keeping separate these two terms. The difference between a serial and a periodical is a matter of who handles what, and what goes where. This leads Andrew Osborn to conclude:

> In keeping with the times . . . a serial can be defined for library purposes as any item which lends itself to serial treatment in a library: that is, to listing in its checking records . . . ; to cataloging and classifying as a serial; and to shelving in the current periodical room or among the bound volumes of serials in the bookstacks. . . . In doubtful cases one's judgment, based on the insights gained through years of handling serial publications, is all that is needed to decide on serial or nonserial treatment.[1]

Definitions

Osborn's pragmatic, final definition of a serial as "any item which lends itself to serial treatment in a library" is the ultimate solution to definitions. Still, for the beginner, it may be helpful at least to give short definitions of the commoner types of serials.

Serial is an umbrella term for any publication issued in parts, with a numerical or chronological designation, and usually published over an indefinite period of time. There are three or four primary types of serials. One type is the periodical and the newspaper. A second is the continuation, or series, which is more elusive because of its generally irregular publication and the beguiling habit of appearing in the form of hardbound books. Still a third type is what is really a separate division—the government document that may or may not be a serial but is likely to be one. Finally, sets in progress may be considered serials when they are to be published over a long period of time.

Were librarian and publisher content simply to leave it at that, there would be enough problems. However, depending upon the library or the publisher, each of the forms has numerous names. So on with it.

Webster defines periodical as a publication that appears at regular intervals, and the English use the term as a synonym for the American "serial." Generally, though, the term periodical is construed to mean *magazine*, which is a periodical containing miscellaneous articles, or stories, or poems, or just about anything that has general or special appeal for a particular group of readers. Most, although certainly not all, are professionally produced. The newsstands are filled with magazines, and one seldom hears the dealer use the term periodical. Depending upon one's training or use of English, the magazine may be subcategorized into mass circulation magazines, business publications, special interest titles, farm publications, and so on. There are numerous subdivisions, such as house organs issued by business and industry as propaganda for in-house employees or for the public (and of some value to librarians because the majority are free). Then, too, there is the controlled circulation magazine, which means the publisher literally "controls" to whom the magazine is sent. Many magazines are supported by advertising, and usually the larger the circulation the greater dependence upon the advertiser.

Journal signifies that the periodical is for a group of professionals (whether they be sanitary engineers, librarians, or doctors). Normally, such a publication contains papers, reports, and articles to meet the needs of specific, well-defined readers. Most journals are published by universities, national societies, associations, and other types of institutions. The majority are subsidized by a sponsoring group, and depend on the subsidy and/or subscribers for survival. Some carry advertising, but advertising is a small part of the financial picture.

The English periodicals expert, D. E. Davinson, nicely expresses the reluctance of some librarians to use "magazine" in connection with a periodicals collection.

> Magazine is (in this text) sedulously avoided on account of the rather unfortunate association, in common parlance, with, for example, the women's glossy weekly and monthlies published purely for entertainment. The term "periodical" is used for all materials worthy of inclusion in the informational, as opposed to purely recreational, collections of the library.[2]

Throughout this guide the terms "periodical" and "magazine" are used interchangeably.

There is considerably more to a definition of periodicals than what has been said about magazines and journals indicates. Some journals are newspapers, reviews, bulletins, quarterlies, or proceedings; some magazines are in newspaper format, some are reports or publications.

The average daily, weekly, or monthly newspaper of general interest is such a familiar part of the American scene that it may seem to need no definition here. Let it be noted that some purists state there is no clear distinction between a periodical and a newspaper; and a glance at such magazines as *Rolling Stone* or *More* will show that, in a furor of economy, many specialized magazines have adopted the newspaper format. Webster's definition of newspaper is quite enough: a paper printed and distributed at stated intervals, usually daily or weekly, to convey news and advocate opinions. As Davinson puts it: "This inclusion of newspapers tends to cut across the [periodical definition] in the sense that it is less a type of periodical than a particular style of editorial policy."[3]

Beyond the familiar magazine, periodical, and newspaper is the *continuation*, or series, or irregular serial. This is a publication issued more or less regularly over an indefinite period. Depending upon the publisher, a continuation may be "closed" or "open-ended." The closed continuation is one published over a fixed period of time, at the end of which it will be complete. Hence, part of the serial definition ("indefinite period") is no longer applicable. An open-ended continuation is one expected to go on indefinitely. Included here are publications such as proceedings and transactions of a corporate body. Further, continuations are often merely supplements issued in continuance of a book, a serial, or a series.

The problem for the serials librarian is to decide if the continuation is a closed or an open-ended title. If the former, should the librarian treat it as a serial; and, if the latter, is it really a continuation or simply another word for a serial? Unless the continuation is completed within a known and limited period of time, librarians tend to treat continuations as serials and incorporate them into the serial records. If the librarian considers continuations as open-ended, the term is often applied by them (and by agents) to mean almost any serial other than a periodical or a newspaper.

Series is a synonym for continuation, and the two terms often are used interchangeably. Usually, though, series is technically more restrictive in that it presupposes a closed-end situation, that is, at some time the publisher's series, whether it be "Rivers of America" or "Outdoor Life Books," will come to an end. Also, series is thought of by some librarians as applicable to book publication. (A *monographic series* is devoted to a single subject. Most are open-end continuations by organizations such as "Cambridge Monographs on Education" or "Monograph on Pottery." These may be or may not be in book form.)

There are certain agents who specialize in series; and here series means all forms of continuations and serials (except for periodicals and newspapers). Within the scope of continuations or series are numerous types of serials other than the familiar periodical or journal. Among them are:

Irregular serials, which is any open-ended continuation or series that appears irregularly, that is, without any definite publishing schedule. Emery Koltay, in his directory *Irregular Serials & Annuals*, includes titles issued annually or less frequently than once a year, or irregularly (*note:* annuals are not usually all that irregular by definition, but Koltay includes them here as an important added service to readers); serials published at least twice under the same title or those first publications that plan to have subsequent numbered issues.[4] The need for such a directory indicates the problems with irregular serials: the confusion between such a serial and a book, frequency of publication, price, and, among other things, change in publisher or change in address of the publisher.

In view of the difficulty of bibliographical control of many of these serials, and in view of the equal difficulty of locating the time and place of publication (not to mention the price), only the largest of agents handle continuations. And even they tend to let other special agents handle the more difficult, the more irregular, items such as, proceedings of "floating" conferences, for example, the International Geographical Congress.

Other terms frequently encountered within the context of continuations, series, and/or irregular serials are:

Annuals. This category includes a book, report, proceeding, etc., that is issued annually and is to be published regularly for an indefinite period. Examples range from the familiar almanacs to annual reports from business concerns to scientific organizations. Most librarians tend to treat annuals as serials for purposes of check in and cataloging. There are numerous problems—from the publisher who issues the annual at various periods throughout the year so no specific delivery date is possible to the publisher who skips one or two years and then suddenly issues the missing "annuals" in a single year. As noted, there are special agents who handle only these types of continuations. However, too many librarians are not aware of the fact that most of the larger and medium-sized agents can supply at least the most often called for, the most popular of the annuals.

Proceedings and transactions. Such titles as "Proceedings of the Section for Linguistics and Literature of the Hungarian Academy of Science" or "Transactions of the Institution of Mining Engineers" indicate the scope of this category. Most are limited to publication of the papers or the discussions presented at a specific meeting or the result of a specific commission or group designated to explore a particular problem in a scholarly or technical area. Because proceedings and transactions depend upon a group exploring a topic, they differ from journals in that they may be irregular, or annuals, e.g., *American Wood Preservers Association Proceeding*. Furthermore, transactions and proceedings may be published in hard cover.

International congresses. In a sense, this is a transaction or proceeding, and, as the term implies, is a report on a meeting of a scholarly or scientific or political or . . . just about any type of group on a regular or irregular basis. Unlike the proceedings or the transactions, though, the papers are not likely to be regularly published in journal form, but usually will appear as hardbound books. The really basic problems are outlined by Brown:

> [The international congresses] are usually held every four or five years in a different country each time. They are usually published in the language of the host country so that one has "Proceedings" for English and American . . . *atti* for Italian, *etc.* Some congresses may only publish abstracts of the proceedings. At times they are published independently with from one to twenty or more volumes for each Congress. At other times they may be published in a number of journals. . . . Every Congress is published by a different publisher and it seems best to rely on a good dealer to follow up on these Congresses rather than try to keep abreast of them as they change their place of publication.[5]

This hardly covers all the variations on the irregular serial or, for that matter, the regular. There are other distinctive types, such as bulletins, business services, reports, memoirs, and so on. Each comes with a built-in problem or two, and each may or may not be ordered from a given type of subscription agent.

Another vast area of serials is the government document. They tend to be treated in separate sections or departments in large and medium-sized libraries, as they present problems of their own. For smaller libraries the more familiar and popular government document will probably be handled as a periodical—at least those that meet the broad definition. (They will often, in fact, be treated in the same manner in larger libraries if conventional cataloging is employed by the large library.)

SOURCES OF SERIALS

Libraries have several sources for periodicals. One such source is the serials subscription agent, a person or a company that acts as liaison between the library or subscriber and the publisher. The agent is described variously as the vendor, dealer, or jobber. Throughout this guide, the term "agent" is primarily used.

Almost all libraries use one or more subscription agents for serials and particularly for the acquisitions of periodicals. The present survey of libraries revealed that of 850 libraries contacted, 95 percent employed an agent.

Types of serials available from a subscription agent depend upon a number of factors, primarily the size and the scope of the agency. The two largest domestic agents—Ebsco Subscription Services and F. W. Faxon Company, Inc.—have access to between 50,000 and 70,000 serials. A small one-man or one-woman field agent may only be able to order sixty to one hundred of the mass circulation magazines for a library. And in between are small to medium-sized agents who have access to most American titles required by the small to medium-sized library.

No agent is able to supply all titles available at either the domestic or the international level. The result is that larger libraries employ several agents for different types of serials and serials from various parts of the world. Even with a half dozen agents, both general and special and both domestic and international, no library can hope to secure all its wants from agents alone.

For numerous reasons discussed in the section on publishers, it is either necessary or economically beneficial for a library to order certain of its serials directly from the publisher. The present survey of libraries indicates that, on average, the library will order approximately 20 percent of its periodicals directly from the publisher. (The percentage may be higher for other types of serials.)

The survey shows that the average library obtains approximately 12 percent of its periodicals as gifts or exchanges. In a small library a gift may mean no more than a few odd issues of magazines from friends of the library, or possibly subscriptions donated by local businesses and groups. However, for the average medium-sized to large library, gifts and exchanges work is an important function, oftentimes carried out in a separate division, department, or section in the library. And much emphasis is on "exchange."

> Among libraries, the term "exchange" is used to cover a wide variety of transactions, such as exchanging of monographs, government documents, serials and duplicate issues of periodicals.[6]

In resorting to interlibrary loan, on the other hand, the item is simply borrowed and so not retained as part of a library's permanent collection. For that reason, interlibrary loan is not considered in this guide. Still, as a source of information for the average user, the importance of interlibrary loan (either via the actual copies or, more likely, via microform or xerography of what is needed) cannot be overlooked.

Few subscription agents handle reprints and back issues. Most are obtained directly from publishers or from dealers who specialize in back issues, out-of-print material, reprints, microforms, etc.

PATTERNS OF LIBRARY SERIALS ORGANIZATION

As with almost any other type of library organization, the parameters of the library serials operation will depend primarily upon the size and the purpose of the library. But even here there are impressive variations. William Huff found in a survey of academic libraries with 5,000 or more serials titles that at least one half of those surveyed had the serials scattered among various departments, i.e., acquisitions, cataloging, and a periodical collection or room. On the other hand

> In 49 percent of the libraries serials acquisitions are administered by a serials department, section or division. . . . Some serials departments also acquire documents. Ten libraries had serial departments which did not include acquisition responsibilities.[7]

In almost every case, Huff reported that there was a desire for more centralization of all serials activities—not simply of the acquisitions process alone. As Osborn points out

> From 1939 on there has been a slight tendency to centralize serial activities to the extent that a full-fledged serials department is created, coordinate with acquisitions, cataloging and other departments. In point of theory it is difficult to lay down hard and fast rules for the location of the primary serial functions.[8]

Whereas there is not total agreement as to the advisability of a centralized serials department, where such departments or divisions do exist it is safe to make some generalizations based, for the most part, on *efficient* employment of automation.

The primary reason for such centralization is that it allows more efficiency, i.e., the consolidation of serials records and routines and the elimination of much duplication of effort. There is also close coordination of the department or division with acquisitions, cataloging, and other related areas in the library. The local table or organization may call for either independent departments or divisions within larger departments, i.e., usually acquisitions or cataloging.

Even where there is no formal centralized organization, i.e., where serials are handled as a part of acquisitions, cataloging, and possibly a periodicals room, the tendency is to centralize records as much as possible. Hence, books and serials may be handled out of one record area, although the two records will likely be used in doing so. Determination of the patterns of operation to be chosen—centralized or decentralized—can depend as much upon the physical layout of the library as upon the administrative philosophy of the librarian. (As more than one writer has observed, it is often unclear as to what is specifically meant by the terms "centralization" and "decentralization." One librarian may mean the bringing-together or scattering of records, another the unifying or dispersing of the periodicals collection.)

Where there is no central serials division or department, periodicals are handled by various other divisions and departments.

Acquisitions is usually responsible for the ordering of periodicals, and as often as not for the maintenance of serials records. The acquisitions department may be favored because here is where the routines of serials and acquisitions overlap most noticeably. This is particularly true because, other than periodicals, many serials (monographs, series, etc.) are often treated in a library as books. Receiving shipments, financial accounts, and the like are part of the work of an existing acquisitions department, and it is easier (or so the argument goes) to place all of these functions in a single department than to create a separate serials unit in which some of the functions of the acquisitions unit are repeated, albeit with a difference. Where the serials are cataloged, they are sent on to the catalog department from the acquisitions department. The catalog department has the essential tools, from the shelflist to the various bibliographies and union catalogs, needed to do the job.

Some libraries may designate part of the previous divisions to a periodical room or center where the periodicals and some of the serials are housed. In this decentralized scheme there may or may not be one or several librarians designated as serials librarians who are responsible for maintaining records and serving as coordinators among the various divisions and departments.

Regardless of size or type of library, one individual should be responsible for the organization and administration of serials. The obvious reason for this is to set up and maintain the unique records and routines that proper control of the collection demands. One person soon becomes able to cope with the routines efficiently and quickly.

In the median situation, where less than 400 titles are coming into the library, a part-time clerk should be able to manage most of the necessary daily routines. Between 400 and 1,500 or 2,000 it is desirable that a separate serials unit be set up. Yet the figures must be modified up or down depending upon how the periodicals are used. If they are simply ordered and shelved for little more than occasional use, a part-time person might well be able to handle over 500 titles. But if an effort is made to utilize the periodicals extensively (which may mean everything from regular routing to abstracting), a full-time person will probably be needed even in situations in which fewer than 500 titles are held.

Given this jigsaw organizational pattern, it is understandable that such variety appears in the handling of serials. A certain amount of difference is commendable, but the degree of difference can be baffling for anyone attempting to standardize procedures. Huff found that in large academic libraries, "Of [those] questioned, only 12 percent had a formal policy for serial acquisitions."[9] Going beyond acquisitions to all aspects of serials and periodicals organization, Brown quickly admits that

> ... Every library has special and individual needs. ... [Therefore] no one set of rules and routines will fit all libraries. ... No outsider can set up an office manual for any and all libraries. ... The variables are too numerous.[10]

The conclusion is by way of a paradox. While other sorts of library work require more attention to detail than does periodicals work, probably no other has become so little standardized. The lack of standard organization and standard routines often has produced a result that comes perilously close to chaos in its effects. At its best, serials work offers the more imaginative librarian almost a free field in the organization of records and procedures—at both the manual and automated levels. At its worst, it accounts in no small part for the failure of communication between some libraries and some subscription agents and publishers.

Osborn, somewhat optimistically, asserts that: "In the hands of experts serials are acquired and processed by efficient, businesslike methods."[11] If libraries, publishing firms, magazine subscription agents, and so on were entirely staffed by "experts" this might be a truism. As it is, one less than alert clerk, one exhausted mailman, or a rushed and harried "expert" can make an error that will shake seriously the "efficient, businesslike methods" in the best of libraries. Even the tireless computer can make mistakes. The net result is summed up by an American Library Association Committee:

> It is . . . necessary to eliminate the staggering number of needlessly generated errors by all parties concerned. Indeed, if this could be done, more would be accomplished than by any other contribution. And to make this possible, each type of organization, the library, the dealer and the publisher should train their personnel properly, supervise them adequately, check the work units for errors, and respond to complaints as quickly as possible.[12]

While this sounds somewhat like a paragraph out of an army training manual or an accountant's textbook, the tone fits the situation. As Brown puts it: "Serials librarians must be able to put up with a great amount of detail and a continual variation of titles, business trends, and financial problems. Many librarians have no patience with these detailed routines."[13]

Ideally, every library would have one or more librarians devoted to serials, just as every library would have an individual reference librarian, a cataloger, an administrator, or a circulation specialist. It is not surprising that a survey of New York State librarians indicated that the vast majority of librarians "appear to know little about what their subscription agents can be expected to do for them."[14] This may seem like an astonishing conclusion to serials librarians, especially those who devote their full time to such work, but its candor is admirable.

SELECTION OF SERIALS

In another publication I have gone into detail regarding a philosophy of magazine selection.[15] Much of what is said there is applicable in dealing in general with serials. It is the intention in this section to mention only some of the more basic bibliographical aids used in selection and verification, and to consider a few brief principles of selection.

One may write at great length on the advisability of this or that approach to selection, but the amount of money available for the purchase of one's collection of periodicals is a factor no philosopher may avoid.

Current budgets superimpose restrictions on selection and acquisitions. Once a subscription is started, the average librarian finds it easier to continue with the subscription than to go through the problems of cancellation or deciding upon renewal. This is particularly so when there is a possibility that at some later date the library may have to order back issues of the same title at a considerably higher price from back-order sources.

Subscription rates are increasing at a faster pace than most library budgets. Just to "stand still," a number of libraries have cancelled so-called peripheral titles and put a virtual halt to the ordering of new titles other than those considered absolutely necessary.

Given such a situation—the reluctance to cancel old titles and the equal reluctance to order new—the emphasis in the first part of the 1970s turns out to be as much on "deselection" as on selection. At first glance, one form of proceeding ought to be no more difficult than the others, but when one considers the problems involved, one realizes that librarians now find themselves in a rather perilous situation. Previously, a large library might simply order any "basic" title indexed or abstracted in a "basic" service, whereas now the librarian must consider that the budget will not allow such choices. This is what one expert calls "a definite trend" in collection development.

If serials budgets are reaching the 70 percent level, then it is safe to say the serials librarians must be heavily involved in the collection development aspects of budget policy formulation, evaluation of the library's serial resources, determination of collection development policy, and development of review programs to cope with massive title deselection projects with all the implications for nonrenewal (always better than the cancellation headache) procedures and extensive record changes.[16]

If the selection trend in the late 1960s and early 1970s was toward meeting the needs of heretofore overlooked audiences and programs, it is now, in the mid-1970s, clearly going in another direction. For one thing, accountants and budget experts threaten to dominate the selection scene. Hopefully, steps will be taken soon to formulate and evaluate selection policies that will not only include considerations of budget but also give equal emphasis to the subjective problems of who uses what, and why and when. There are some signs that librarians are not about to give up the periodicals ship to the navigator who sights the course for the coming year on the dollar alone.

Searching and Verification

At its most modest level, the librarian may verify a title, including publisher, address, and price simply by consulting the average index or abstract (all of the H. W. Wilson indexes give this information in full for each title indexed).

There are two other useful general directories or guides:

Ulrich's International Periodical Directory (New York: R. R. Bowker) is updated every two years. *Ulrich's* lists approximately 55,000 in-print periodicals published throughout the world. Arrangement is by subject, and there is a definitive index. Each entry includes complete bibliographical information, International Standard Serial Numbers for titles, and the Dewey Decimal Classification number. Further features list major indexes and abstracts where a title is analyzed, notes on book reviews and illustrations, and variations between the publisher's address and the subscription address.

For verification, purposes, *Ulrich's* generally can be trusted to provide accurate and complete information. Since prices and publishers obviously do change, the biennial revision and annual supplements include both new and older titles.

For selection purposes, the directory breaks down by subject the major and many minor titles in every area from accounting to veterinary science. The listing is inclusive, not evaluative. By checking such things as circulation, the degree of indexing and abstracting, the sponsoring publisher, the editor, etc., the librarian can achieve a general idea of the relative importance of a title.

The Companion to Ulrich's, *Irregular Serials and Annuals: An International Directory* (New York: R. R. Bowker) lists other than periodical serials by subject. Not all periodicals are irregular, for a number of regular annuals and continuations are included. It serves much the same purpose as *Ulrich's* for nonperiodical serials.

Of particular value for ephemeral materials, as well as for such publications as newsletters, government periodicals and series, house organs, etc., published in the United States and Canada, is *Standard Periodical Directory*, 3rd ed. (New York: Oxbridge, 1973). Entry information is complete in this subject-arranged guide. And while there is not a subject index, titles are classified under more than 200 major subject headings, a feature that makes it relatively easy to use.

For newspapers of the United States and Canada, the old standby is the *Ayer Directory: Newspapers, Magazines and Trade Publications* (Philadelphia: Ayerpress, annual.) Here arrangement is geographical by state or province with complete information given about daily, weekly, and other frequency newspapers. Major periodicals are listed in a similar fashion, although emphasis should be on "major," because not all titles published, say, in New York or North Dakota, are included. A classified index helps to isolate black, religious, and trade and technical publications.

Beyond these directories are the most specialized subject-oriented works, such as *The World List of Social Science Periodicals, the Directory of the Jewish Press in America,* and *Selected List of Periodicals Relating to Negroes*. Most of these are reviewed as they appear. For an ongoing check on American entries the best single source is the annual *American Reference Books Annual* (Littleton, Colo.: Libraries Unlimited, 1970 to date), which annotates American published reference titles, including those in the serials and periodical directory area, by subject. The *ARBA* should be backed up by *Winchell's Guide to Reference Books* and Walford's *Guide to Reference Materials*—both of which are helpful for retrospective titles.

When the librarian turns to international serials and periodicals, there are an equal number of specialized directories by area and country, for example, Woodworth's *Guide to Current British Journals*, 2d ed. (London: The Library Association, 1973), which cites and briefly annotates British periodicals by subject. The bibliographical control is good to excellent in Western Europe, but falls to less than satisfactory for other parts of the world (a reason, by the way, that many libraries depend so heavily upon reputable international agents for foreign periodicals).

Union Lists

Almost all the directories are concerned with in-print titles, but how does the librarian verify a title no longer published? Equally important questions are How does a librarian locate a title in another library, or determine when a given title began publication, stopped publication, changed title, changed publishers, etc.? There is no definitive answer, no single source to which one might refer such questions. The single most useful and most often used, however, is *New Serial Titles* (Washington, D.C.: Library of Congress, 1961 to date), issued eight times a year and cumulated quarterly, annually, and every ten years. This continuation of *Union List of Serials in Libraries of the United States and Canada*, 3rd ed. (New York: H. W. Wilson, 1965, 5 vols.) carries on the listing of periodicals that are added to major American and Canadian libraries. The series constitutes a finding list of almost every conceivable title, domestic and foreign, in-print and out-of-print, to be found in libraries. The majority of librarians use this list to locate libraries with a title requested by a user that is not in the parent library, or to verify titles, beginning date of publication, date of cessation, suspension, etc.

While a subject approach to the contents of *New Serial Titles* is offered in *New Serial Titles—Classed Subject Arrangement* (a separate monthly publication that is not cumulated), no indication is given of relative value of the title. Hence, the librarian uses this list in the selection process only as an alerting device. The librarian will then find further information about the title in examining a sample copy or by questioning subject experts or agents about it. All in all, this constitutes an awkward and time-consuming arrangement, and one not often used by librarians. True, Osborn and others advise librarians to "go through carefully—not scan—twelve monthly issues of *New Serial Titles—Classed Subject Arrangement*,"[16] but this is suspect advice because of the limited result that such a search provides.

There are other national, regional, and local union lists—again listed in the basic guides to reference titles as well as in compilations such as Ruth Freitag's *Union List of Serials: a Bibliography* (Washington, D.C., Library of Congress, 1964). Their number is likely to increase as more and more librarians engage in the cooperative purchase and storage of periodicals and serials.

Selection Principles

With due respect to the necessity for serials budget allocations, and for the new trend towards "deselection," we wish to conclude this section with a few words about selection principles—principles easily overlooked in the rush to equate serials and periodicals routines with measurable and sound business practices. Given the limited holdings of periodicals and other types of serials in all but the largest libraries, it can be said fairly conclusively that the furor over collection development and budget is likely to be a problem only in the largest of research and academic libraries. The average librarian does well to hold his or her own in a situation in which the budget pays for under 500 titles. What follows is addressed primarily to this librarian.

Much has been written and will be written on the fine points of selection. However, most of what has been said may be reduced to some relatively simple fundamentals. The majority of librarians select periodicals according to the following:

Expectations of users. In all libraries the periodical holdings will contain basic titles, i.e., those that have gained wide acceptance. These range from the

Readers' Digest, a publication with a circulation equaled only by that of *TV Guide*, to such socially and educationally certified titles as *Harper's Magazine*, *Atlantic Monthly*, *Newsweek*, *Time*, and the inevitable *Saturday Review*. In these cases, and in those of another fifty to one hundred relatively popular and well-known newsstand titles, the decision to purchase is not so much a conscious choice as a desire to meet the expectations of readers who have come to expect that certain titles belong in a library. Much the same can be said for other perhaps more auspicious serials, such as the *World Almanac* and the *Yearbook of Agriculture*.

The pros and cons of the librarians meeting the expectations of the public are subject to unending debate. Essentially, the question reduces itself to the timeless argument as to whether a library is first and foremost an educational institution or rather a source of recreational reading, or both of these things. Most librarians, quite wisely, offer a periodical collection that represents, or its composition is a compromise between, the two extremes. Hence, this side of the smallest library, the average reader is likely to find both the *Readers' Digest* and a run of *Daedalus*. While the argument is less heated in academic libraries, an echo is heard when the librarian must decide whether to purchase such titles as *Rolling Stone*, *Mad*, or a leading "little" magazine in the arts, alternate culture, literature, etc. Add to this the dimension of the "storefront" library trying to meet the expectations of the poorly educated child, teenager, or adult, and questions arise as to the advisability of "salting" the periodical collection with everything from a popular teenage magazine to a man's magazine. Finally, social, scientific, and political change too often are not adequately represented, particularly by those magazines that reflect any aspect of the rejection of established viewpoints.

Another type of user expectation is less argumentative, although equally puzzling. The "expert," whether he or she be a college professor or an antique collector, expects certain "basic" titles in his or her own interest area. When the title is not too esoteric, or when the library is particularly geared to meet the needs of a specific type of expert or student, selection is based upon the expressed (and often unexpressed) needs of the specialist or would-be specialist. Certain basic titles are so well known as to present no problems, but what is to be done about the expectations of the user for so-called peripheral titles or for new, yet untested journals? Precisely how many journals are "basic"? And of the "basic" titles, how many are really used? Such questions become increasingly important as inflation grows and budgets decline.

Expectations of librarians. Davinson fairly well sums up this situation: "There are those periodicals which are absolutely indispensable in a given library situation which it would be inconceivable to be without. . . . Given reasonably adequate resources it is not difficult for the librarian to recognize what are the core periodical titles."[17] The collection is shaped by the expectation of the librarian as to what the user will need for both recreational and educational purposes. Guided by knowledge of the public served and by familiarity with similar titles, the librarian always should be aware of an insidious bias: the choosing of materials only in terms of patron acceptance or rejection. Most librarians recognize this quite human reaction, and seek to temper it as they can.

Use of the title. It is a foregone conclusion that *Time* is a popular magazine in terms of frequent use for both recreational and informational needs. *Proceedings of the Virgil Society* is a serial that the librarians know will not be consulted as often as *Time.* If a decision must be made between the two, the librarian has no difficulty in making it. In less extreme cases, however, a real problem exists in making individual choices.

How does the librarian evaluate a title that may have only a small number of regular readers? The question has built-in complications, e.g., if the periodical is little used, how important is that use? The answer may be self-evident by the amount of dust gathering on a magazine or, more likely, by such objective tests as circulation counts, citation studies, experience of other libraries, and the amount of indexing and abstracting accorded the title. A more meaningful and certainly individualized answer may be found by interviewing the people who do, or do not, use the magazine.

Despite a vast literature in the methodology of evaluating the present and potential use of titles by both generalists and specialists, no definitive answer is to be found. It is small wonder, then, that librarians are haunted by the notion that sooner or later a user will ask for a title that has not been subscribed to by the library only because of the librarian's failure to assess its value properly.

Selection Aids

Although librarians are able to select a given number of titles based upon personal knowledge of the title's use and worth, most add three other devices to their acquisitions armory.

Advice from subject experts. In academic libraries, the advice may be in the form of a virtual command dictated by division of budgetary allotments among departments, i.e., a given department, such as philosophy, is allowed so much for periodicals and the members of that department request the library to order X to P titles. In other kinds of libraries, the advice tends to be less formalized, and may range from the hypothetical little old man's or teenager's inquiry about "everything on a subject" to the scientist's or business person's request for specific titles.

Abstracting and indexing services. Periodicals of great potential use to everybody are those that are abstracted or indexed. At one time, the number of abstracting and indexing services was limited to those issued by H. W. Wilson and to a few others of a highly scientific or specialized kind issued elsewhere. Today there are several thousand such services. The result is that other than new or purely recreational periodicals, most magazines are now analyzed in one service or another. Many are found in not merely one but in as many as a dozen or more. Considering this situation, the librarian can no longer simply accept (or reject) a title on the basis that it is listed or not listed in an index. Today the name of the indexing game is to select and choose abstracts and indexes as much by subjects covered as by titles analyzed—titles that the library has acquired over the years.

Even so, one common selection situation in all but the largest libraries is to order the Wilson indexes and a few other well-established services, and order (or not order) titles based upon what is found in those indexes. This apparent working of the selection process in reverse is a subject of later discussion.

Current sources. Although experts and abstracts and indexes are valuable resources for retrospective titles, the average librarian must have some consistent method of keeping up with the publication of new titles. This is a problem for the small to medium-sized public or school library in its effort to keep its collection reflective of current trends and tastes. The problem is of another sort in academic and special libraries where fast-breaking developments in new fields of interest must be noted—both at the domestic and the international levels.

Among sources of current reviews of periodicals are Katz's column in *Library Journal* and the equally excellent notes on magazines in *Booklist, Top of the News*, and the *AB Bookman's Weekly*. Literary and "little" magazines are regularly reviewed in Tom Montag's *Margins* and Len Fulton's *Small Press Review*. Less obvious sources include notes in the leading scholarly journals, as well as roundups in such popular magazines and newspapers as the *Village Voice, Ms.*, and *New York*. *Folio* regularly lists and annotates new titles of general and business interest, as does the *Media Industry Newsletter*. One can conclude that an increased awareness of the importance of magazines is reflected in the proliferation of reviews evident from the early 1970s on.

Several agents, such as Faxon and Stechert-Macmillan, regularly issue information in the form of bulletins and notices about new titles and ceased titles. While useful, these sources lack comprehensiveness, and cannot stand as a substitute for *New Serial Titles* (they are, all the same, considerably useful for purposes of selection). What is needed is something equivalent to the *Publisher's Weekly* compilation of new books (and many book-type serials), i.e., the "Weekly Record," coupled with the magazine's equally excellent "PW Forecasts" of titles to be published. Given the nature of serials, such a service is not likely to be made available. The alternative could be an increase in the amount of information (from short descriptive annotations to publisher's addresses) offered by *New Serial Titles*. Unfortunately, the cost factor here militates against such a possibility. Meanwhile, the best hope is that the reviews of new titles will continue to expand in number and, further, that specialized magazines will adopt to a greater extent than now exists the practice of reviewing new titles in their respective fields.

Other channels of assistance may be found in Katz's *Magazines for Libraries*, 2nd ed. (New York: R. R. Bowker, 1972) and its supplement issued in 1974; Evan Farber's *Classified List of Periodicals for the College Library*, 5th ed. (Westwood, Mass.: F. W. Faxon, 1972); and Marian Scott's *Periodicals for School Libraries*, rev. ed. (Chicago: American Library Association, 1973). Then, too, specialized subject lists with annotations appear from time to time as books or as review articles. While useful for selection of retrospective and fairly current titles, none, of course, of the mentioned aids solves the problem of what was published "yesterday."

REFERENCE NOTES

1. Andrew Osborn, *Serial Publications*, 2nd ed. (Chicago: American Library Association, 1973), p. 13.
2. D. E. Davinson, *The Periodicals Collection*, 2nd ed. (Elmsford, N.Y.: London House & Maxwell, 1969), p. 37.

3. *Ibid.*, p. 40.
4. Emery Koltay, *Irregular Serials & Annuals* (New York: R. R. Bowker, 1967), p. vii. This is frequently revised and updated.
5. Clara D. Brown, *Serials: Acquisitions and Maintenance* (Birmingham, Ala.: Ebsco Industries, 1971), pp. 69-70.
6. John E. Galejs, "Economics of Serials Exchange," *Library Resources & Technical Services*, Fall 1972, p. 511.
7. William H. Huff, "The Acquisition of Serial Publications," *Library Trends*, January 1970, pp. 297-98.
8. Osborn, *op. cit.*, p. 51.
9. Huff, *op. cit.*, p. 298.
10. Brown, *op. cit.*, p. 2.
11. Osborn, *op. cit.*, p. 89.
12. ALA/RTSD, Acquisitions Section, "Guidelines for Publishers, Agents and Librarians in Handling Library Orders for Serials and Periodicals" (Chicago: American Library Association, 1973), p. 2. This is a processed report that is frequently cited throughout this work as the ALA *Guidelines*.
13. Brown, *op. cit.*, p. 9.
14. "Report on a Survey of Subscription Agents Used by Libraries in New York State" (New York: New York Library Association, 1970), p. 3. A processed 12-page report.
15. Bill Katz, *Magazine Selection* (New York: R. R. Bowker, 1971).
16. Osborn, *op. cit.*, p. 69.
17. Davinson, *op. cit.*, p. 103.

2.
THE PERIODICALS PUBLISHER

According to agents, and not a few librarians, the villain in their midst is the periodicals publisher. The agent often explains failures on his part as a consequence of an uncooperative publisher. And the librarian who makes a claim now and then must realize that a good deal of difficulty comes from a less than avid interest in the problem by the publisher.

But are all publishers really that bad? How many are the unwitting fall guys for the agent's errors or lack of efficiency? The purpose of this chapter is to explore such questions. Most of the discussion is limited to periodicals publishers. This limitation is necessary to keep the chapter within a manageable size. However, a good deal of the information presented here is as applicable to other types of serials publishers of any sort as to magazine publishers.

ORDERING FROM THE PUBLISHER

Even the most ardent advocate of the subscription agency–library relationship has some occasion to order directly from the publisher. At least six reasons can be given for resorting to the direct order.

The publisher of X title refuses to work through an agency; only orders received directly from the library are accepted. This is frequently the case with national societies, institutions, or associations. To compound the headache, some publishers will accept subscriptions only from individuals, not from libraries.

The agent's service charge is considered for a given title, and the library believes it more economical to order directly. This arises in several situations, the most basic and common being cases in which the library takes most or all of the titles a publisher puts out. In this instance the publisher may offer a discount, as well as other services ranging from a "till forbid" contract to quick accountability in claims matters. Furthermore, in the case of membership organizations, substantial price benefits go to members, as do occasional monograph bonuses. Unfortunately, not all such organizations will sell subscriptions to libraries. Special institutional rates, always higher than the personal rate, sometimes obtain. Osborn explains how the higher rate can be avoided without compromise of the niceties of the situation:

> Membership is often taken out by a library in the name of a professor or staff member when institutional membership is not possible, but sometimes the individual himself must join and be reimbursed by the library. It is virtually only *Chemical Abstracts* which considers the latter practice unethical. In addition [this enables] the library to procure publications which would not otherwise be available or which would cost appreciably more. . . . [1]

The publisher encourages direct library orders by establishing special subscription departments that deal only with libraries. Where this situation exists, speed and efficiency may be greater than dealing through an agent.

The time span between sending an order to the agent and actual receipt of the first issue of a serial may be too great in given situations. Thus, in order to avoid the delay caused by channeling the order through a third party, the library orders directly from the publisher—a reasonable, though not always foolproof, way of speeding along the title.

Many government and institutional serials are available only as gifts and/or exchanges. As these items are free, subscription agents do not handle them. However, the ordering and checking in of such serials can be as time consuming as in the case of any other type of subscription, whether or not an agent is used as supplier.

> Many librarians feel that domestic exchange is not as free as it looks. Money and personnel are needed to conduct the routines. Often the library does not have sufficient publications available of its own and has to purchase them. The value of the material received is uneven and some is very ephemeral. Service with other libraries may become erratic, taking much time in claiming, with small returns.[2]

Materials not handled by an agent include free publications; services, particularly of the investment and business sort, which are often available only from the publisher; controlled-circulation items sent by the publisher to a "select group of readers" chosen by the publisher to justify his argument to would-be advertisers that they are getting the most for each dollar they spend; some university periodicals; publications such as school papers that are available only in bulk quantities; and many irregular serials, especially those of infrequent appearance and variable price, such as "little" magazines, underground newspapers, and counter culture political titles.

The average agent does not handle such "fugitive" publications for a number of reasons. Most of the reasons are familiar enough to librarians who may have tried to order such works directly from the publisher. Many publishers of these works are often less than businesslike in their dealings with subscribers. They might or might not answer correspondence about subscriptions; they tend to have an irregular publishing schedule, with resulting frequent claiming; and they balk at replacing or making adjustments for missing issues. A good many of these firms, of course, are one-person operations. The editor is printer, distributor, and often principal or even sole contributor. He or she neither understand nor appreciate the role of the agent in the process of getting the title into a library. In the past two or three years, however, a number of "little" magazine publishers have become considerably more sophisticated in business and now operate efficiently through agents or such special distributors as DeBoer.

PUBLISHER-AGENCY RELATIONSHIPS

Why does the average publisher work through a subscription agent? The agent batches the library orders, and sends the publisher one order for, say, ten or more libraries. The agent makes advance payment to the publisher, which saves the publisher the work and expense of billing individual libraries. Advance payment for multiyear subscriptions often give the publisher a considerable amount of working capital. The agent handles renewals and long-term subscriptions, procedures that constitute a considerable problem so far as the publisher is concerned. For this service the publisher allows the agent an average discount of about 9.3 percent on a title. (This discount may go as high as 50 percent or descend to zero.)

A summary of why the majority of publishers work through agents is given by Huibert Paul, formerly of the *PNLA Quarterly*:

> ... I appreciate subscription agents. It is very pleasant to see subscription monies roll in via agents without having to bother about sending invoices or renewal notices. The *PNLA Quarterly* gives agents a discount of 10 percent and it is well worth it. As a publisher I especially long for the services of subscription agents whenever I deal with libraries that either will not or cannot use them. Such is not infrequently the case with school, college or university libraries. After waiting in vain for money to come in, I find myself forced to write tedious invoices. As a reward for my labours I then do not receive money but rather a form, to be filled out in triplicate or quadruplicate. These forms do not differ a whole lot from state to state, but they differ just enough to make the publisher's life miserable.[3]

Here it should be noted that not all publishers are any more satisfied with the agent than are some librarians. A librarian submits the following comments received recently on this topic from a publisher:

"By the time orders are re-channeled to us thru subscription agencies, we oftentimes cannot begin with requested issue. Orders are processed to begin with the current issue on hand at time order is received. ... We find direct service is sometimes more satisfactory to client. It is definitely quicker. ... We much prefer direct orders; libraries using agents [*sic*] 'service' pay more for being a nuisance. ... We prefer direct subscriptions but accept subscriptions placed through agents in that agents receive a standard discount for their services. Also, routing correspondence through agents often is slow and cumbersome. ... But it works out more efficiently when done directly. ... We much prefer libraries to place their subscriptions directly with us, because we are paid in full instead of only 85 percent."

THE PUBLISHER'S VIEWPOINT

The problem in respect to the publisher is the unexpressed assumption that "the publisher" is a monolithic giant from whose mouth pours 50,000 to 70,000 titles every year. Publishing, as most human activities, is extremely pluralistic. While periodicals publishers obviously do share certain similarities, such as their use of the United States mails, most defy categorization by type or function. The simple descriptor "publisher" does not, by any means, tell the whole tale.

The activities of the 20,000 or so American periodicals publishers present a constant threat to the sanity of agents and librarians. Still, year-in and year-out the average library has difficulty with only 4 to 8 percent of all titles—hardly an indictment of publishers as a whole. Of the troublesome few, most are publishers of large circulation titles. Clearly, there is a correlation between the size of a publisher's subscription list and the potential for problems.

This is not to suggest that the man or woman who may be using a mimeograph machine to issue a magazine from a basement cannot be an equal headache. Every agent or librarian is familiar with the "nonpublisher" who issues magazines and journals. Few of these people have any knowledge of publishing, whether they are scholars producing recondite journals or young enthusiasts plugging music or diet in a mimeographed newspaper. The failures of this group, at least as far as agents and librarians are concerned, are topics of conversation at many a conference.

The vast majority of publishers are neither very large nor very small. These average-sized publishers represent the better known, lower circulation periodicals of popular interest, such as business, technology, science, the humanities, etc. Most make a conscientious effort to publish on time, solve subscriber complaints, and, generally, this side of a natural or technical disaster, function in such a way as to cause no subscriber or agent much pain.

The majority of difficulty comes from the mass circulation magazine or journal. And there are reasons that size breeds problems. In general, size or relative importance in terms of acceptance by members of a discipline results in distance—distance from the individual subscriber, whether this be the individual down the block or a large research library across town. The problem is not simply a matter of indifference on the publisher's part, but more properly one that has to do with operational realities of the big firm.

Small publishers exercise direct, personal control over subscriptions and their servicing. The usual situation is well described by Asher Birnbaum, publisher of *Tennis* magazine (sold in 1973 to the *New York Times*). And while *Tennis* is a commercial venture, what Birnbaum has to say about his circulation situation is true in the case of any sizable journal periodical:

> Our first print order was 10,000. One day I arrived home from a sales call and found 10,000 issues of *Tennis* stacked in our living room. So my wife, my sons, my daughter, a lot of neighborhood children and I sat around wrapping and pasting labels on 10,000 issues.... I'd never do that again [but] we always handled our own list updating and claiming.... But once we had entered the change data on 3 × 5 cards (using an increasing number of part time women) we'd hand it over to a fulfillment company to handle.[4]

The point here is that small and even many medium-sized publishers have direct involvement with subscriptions and subscribers. Letters are answered, subscriptions are updated, and confusion over missing issues is normally straightened out promptly. This is possible because "a part-time employee" or the editor himself or herself, with a stack of addressograph plates to work from, can immediately locate the problem.

As the magazine grows, the publisher maintains control over circulation problems by hiring a circulation manager. Now the actual pasting of labels may be done at a printing plant or by a distributor, but the subscriptions and problems are handled by the circulation person. In other cases, the publisher may establish reader service departments; these may be no more than one man or woman or a small staff. Conversely, they may grow into giant departments, which along the way often seem to lose the old personal interest in keeping things running smoothly.

This is not the place to discuss either circulation managers or readers service bureaus. Many medium-sized publishers of both commercial and noncommercial titles have such departments. Most operate with considerable efficiency and courtesy. The situation leads the committee of the ALA *Guidelines* to note: "Be aware that some major publishers of periodicals have established subscription departments which may provide the best service for their own publications."[5]

Whether or not there is a circulation manager or a part-time person, the larger the publisher grows, the more likely he or she is to enter into an agreement with a fulfillment agent.

The specific duties of the independent fulfillment agent differ according to the employing publisher. For example, one publisher may require the fulfillment agent to do nothing more than print and affix labels to copies of a magazine. Another may expect the agent to carry on a "mail-cage operation," that is, to handle all aspects of the processing of subscriptions.

Most large publishers use such arrangements in handling subscriptions, and, in many cases, a letter or claim sent to a publisher really goes directly to a fulfillment agent, who then must decide what is to be done with it. Unfortunately, in some cases, the fourth party is often no more than a computer with stock answers—mostly negative—to the questions and claims that come along.[6]

Some difficulties arising at the fulfillment stage may be illustrated by a change of address:

> When publishers receive a change of address, they must locate the subscription whose address the customer wishes to have changed. When they attempt to do this, three things may happen.
>
> The first is that they may locate the subscription, remove the old plate (or punch card or magnetic tape or disc record) and substitute the new one. If these two things are done concurrently, service should begin at the new address. However, if the publisher's procedure is to cancel the subscription at the old address and then start one at the new address, it is possible that the cancellation of the old subscription may take effect prior to the inauguration of the new subscription and if labels for a given issue are being prepared during this time, an issue may be missed.
>
> If a customer has more than one subscription to a journal and if he is not very precise about which subscription to change, there is a possibility that the address will be changed on the wrong subscription but that in checking the

file, a clerk will discover another subscription at the old address and change that one too. There is also the possibility that the fulfillment clerk may not be able to find the original subscription in the file, may assume that it has already been cancelled and start a new subscription. In this case, two subscriptions will be received. Therefore, it is urged that addresses not be changed except at renewal time.[7]

When the publisher is small, most problems with change of address are likely to be isolated quickly, but in Greenfield's example the emphasis is on the large publisher. Equally important, he stresses the problems of the faceless clerk and "punch card or magnetic tape or disc record," all familiar devices in the fulfillment agency operation.

The change-of-address syndrome illustrates one difficulty in dealing with larger publishers, but other common problems exist. One such problem is the failure to start service promptly. Response to the questionnaire used in our survey indicates that most agents believe a publisher takes twenty-one to sixty days to process a library order. Ebsco, at the low end of the scale, says it needs only twenty-one days to establish an order, but others ask for ninety or more. In 1971 the Magazine Publishers' Association established guidelines for magazine and subscription fulfillment and services practices. It was recommended that a publisher of monthly or less frequently issued titles should mail the first copy within forty-five days after receipt of the order. For magazines published weekly or biweekly, the first issue should be mailed within twenty-five days. Some publishers simply cannot be that obliging. A large publisher has to forward an instruction to a fulfillment agent. This, of course, creates delay, and a common result is that the library subscription begins with an issue later than the one requested. In such an event, the library is often at pains to get the earlier numbers it needs.

Late receipt of titles is often a failure on the part of the United States mails. In one study made for magazine publishers it was found that: "Postal service today [late 1973–early 1974] is providing less than 60 percent on time deliveries."[8] At the same time, the expert on mails observed that publishers "making the effort *do* get better than average deliveries."[9]

Furthermore, the printing of the issue may be tardy. Large publishers have considerable control over printing either because they own their own plants or because they represent such a large part of the business of the printer they employ that every effort is made to get the title out on time. The smaller publisher rarely has such leverage, and in the case of a monthly publication, a leeway is allowed in most printing contracts of from ten to fifteen days during which the periodical may be printed. This, then, is one area in which the large publisher has a distinct advantage. But there is a catch: usually, once off the press, the magazines, have to be forwarded to the fulfillment agent, a procedure that more than cancels out any time advantage. Other factors causing schedule delays are strikes, mechanical breakdowns, and unforeseen shortages of paper or ink.

Moreover, as is the case with many small publishers seeking inexpensive printing, the printer can be located in an out-of-the-way place. Thus, delay occurs in mailing the publication back and forth between printer and publisher.

The "dating game" is a publisher's idiosyncrasy of some size. The "game" is explained by publishing expert, J. J. Janson:

> Some publishers do a good job of getting their magazines out on time, others do a lousy job. The audit statement should reflect and advise the advertisers about this.
>
> Not long ago I was walking through a printing plant and picked up a copy of a magazine with a cover date of January 15. The cover referred to a major industry show with which the issue was supposed to coincide. But the date on which I took the plant tour was February 2 and the magazine wasn't even bound yet. I'm sure that many advertisers in that issue bought space because of the timing with the show. I'm equally certain that they were sadly disappointed—if in fact they ever learned of the delay.
>
> And while I'm on the subject of dates, why don't publishers include subscription expiration dates on their renewal offers? There's nothing that bugs me more than being told that my subscription to a magazine is up soon. What does soon mean? If I knew, maybe I would renew immediately instead of waiting around for the third renewal notice.[10]

Missing issues are a particular headache for librarians, and made even more painful by the policy of large publishers. When a library claims a missing issue, many large trade publishers solve the problem by extending the subscription an extra week, six weeks, or six months depending upon circumstances. No effort is made to supply the missing issue. The ALA *Guidelines* notes this procedure is "unacceptable," and that the library is "better served by refunds rather than extensions of the subscription period, because it will have to buy the missing issues anyway."[11]

The procedure is unacceptable, but the librarian or the agent who seeks refunds rather than an extended subscription is usually fighting a losing battle. An experienced agent, who did not want to be identified, explains why the publisher extends subscriptions rather than supply missing issues:

> Why is a publisher of a major publication reluctant to send claimed missing issues? The answer is simple. They have several million circulation with an average of 100,000 missing issue claims per issue. Legally they can extend your subscription one issue (or more) upon your claim. It costs them only 15 cents to keypunch a card for their computer to extend the subscription. On the other hand it costs an average of $1.15 to overprint say 100,000 issues for claims. The $1.15 includes the printing, holding extras in a warehouse, processing the claim in the warehouse, retrieving the issue from the shelf, wrapping and mailing it to the claimant. You can see why a circulation manager will choose to spend $15,000 against approximately $115,000 per month.[12]

Rising costs for paper, ink, printing, labor, binding, processing claims, warehousing, etc., no longer make it feasible for the publisher to overprint. On the contrary, this practice is regarded as a luxury only a few large publishers can afford. Where it is a matter of cutting corners to survive, the average publisher cuts corners. One way of doing this is, of course, to eliminate costly warehousing and overprinting charges by ignoring the matter of missing issues and their replacement.

Rising costs are, in fact, leading to technological changes in operation procedures. For instance, it becomes common to eliminate all overprinting, and to supply missing issues on microform; or, as suggested to replace hard copies altogether, except in the case of the more popular titles, with some form of micropublication.

In the meantime, the librarian is faced with the problem of claiming issues that the publisher does not have and the agent cannot locate. As one agent puts it: "Some few publishers check their list of subscribers to see if the claimant's name was on the list for that issue and, if so, merely state that the issue for that subscriber had been turned over to the post office and that ended their responsibility. I can see more and more of that happening in the future."[13] What is the agent or librarian to do in such cases? Nothing short of canceling what may be a needed subscription.

A related problem concerns the effort publishers make in cutting out "fat" in the overprinting they do. Here, it is imperative to have an accurate knowledge of how many copies will sell. This is done through control of sales and subscriptions; and while the former cannot be carefully controlled, the latter can be simply by requiring that subscriptions be placed further and further in advance. This may not be in keeping with library procedures, but if the library wants the subscription to begin with the first issue of a volume or the first issue of a year, the librarian must comply with the publisher's demand for advance subscriptions. Otherwise, of course, the necessary issues are missed and the publisher has no overprint copies with which to meet claims for these issues.

A further source of misunderstanding is that publishers often change their rate schedules without notifying the agent in advance or without considering standard renewal periods. The ALA *Guidelines* notes that, "Publishers should advise dealers of rate changes in advance of renewal time, if possible by August or September of each year."[14] Publishers with any sense of business procedure usually do make such announcements in advance, although in times of rapidly rising costs and inflation advance notice becomes virtually impossible. Price change follows upon price change and such changes can and do occur at any time of the year. It is even possible to have more than one change in a year's time, although this is not yet common.

Sudden price hikes result in the "bill backs" discussed elsewhere. Sad to say, such happenings are not confined to the workings of large publishers. The unannounced rate increase can be made without warning by any publisher at all, regardless of size or type of publication issued.

THE AGENT AND THE PUBLISHER

Why are there delays in subscriptions? Why are claims for missing issues ignored? Why, indeed.

The librarian usually puts the blame upon the agent. Direct experience and frustration with the publisher may bring the librarian to reconsider where the blame belongs. Certainly, some part of it can be ascribed to the publisher.

Fred Roessler, formerly of Maxwell International Subscription Agency, puts the matter this way:

> Please try to get across . . . that an agency is only a middleman and cannot control a publisher—that an agency in reality is just an extension of the acquisitions department of any library and really works for them, not the publisher. We get just as frustrated as the librarian who can't get service started or get that missing issue for them.[15]

The frustration is real enough. All efforts of a conscientious and hardworking agent to satisfy a library claim are frustrated by indifference or carelessness on the part of the publisher. It is true that the agent is a middleperson between the library and the publisher. It is true also that the agent has no legal way of forcing the publisher to honor a claim. The net result is the agent getting a good deal of unwarranted flack from librarians who fail to appreciate that sometimes even the best agents cannot make a publisher understand why the library needs or, for that matter, should receive a missing item. Clasquin states the agent's case in no uncertain terms:

> In behalf of the library client, the subscription agency can promise to forward to the publisher claims for materials not received. Note here that agency performance is limited to notification. In fact, any promise by the agent which implies performance beyond notification is illusory, because ultimate performance, i.e., the supply of the issues, is under the control of the publisher only.[16]

While it is only fair to recognize the position of the agent in relation to the publisher, one has a right to expect more than excuses from the agent. One major reason libraries employ agents is to expedite and speed claiming. Agents, on the whole, make a point of their services in this important area. And the majority of agents do make a considerable effort to satisfy claims. Possibly the average agent is a trifle defensive in the claims area because he or she has been cursed so many times by both librarians and publishers, and because good and bad agents sometimes use identical arguments for doing nothing. The excellent agent is, understandably, trying to get across the point that he is not a latter-day Mandrake the Magician who can produce missing items with a wave of the wand. The inept agent simply adds "Me, too," hiding his lack of action behind the better agent's well-constructed argument. The problem is that the librarian, whether of a skeptical frame of mind or not, can never be sure whether delay is attributable to lack of vigor on the part of the agent or to lack of interest on the part of the publisher.

Advice that better agents might well heed is to strengthen the arguments they use to justify claiming botchups, and the one way they can succeed in this is to reduce by whatever means the botchups that occur.

It has been pointed out that the agent has no direct control over the publisher. Yet the good agent exerts pressure on the publisher to supply missing issues, to straighten out snags in new subscriptions, etc. This can be done by thorough and timely follow-up by the agent on library claims for the missing items. The follow-up may take every conceivable path from standard forms to telephone calls to even, in extreme cases, threat of legal action.

The unspoken premise of the agent argument is that many publishers simply couldn't care less about the way their subscribers feel. The agent makes the point strongly enough showing what publishers fail to do when claims are entered. The reverse side of this position is that many publishers do want to please their subscribers, are, in fact, deeply concerned with keeping them happy. Here, for example, is circulation expert James Kobak speaking to publishers:

> My thesis is simple: subscribers are customers—and should be treated like customers. In fact, they are probably the most important customers you (the publisher) have. . . . Subscribers pay you money so that they can read your magazine, and they pay in advance—which helps your cash position. If they renew, they pay you again and again—and the expense of obtaining that renewal is much less than that of obtaining a new subscription. They are a source of other subscriptions. They form the loyal readership which you work so hard to sell to advertisers.[17]

Further proof is the feeling by a majority of agents who, conscientious in following through with claims, find that most publishers meet, or attempt to meet, these claims.

This is not to suggest that all publishers are conscientious and aware of library problems. Some, and more particularly the large publishers of commercial and general consumer magazines, are less than concerned about library problems—a small percentage, after all, of their millions of subscribers. The large publisher or the society or organization that supports nonprofit journals may be equally blind to the needs of libraries. Still, the publishers simply cannot be asked to take all of the blame for what failures occur. It is possible that some of the time, at least, the agent (or even the librarian) is to blame for the snags that come along.

REFERENCE NOTES

1. Andrew Osborn, *Serials Publications*, 2nd ed. (Chicago: American Library Association, 1973), p. 99.
2. Clara D. Brown, *Serials: Acquisitions and Maintenance* (Birmingham, Ala.: Ebsco Industries, 1971), p. 119.
3. Huibert Paul, "The Serials Librarian and the Journal Publisher," *Scholarly Publishing*, January 1972, p. 181.
4. "The Ultimate Do It Yourself," *Folio*, April 1973, p. 38.
5. ALA/RTSD, Acquisitions Section, "Guidelines for Publishers, Agents, and Librarians in Handling Library Orders for Serials and Periodicals" (Chicago: American Library Association, 1973), p. 4.
6. The interested librarian who would like to know more about fulfillment agents will find complete information, including an annotated directory of such agents, in *Folio*, January–February 1974, pp. 40–67.
7. Stanley Greenfield, "The Librarian . . . and the Subscription Agent," *Special Libraries*, July 1972, p. 299.

8. Henry Zwirner, "Can You Expect On Time Magazine Delivery," *Folio*, March–April 1974, p. 54.
9. *Ibid.*, p. 49.
10. J. J. Janson, "The Dating Game," *Folio*, June 1973, p. 6.
11. ALA/RTSD, *op. cit.*, p. 15.
12. Subscription agent (name withheld), letter to author, February 15, 1974.
13. Subscription agent, *op. cit.*
14. ALA/RTSD, *op. cit.*, p. 15.
15. Fred Roessler, General Manager, Maxwell International Subscription Agency, letter to the author, March 5, 1974.
16. Frank Clasquin, "The Claim Enigma for Serials and Journals," in *Management Problems in Serials Work*, ed. by Peter Spyers-Duran and Daniel Gore (Westport, Conn.: Greenwood Press, 1974), pp. 66–67.
17. James B. Kobak, "My Good Customer . . . ," *Folio*, January–February 1974, p. 41.

II.

SUBSCRIPTION AGENTS AND WHAT THEY DO

3.
SUBSCRIPTION AGENTS

Our survey of 850 various types of libraries throughout the United States revealed that some 95 percent employ one or more subscription agents. Why? There are numerous reasons, but essentially the agents' main purpose is to reduce the amount of paperwork the library must do in ordering and maintaining its subscriptions.

Instead of entering orders with hundreds or even thousands of individual publishers, the library uses one agent. This means a single order, a single invoice, a single payment, and a single source of most, if not all, periodicals. Furthermore, the agent renews subscriptions, offers a variety of purchasing plans, handles claims for missing or slow material, and proportionately offers a number of other services (enumerated throughout this guide). So much for the advantages. A number of librarians point out there are also a few drawbacks to the agency scheme of things. Cost is increasing and could eventually overtake any saving offered by the agent by way of discounts and the like. Again there is loss of contact with the publisher, and, beyond this, the dependence of the library on a single source can sometimes be a disaster, as when that source disappears (as with Richard Abel and Company). Other drawbacks will be pointed out later in this guide.

No matter how the librarian evaluates the advantages and disadvantages of the agency relationship, one major factor to be considered is method of operation of both librarian and agent. This factor, not often stressed, deserves attention. A university librarian fairly well sums up the matter of "personality":

Reaction to jobbers or dealers is both personal and accidental. Some librarians have excellent results, and others wish they had never run across a particular firm. I know that I have had that result myself. Some dealers have area managers who vary in quality and ability. What may be excellent in California may be inadequate in New York. . . . Other factors may include: change in library staff, promotion, or other separation from dealers, mergers and splits among and within individual jobbers, individual internal library administrations, and the lack of communication of dealer changes.

The variables outlined by this librarian are echoed in the response to the questionnaire used in the present study to determine the service capabilities and quality of various agents. While there was considerable consensus about one agent or another, a check of the findings will show that while 80 percent or more of librarians queried may rank an agent good to excellent, another 20 percent or so may find this same agent only fair to poor. Furthermore, no definite correlation can be established between size and type of library in the evaluations that are made. The only conclusion arrived at was that the personality—and all that implies—of the librarian and the agent is a dominant factor in satisfactory or unsatisfactory agent-library service.

Despite the apparently hopeless quest for the perfect subscription agency, the following statement is fair enough: "In general, an abundance of goodwill characterizes the relationship that exists between libraries on the one hand and the publishers and agents on the other."[1] This side of a total breakdown in the relationship between the agent and the library, what rifts there are tend to stem more from a moment of generated heat than a substantial and prolonged difference in point of view. It seems clear that the quality of service given the library by the agent is generally acceptable.

LEGAL RESPONSIBILITIES OF THE AGENT

Unless otherwise stipulated, the agent is legally bound to consider the order for the periodical from the library. Once accepted, the agent must enter the requested order with the publisher, and pay the publisher for the subscription. The library's legal responsibility is to pay for the subscription and to accept any additional charges levied by the agent for the service of entering the subscription with the publisher.

As Clasquin points out:

It is generally conceded that the agency-library relationship is only a contractual one and that any service above the normal contractual agreement of placing subscription orders, paying the publisher and billing the library, is merely a promise.... Once the subscriptions are placed, the publisher paid and the library billed, the agent most likely has fulfilled his contractual obligations, in which case his legal responsibility would end here.[2]

Somewhere in their advertising pieces, most agents include a statement similar to that of Ebsco Subscription Services:

Our Responsibility: Ebsco's obligation is to order subscriptions and service delivery or, if obtainable, substitution or refund. We guarantee entry and service of your order excepting publisher bankruptcy and other non-agent responsibilities. We cannot accept responsibility for government mails or final delivery. Our service after entry is prompt and exhaustive in securing timely delivery.[3]

Other agents produce similar statements not only to explain the scope of their responsibility but, in a real sense, to outline their legal obligation in the relationship with the library.

Agent legal obligations are important on two major counts. One, when a library or a governing authority insists on competitive bids from agents for serials, awareness is needed that the lowest bid generally represents an undertaking by the bidder to do nothing more than minimum legal requirements. Given no responsibility other than placing the order, the agent's overhead will be considerably lower than that of the agent who offers services that extend beyond legal requirements. And with a low overhead, it is not surprising that such an agent can undercut his or her competition. Two, reputable agents offer considerably more than is legally required. In this case, it is important for the library—whether it be bound by a bid system or not—to know precisely what those extra services consist of in terms of library needs. The low bid will have real meaning only when agents of equal repute offer equal services in their bidding.

The agent is *not* legally responsible for, among other things

1. Delivery of the item from the publisher, i.e., once the publisher is paid by the agent.
2. Refund of subscription money because the publisher fails to deliver, goes bankrupt, or abandons the wanted publication.
3. Timely delivery of any item from the publisher.
4. Delivery of missing issues in an otherwise continuous subscription-renewal situation.
5. Acting directly in claiming missing items or in claiming items that are not delivered initially after a subscription or order has been entered.

Because the publisher (as well as the mails) represents a third, even a fourth party, in the agent-library arrangement over which the agent has no control, no agent can guarantee items 1, 2, or 3. Conversely, some agents will promise, where available, to find missing issues, i.e., 4.

No law, however desirable from the librarian's viewpoint, is possible that covers the points enumerated above. There are too many variables, too many different areas of responsibility that are beyond the agent's control. For example, no law can guarantee timely delivery of an item when variables like the following exist: publisher's problems with the printer, mailing irregularities, the overlooking or skipping an issue by the publisher, mail delays, and errors in the addressing of an item.

One more major point: No agent is legally bound to supply the periodical ordered by the library. Many agents make a major effort to secure lost or otherwise not received titles for the library. On the other hand, the agent's responsibilities end when he pays the publisher. This point has led to more confusion and grief than almost any other in the library-agent relationship.

TYPES OF AGENCIES

In America, in the old days, serials were supplied primarily by book dealers. Beginning in the latter half of the nineteenth century, a few dealers began to add periodicals to their lists. By the end of World War I, interest in periodicals, grew, and certain bookmen gave an increasing amount of attention to their procurement.

Serials agents were operating at peak numbers in America in the period immediately following World War II. By the mid-1960s, however, higher costs of operating, coupled with fewer publisher discounts and the necessity for automation, drove many serials agents out of business or into mergers with larger concerns. The trend in the 1970s is toward fewer and fewer agents of larger and larger size, these providing more and more materials. For example, it was announced in the early part of July 1974 that Maxwell Scientific International had been purchased by Moore-Cottrell Subscription Agencies. Yet, while the number of existing domestic agents is not as great as it once was, considerable latitude remains to librarians in the choosing of agents.

Large Agencies

There are two giant library service subscription agents in America: Ebsco Subscription Services and F. W. Faxon Company. Between them, they handle approximately two-thirds of all subscriptions sold to libraries through agents. Of the two, Ebsco is the larger. Lacking any statistical data, our assumption of the difference in the amount of business is based pretty much on returns from librarians in the questionnaire and conversations with agents.

Faxon is primarily a subscription agency, although the firm publishes a number of books and the well-known magazine *Bulletin of Bibliography*. Established in 1886, Faxon has "been under the same family management for the last fifty-four years," according to a brochure on the firm's services. It, as does Ebsco, handles both American and international periodicals and a wide variety of other types of serials. The firm includes over 18,000 libraries among its customers.

Both Faxon and Ebsco serve all types of libraries, although Faxon tends to concentrate its efforts more strongly in the area of research and academic libraries than does Ebsco. The latter, however, has more customers among small school and public libraries. And both fairly well divide the business of the medium to large public library.

According to a recent brochure, Ebsco "evolved from a door-to-door magazine sales agency," begun in 1930 by Elton B. Stephens. It is now truly a conglomerate, having acquired along the way the Franklin Square Agency, a binder and cover operation, a point of sales division (bookcases, magazine racks, etc.), a printing and binding plant, a military service company, a field subscription agency, and an indoor advertising operation. It also has a door-to-door operation, Periodical Sales. In a letter to J. T. Stephens, president of Ebsco, observes that: "Our company is diversified and active in a number of fields. This gives us a financial strength which has enabled us to broaden our service to libraries."[4]

The key phrase here is "financial strength," and this is what sets both Ebsco and Faxon apart from other agencies. They have the resources to handle large numbers of subscriptions and an equally large number of serials. Furthermore, both have become leaders in automation of subscription services, and both have staffs considerably larger than those found in other agencies. The understandable result is that between them they control the vast majority of medium to large library accounts, and not a few smaller accounts.

Medium-Sized Agencies

There are approximately eight medium-sized domestic agents. The difficulty here is defining "medium-sized," although in broad terms the definition is used here in referring to agents mentioned most frequently by librarians after Ebsco and Faxon, and to those in whose catalogs or service brochures a considerable number of titles appear.

All medium-sized agents have two things in common: they offer a wide variety of services; and they serve all types of libraries everywhere in the United States. They differ from the two giants only in that some are automated and others are not and they tend to have smaller staffs. Nor are they likely to be able to supply as many titles—more particularly serials other than periodicals and international titles—as do the larger agents.

Medium-sized agents fall into two categories: international and academic and popular and domestic. The former consists of only one agent.

Stechert-Macmillan, founded in 1872 and until two years ago known as Stechert-Hafner, is particularly strong in series and nonperiodical serials. The firm is often used by academic and research libraries for international orders. However, in the past two years, it has made an effort to increase the scope of its business; and it now offers an increased number of services for purely domestic consumption.

Another medium-sized agency is Moore-Cottrell Subscription Agencies, a firm that has consolidated its position greatly through acquisition of Maxwell International Subscription Agency in mid-1974. Since the Moore-Cottrell takeover, three American agents continue to operate under the name of the Maxwell group of companies: Maxwell Scientific, Maxwell International, and Microforms International. As a whole, the company remains a force among firms with international dealings. It has branches in Canada, Mexico, Australia, France, England, and Germany. (Note: Where Maxwell is considered throughout this guide, the primary reference is to Maxwell International as a separate firm.)

Other medium-sized domestic agents are considerably less involved in international sales, although all do handle to a limited degree more popular international titles. Most concentrate on domestic sales. In order of relative size, they are Moore-Cottrell, Universal Periodical Services, McGregor Magazine Agency, Read-More Publications, Instructor Subscription Agency, and Turner Subscription Agency.

Small Agencies

Between the smaller medium-sized agencies, such as Turner, and larger small agents, such as Aquinas Subscription Agency, no firm line drawn until "small" is used to describe an agent with a limited number of titles; a staff of only the agent plus a clerk; and service limited to a specific geographical area and, usually, type of library. There are various estimates on the number of one-person agencies in America, but as of 1974 a fair figure would be between 150 and 200—about two or three per state, with a higher concentration in large urban areas.

International Agents

Larger libraries rely upon international agents for foreign subscriptions and other types of serials. The survey of librarians revealed that certain international agents or, more particularly those in Europe, enjoy a good to excellent reputation for service. Those mentioned most often are considered in detail in the Checklist; others are listed in the Directory.

Few nonacademic or small to medium-sized American libraries employ foreign agents "because of currency-exchange problems and language used in correspondence and on invoices. The problems do not, in actual practice, exist to any substantial degree."[5] Which is quite true, but it should be observed that in most cases foreign agents are not used because the larger domestic agents handle the foreign titles needed by all but the largest research library. More importantly, agents like Stechert-Macmillan—offer European service in considerable depth. Thus, the need to go overseas is felt by only very large libraries.

Ordinarily, when a library does employ a number of international agents it is because the library requires many non-European serials. There is without doubt some point in this instance in going directly to the country of publication. Foreign agents are excellent, and they often serve the dual purpose of acting as general subscription agents within their own countries and as exporters to foreign libraries.

By the same token, certain large American domestic agents serve foreign librarians with American titles. McGraw-Hill Export Subscription Agency, for instance, is one of these.

Special Agencies

Specialized subscription agents tend to concentrate upon one type of serial or serials limited to a certain subject area. Almost all of these agents depend upon academic and research libraries for business. Bernan Associates, for example, specializes in government periodicals and documents.

An equal number of international agents have specialties in terms of the country of issue or of subject area. Agents of this sort tend to be medium to large organizations, with complex, sophisticated systems of ordering and servicing serials. Also, many, such as Harrassowitz or Blackwell's, do an equally impressive business in other types of materials, more specifically, books.

There are still other agents, such as Kraus Periodicals Company, who deal in reprints and back issues. For the most part, these agents are not considered in this guide unless they offer a subscription service. This does not imply that they are unimportant; they are of great importance in their own area of operation.

Field Selling Agents

The Audit Bureau of Circulation, which literally audits the circulation claims (among other things) of major American magazine publishers, breaks down subscription agents into five categories: (1) catalog agencies and individual agents (the type discussed to this point); (2) a publisher's own salesmen; (3) independent agencies' salesmen; (4) newspaper agencies; and (5) members of schools, churches, fraternities, and similar organizations. All of these, with the exception of the first, go under the general name of "field agencies," and while differences in organization and method of operation exist among the four, essentially there is little to draw between one and the other.

Scope of titles. Most limit themselves to the sale of from fifty to one hundred mass circulation or semipopular titles.

Price of titles. All sell their fifty to one hundred titles at a discount of from thirty to fifty percent below the publisher's retail net price. (The average agency discount on periodicals is about 9.3 percent.)

Scope of business. Estimates vary, but approximately 42 percent of all subscriptions to the one hundred mass circulation magazines in America are handled by these subscription agents. Sales by such agents exceed $300 million a year.

There are literally thousands of door-to-door salespeople who qualify as field agents, but in library terms three types stand out.

1. Field agents that are subsidiaries or divisions of catalog agencies:

Ebsco Subscription Services. This firm has a three-part organization setup. The first consists of the field crew that saturates a neighborhood with door-to-door sales. The second is the part-time worker who sells to neighbors and friends. The third division sells a magazine-reading service consisting of magazine subscriptions, protective magazine covers, and magazine display stands. Examples of areas covered are doctors' offices, high school libraries, barber shops, beauty salons, hospitals, and sometimes public libraries. In the last instance, the library accepts the service as a gift of a local business, which agrees to pay for the subscriptions included in it. A 1972 report placed the volume of subscription sales of this division of Ebsco (then called Franklin Square Agency) at $25 million.[6]

Moore-Cottrell Subscription Agencies. This agency is a subsidiary of Perfect Subscription Company, which, in turn, is part of the Cadence Publishing & Publishing Services, which itself appears to be a division of Perfect Film and Chemical Company. Here, unlike Ebsco, the field agents operate under distinctive names, such as Solle's, Inc. of Minneapolis and Craig Farnsworth of Elnora. These are the only large to medium-sized catalog agents identified as having field agents, but there are others. It is important to stress that the agents are not making any secret of the work they do. Quite the contrary, both Ebsco and Moore-Cottrell (or, more properly, Perfect Subscription Company) are willing to explain in detail their operations.

2. Field agents whose primary effort is working directly for the publisher, although as independents.

Publishers Clearing House is by far the largest, and according to one report: "It mails estimated 150 million pieces annually. Grosses estimated $35 million in cut rate orders."[7] And in a *New York Times* advertisement directed to publishers the firm claims to "sell more magazine subscriptions than anyone else in the country."[8]

Educational Subscription Service. This agency is well known, as it floods schools and colleges with cards and brochures offering cut-rates on magazines. This firm has invented such terms as the "student courtesy rate" and the "faculty courtesy rate." It grosses some $1 to $2 million a year. In one respect, it differs radically from most field agents in that sales are made through the mails, not on a door-to-door basis.[9]

3. Field agents who work as a part of a publisher's sales force. Here, the publisher literally sets up his own field agent, rather than hiring an independent field agent, such as Ebsco or Publishers Clearing House.

An example is Family Publications Service, Inc. This is a subsidiary of Time-Fortune-Sports Illustrated, etc., and is responsible for special offers made through the mails or by phone or by door-to-door campaigns. Others are Periodical Publishers Service Bureau and International Magazine Service—both field agents specializing in Hearst publications.

Variations on the same theme go on indefinitely. It is common, for example, for a field agent to set up an arrangement by which magazines are sold on behalf of churches and fraternal organizations, and common, too, to create a sales force consisting of part-time salespersons such as housewives or students.

The average discount to the field agent is 80 to 90 percent of the publisher's retail net price. Given this huge discount, it is little wonder the agent can then sell the magazine at a 30 to 50 percent discount to an individual or library. Further financial ramifications depend upon the ingenuity and responsibility of the field agent. For example, X agent receives a title for $1, or 10 percent of the publisher's net price of $10. The agent then "fields" it to another individual agent or to a door-to-door salesperson for $2. That agent or salesperson may sell it directly, or set up a program to sell it to still another agent or salesperson who then sells it to the subscriber. And so it goes. Somehow the subscriber finds himself or herself paying only $5 for the title, or 50 percent of the regular price, and the agent receives $4 along the way for his efforts.

What is the value of this type of arrangement to the publisher, and what consequences does it have? The publisher of *The New Republic* (who does not give such discounts) replies:

> The value of this arrangement to publishers is that they don't spend any money to get a subscription, but they do have to fulfill the subscription. Taking into account only the production costs of the magazine (printing and paper) and ignoring other cost factors, fulfillment might cost 20 cents or so an issue, or for a weekly, over $10 per year on a $1.40 order (20 percent or $7). But why complain about it? Just don't do it, they say. All right, but this flood of half-price offers conditions the public, and makes it hard for those who need to sell at a sensible price. Fifty-nine years ago *The New Republic* sold at $5 per year, and since 1972 at $15. Has anything else gone up in price just 3 percent a year?[10]

Not only does the field agent's prices make it difficult for smaller magazines to compete with the big ones, but it sometimes makes it difficult for librarians to understand why only a minority of magazines (from sixty to one hundred) offer reasonably large discounts.

Catalog agents, i.e., those who serve libraries, receive similar discounts from publishers, although usually these are smaller than those granted field agents. However, the catalog agent is selling more than price. He or she is selling service, and while some small agents can pass on a 30 to 50 percent discount, most medium to large agents cannot compete in this way with the field agent.

Interestingly enough, the discount to an individual or a library on a title is unlikely to surpass 50 percent. The reason is that most periodicals use second-class mailing. In order to qualify for such a mailing, the publisher cannot offer his title at a discount of more than 50 percent of the net subscription price. But he can discount it in any amount when he "sells" it to an agent who sells it later to an individual.

That there is something wrong with this practice is discussed in some detail later. Suffice it to say here that this practice has backfired in the case of such mass circulation magazines, as *Life*, *Look*, and the *Saturday Evening Post*, all of which had hugely inflated circulation figures as a result of their almost literally giving subscriptions away.

The average field agent is called just that because he or she secures business by telephone or door-to-door visits. Most such agents do not call on libraries. Still, because of complex corporate relationships and the involved system of field selling agents, the librarian may never be sure in dealing with a one-person agency whether the agency is a catalog agency or a field agency. What difference does this make?

The typical field agent is interested only in entering an order, receiving payment for it, and departing. Service in such an instance is, to say the least, minimal. The arrangement tends to slow down the entry of subscriptions, as a fourth party, the field agent, has entered the picture. The usual triangle—library-agent-publisher—now becomes library-agent-agent-publisher. Moreover, the average field agent has even less control over a subscription than the smallest of independent agents who deal directly with the publisher.

Still, there are advantages in using field agents. One, of course, is that the librarian may expect rather substantial discounts, normally in the range of 30 to 50 percent. Overhead prevents larger agents from offering competitive discounts. Thus, if the library is interested primarily in having an order entered quickly and simply and can do without any additional service, the field agent may suit its purposes well enough. ("May" is used advisedly because the same discounts usually are available from small independent agents who offer something more in the way of service.)

When is a small independent agent (i.e., one working directly with a publisher) not a field agent? Unless otherwise indicated, most of the agents listed in this guide's Directory are independents. However, where there is any doubt the librarian should not hesitate to ask, particularly if he or she wants some assurance of good service.

The Deceptive Agent

The large, medium-sized, and most small subscription agents are honest, if not invariably the epitome of efficiency. Certain small agents (and more particularly the publisher's or the field selling agent), however, have been known to follow suspect business practices. It is not unheard of for some to take individual or library orders—including payment—and disappear without further word. Others have overcharged their customers flagrantly. And still others have promised a thousand and one services, yet found it difficult even to trace a single strayed subscription. The librarian who is *not* dealing with a well-known and reputable agent (most of whom, but certainly not all, are listed in the Directory) should automatically be on his or her guard to ward off fraud.

In the early 1970s, the Federal Trade Commission charged a number of publisher's agents with using "deceptive tactics to sell long term magazine subscriptions." Some of the deceptions practiced are

Misleading subscribers to believe they are getting free subscriptions.

Selling two- to five-year contracts for magazines at substantially higher than the retail rate.

Harassing nonpayers by threat of court action or adversely affecting the subscriber's credit rating.

Assuring buyers that subscriptions can be cancelled when, in fact, this is not permitted.

General failure to disclose the real cost of a magazine.

It is of interest to know the names of the companies involved: Civic Reading Club, Inc.; Educational Book Club, Inc.; Home Reference Library, Inc.; Home Reader Service, Inc.; Mutual Readers League, Inc. (all agents for Cowles Communication Company); Family Publications, Inc. (a *Time* publisher's agent); Periodical Publishers Service Bureau, Inc. and International Magazine Service (both agents for Hearst); and Perfect Film and Chemical Company and two of its agents, Perfect Subscription Company and Keystone Readers' Service, Inc. All the publishers involved denied the FTC charges.[11]

Other agents named in an FTC magazine sales inquiry in late 1970 were Interstate Publisher's Service; Local Readers Service and an affiliate, Literary Readers Service; Universal Reader's Service; Publishers Continental Sales Corporation; Subscription Bureau Ltd.; and Public Circulation Service. Again, denials were issued.

Much of this is reminiscent of the inquiry the FTC made previously into encyclopedia sales. The door-to-door salesman, who is sometimes described in brochures as giving Americans the "opportunity to subscribe to most of America's finest magazines," may or may not be the finest thing to happen to a reader.

AGENCY-LIBRARY RELATIONSHIPS

(*See* Section I of the checklist)

The single most frequent complaint librarians bring against agents is the lack of meaningful communication in the encounters they have with one another. This noncommunications takes many forms: the agent's apparent lack of interest in the library and its problems; the agent's failure to answer letters promptly; the agent's failure to acknowledge claims; the agent's failure to explain his other charges clearly; the agent's failure to . . . well, generally communicate with the librarian in a meaningful and useful way.

The agent, for his part, has a few complaints too. The librarian fails to notify the agent of claims on time to do anything about them, or enters needless claims. The librarian fails to keep records properly, and makes unnecessary and costly inquiries of the agent. The librarian holds up payment of an invoice. The librarian blames the agent for publisher vagaries and mistakes over which the agent has no control. The librarian fails, in turn, to communicate with the agent, especially about real problems as opposed to imaginary ones.

There are as many reasons for this communication breakdown as there are librarians and agents. Four broad explanations account for much of the trouble.

Automation has resulted in the all too familiar machine answer to queries from the librarian. If the agent's system accepts such questions, fine. If it does not, the librarian is left without a reply or a punched-card type of answer.

An agency is usually operated on a small profit margin. This can, of course, be eliminated if too much time and effort is spent in answering questions from libraries, even when the questions are good ones. On the other hand, too many agents tend to think of any question as needless and an expense to themselves that can be avoided through recourse to the wastepaper basket.

The agent, who understands and appreciates the third partner in the relationship—the publisher—does not always understand why the librarian is not equally familiar with the agent's difficulties in dealing with the publisher. Feeling that the librarian should be aware of the niceties of the case, the agent himself or herself offends by paying scant attention to such things as starting dates of orders, duplicates, missing issues, back orders, etc. The agent tends to respond to complaints about disruptions of any sort with the general excuse that the fault is not his, and nothing can be done to correct matters. There is some truth in such a reply, but the average librarian, anxious to get what users want, can hardly be expected to see it that way.

Finally, while major benefits are inherent in a library's working through a large, well-organized agent, there is also a penalty to be paid. The larger the agency, the less attention the average library problem is going to get, when that problem is only one of hundreds or thousands in a week's or month's work.

Agency Representatives

One of the major recommendations of a study of agents made by the New York Library Association was:

> That subscription agents make regular visits to their library customers or that they have area representatives. If they are unable to have an area representative, that they urge their customers to call them "Collect" when they have an emergency or pressing problem.[12]

Silence on the agency's part is a major complaint of librarians. Nientimp observes that in eight years of work with serials she talked to "several dozen representatives of library supply companies and binderies," but in that time only two came to see her in person about the services they had to offer.[13] Librarians do not want agents popping in every other day, but the vast majority would like to feel that representatives are available to help solve particular problems and to keep them posted concerning new developments and services as these appear. Such noncommunication produces a feeling among librarians that "the emphasis of the agency may be on obtaining new accounts rather than on keeping old clients happy."[14]

One librarian, responding to the questionnarie on agency services, adds a note that fairly well sums up why it is that many librarians equate good service

44 Guide to Magazine and Serial Agents

with personalized service. The librarian, who obtains some 500 titles through agents, states:

> Maxwell is excellent. Our satisfaction is due to the work of Mr. Fred Roessler, the local agent, and his office manager Mrs. Bertha Lane. They are both very, very good—hard workers who really care. Mr. Roessler and Mrs. Lane have served in this area as representatives of several different companies. If services get poor (as often happens when a company gets taken over by a conglomerate) Mr. Roessler takes himself and Mrs. Lane to another company, and continues as good a service as he can give.

Other librarians add such comments as "Our relationship with Ebsco is a little better, probably because of closer proximity to the agent." A public librarian observes: "Ebsco is responsive to complaints and attentive to requests." And a large university noted that "Faxon's direct dial, no toll service is very good."

Despite what seems to be a general complaint by many librarians, agents counter that they have representatives who call upon libraries at regular intervals. Precisely how often the representative calls and how personalized the service he or she gives depends upon the type and size of the agency.

The two largest agents, Faxon and Ebsco, have district offices. Ebsco, in fact, has a network of ten such offices throughout the United States. And, to be sure, the representatives of both firms spend a considerable amount of time and effort in calling on libraries and in attending library meetings of all sorts. Of the other half dozen medium-sized to large agents, each has account executives and representatives who periodically call on customers. As for the agents that are neither very big nor very small, such as Turner Subscription Agency and Instructor Subscription Agency, these do not hire area representatives. Nor, for that matter, do the specialized agents, such as China Books. The small agent who accounts for about one-third of the orders entered by the librarians tends to serve only a limited geographical area. Here business is built upon personal contact with librarians.

Parenthetically, no librarian expects an international agent to have representatives calling on him or her regularly. Still, Swets & Zeitlinger and Blackwell's are represented in the United States, although on a limited scale.

Under the circumstances, the librarians might consider how the agent views representation, or its lack. Representation is expensive, particularly when it requires regularly scheduled visits. It may be a necessary item for the small one-man and one-woman agencies, but larger agents must ask themselves whether it is better to spend X dollars for what is essentially public relations or X dollars to improve services. Most, naturally enough, opt for the latter decision—and, if anything, the number of representatives working for large agencies in the years ahead is likely to decline rather than to increase.

Direct Calls

Eliminating or drastically cutting back on personalized service through a representative is balanced by the larger agents in permitting the library to make collect telephone calls to the agent (in some cases, the process is reversed). Add to this the convenience of TWX, Telex, etc., and the real need for a representative, or so the argument goes, is negligible. Interestingly enough, agents who fall between the largest and the smallest in size are not likely to accept collect calls. The small agent, in serving a limited area, is quite likely to offer collect calls as a regular service.

In many ways, the ability of the library to contact the agent by telephone is preferable to having a representative of the agent at hand. Why? Well, as one large agent explained:

> All of the records of orders, claims, etc., are at the headquarters of the agency. The local rep can do little for the library with a problem until he or she, in turn, has called his office. Why not simply have the librarian call, and eliminate the confusion of the middleperson? The local rep may personalize service, but usually he or she is not going to make it any better.

Add to this service a procedure whereby the librarian is given the name of an individual to call—and not simply an unnamed voice at the end of the phone—and the argument has considerable merit.

Still, as rational as is the argument for the substitution of a telephone, TWX, or some other technological device for the appearance in person of an agent's representative, it lacks conviction for the serials librarian who wants to think of herself as something more than a name on an annual order.

Agency Correspondence

One of the commonest complaints librarians make is that the agent fails to answer their mail promptly. If the agent is to be believed, this is not the case; or, to be more precise, this is not the case in terms of general agent policy and procedures. All agents claim to answer all inquiries from libraries. Still, when the "inquiry" concerns specific orders or claims, the quality of the answer is often suspect. A computer acknowledgment that the inquiry is being attended to, for instance, is not precisely what the librarian wants.

There is no real consensus as to when, or to what type of inquiries, the agent will respond or how long it takes to get a response. The librarian who wants an answer to a specific question should so indicate in the query, and yet be aware that some agents are more prompt in replying than are others. In no case—this side of years of experience with the agent—should the librarian take it for granted that an answer to a query will be forthcoming from one day to the next.

> It is very disconcerting for a serials librarian to see so many unanswered letters in the open correspondence file. When two or three letters are sent to an agent and four to six weeks elapse without a reply, the librarian begins to wonder if the agency is really still there.[15]

Record Information

Every agent agrees to provide certain record information, such as the library purchase order number, in all letters, invoices, etc., he sends out. In general, however, requirements of this sort should be specified by the librarian, if possible at the time the initial order goes out.

When a question arises as to whether or not a publisher has been paid for a subscription, or as to when payment was made and for what period, the agent should be able to provide all necessary information. This usually includes the library and agent check numbers and dates, and may also include, if necessary, photocopies of both back and front of the cancelled checks. It is of considerable importance that this service be available to the librarian on demand. It is not unknown for a less than reputable agent or publisher to deposit a library check to his or her own account without the necessary next step of supplying the paid-for titles. The possibility cannot be ignored either that employee incompetence, or even dishonesty, may exist in the publisher's or agent's office.

Where a bid is required, the librarian should make certain that provision for supplying such information on demand is included in the bid requirements. This is particularly necessary, of course, when the librarian is dealing with an agent who is not known to the librarian.

Another type of record information is important to librarians. Agents undertake to assist in straightening out the fill in information such as the name and address of the publisher, inadvertently omitted from library orders or claims. Agents who have catalogs listing the requested titles encounter little difficulty in doing so. In cases where the agent's catalog is small or the item being ordered is new or obscure, however, the librarian should be aware of just what the agent is able to provide by way of bibliographic verification.

All agents say that they do quite a bit of such work. But how much "quite a bit" really amounts to depends upon the number and kind of reference works to which the agent has access.

REFERENCE NOTES

1. Peter Gellatly, "Acquiring Serials in Large Libraries," *Serial Publications in Large Libraries*, ed. by Walter Allen (Urbana: University of Illinois Graduate School of Library Science, 1970), p. 44.
2. Frank Clasquin, quoted in Timothy W. Sineath, "Libraries and Library Subscription Agencies," *The Library Scene*, Summer 1972, p. 30.
3. *Librarians' Handbook*, (Birmingham: Ebsco, 1973), p. 3.
4. J. T. Stephens, President of Ebsco, letter to author, February 8, 1974.
5. *International Subscription Agents*, 2nd. ed. (Chicago: American Library Association, 1969), p. 3.
6. Robert J. Myers, "Cancelling Cut Rate Subscriptions," *Folio*, November-December 1972, pp. 68-69.
7. *Ibid.*
8. *New York Times*, May 23, 1974, p. 47.
9. *Ibid.*, August 10, 1971, p. 41.
10. Myers, *op. cit.*, p. 69.
11. *Wall Street Journal*, June 2, 1970, p. 40; August 24, 1970, p. 22. See also *New York Times*, December 17, 1970, p. 49; July 2, 1971, p. 61.
12. "Report on a Survey of Subscription Agents Used by Libraries in New York

State" (New York: New York Library Association, 1970), p. 12. A processed 12-page report.
13. Judith Nientimp, "The Librarian . . . and the Subscription Agent," *Special Libraries*, July 1972, pp. 296-297.
14. *Ibid.*, p. 297.
15. *Ibid.*, p. 294.

4.
AGENCY SERVICES

Every subscription agent is understandably convinced that he or she offers better service than his or her competitors do. And, in fact, some agents do offer special services. Most of these services offered are, to be sure, an outgrowth of size and not necessarily unique to this or that agent. For example, annual review lists are desirable, as are various special order plans, but these are offered almost as a matter of course by medium-sized and large agents. The question the librarian must ask when agents correspond in size and quality of service offered is: What does X agent offer that Y does not?

While this question is answered in many ways throughout the book (in point-by-point detail in the Checklist), we are tackling the question in preliminary style here. What follows are unique services in that they are offered usually by one agent and by never more than three—at least in the way described. Hints are given also as to desirable services not offered by agents, or by so few as to limit severely the choice librarians have in selecting an agent.

SERIALS CATALOGS

Only two domestic agents, Faxon and Ebsco, issue *comprehensive* catalogs of periodicals. (Richard Abel & Company, now defunct, issued an equally fine catalog of nonperiodical serials.) Other agents tend to concentrate on the more popular titles in their catalogs, or, in the case of specialized agents, issue catalogs of specialized materials. The annual Ebsco and Faxon catalogs list alphabetically from 50,000 to 60,000 titles. They contain considerable information and, as such, can serve as valuable bibliographical aids. (The Faxon catalog is free to all librarians; Ebsco charges noncustomers a fee.) Both catalogs list the following information: full title of the periodical, retail price (in cases where two- or three-year rates are available, these are given), and frequency.

Ebsco supplements the above with nation of origin (Faxon simply indicates "F" for foreign); additional postage charges; and information on renewals, title pages, supplements, indexes, "no cancellations," etc.

The Faxon catalog offers slightly different information. A note is given on availability of title pages and indexes. (This information may or may not be found in the Ebsco catalog. Faxon's procedure is more systematic.) Volume information, i.e., the beginning date of a volume, is listed, as is information concerning indexes and abstracting services in which an item is taken account of. In each case, the item is described in fully up-to-date fashion. A "key code" (which, incidentally, provides access to much of the special information found in Ebsco) elicits such comments as "annual bill later periodical" and "slow bill later periodical."

Both catalogs are products of computer files. Both are easy to use, and as each has particular contents not found in the other, large libraries do well to have both on hand.

McGregor's catalog, among those of medium-sized agents, although smaller, yet contains a considerable amount of information, from index data to cancellation policies of publishers. Universal Periodical Services follows suit fairly much in its catalog, as do, for that matter, most other middle-sized agents.

Small one-man or one-woman agencies, when they do issue catalogs or lists (not all do), usually limit information to title and price.

MISSING AND BACK ISSUES

The majority of agents, will not, cannot, or, so they say often enough, should not be responsible for filling in missing issues when their claims fail. Normally, the librarian can only fume in such a circumstance. He or she may

1. Request the agent to try to secure the missing item from the publisher, and pay the publisher, if necessary, for the item. This rarely works because the publisher who could not meet a claim is not likely to meet a request—even with the prospect of collecting an added fee—for a back issue.

2. Ask the agent to try to secure the missing title from a back-issues dealer. Most agents will not do this. The Checklist indicates which agents will attempt to supply back issues.

3. Forget the agent and go directly to a back-issues dealer.

Other alternatives are to order the item in microform or to wait until the volume is complete, and then order the whole volume in microform or in reprint, if either is available. (Some agents will order microforms or reprints of missing items, but they invariably charge the library for this service.)

Many agents argue convincingly that it is practically impossible for the agent to guarantee replacement of missing items. This is the response from all large domestic and most large international agents.

The agent is, of course, free of any legal responsibility to reimburse the library for missing issues. No agent will make such a reimbursement unless error on his part can be shown or unless the publisher reimburses the agent in the matter. In the latter instance, it is usual for the agent to pass the refund along to the library. But both conditions are rare. Any financial loss incurred must be borne by the library.

The librarian asks: Is there not at least moral responsibility on the part of the agent here? The agent has accepted the order and, coincidentally, the profit the order brings. Should not then the agent make an effort to do more than generally happens to locate and pay for missing issues? These are reasonable questions. Most agents reply with what they consider equally reasonable answers. They will assist the library to enter claims through the agency. Indeed, when pressed themselves, they press the publishers to meet the claims. Furthermore, they act as the middleperson between the publisher and library in straightening out misunderstandings that arise over claims.

Just how vigorously the agent proceeds in these matters accounts for the difference between good and excellent service. At the time the Checklist was compiled, only three agents offered to replace missing issues: Maxwell, China Books and Periodicals, and Chinese Materials and Research Aids Service Center. With Moore-Cottrell purchase of Maxwell in mid-1974, its service is likely to be discontinued. The other two agents are able to make the offer only because the number of titles they supply is small.

Back Issues[1]

(*See* Section VI F of the Checklist)

At one time or another, almost every library finds that it requires back issues of periodicals. The need comes about as a result of losing or missing issues in an ongoing subscription or of subscribing to a title only after the early issues have gone out of print.

Of what help is a subscription agent when either of these conditions holds? Most agents, as indicated in the section on claims, make an effort to secure missing issues lost as a subscription proceeds. However, only Maxwell International guarantees to supply such issues free of charge. Most agents, too, will attempt to secure the earlier issues of a volume that a library misses when the subscription begins with the second or third issue of an ongoing volume.

Beyond this point, very few agents are willing to go. The back issue, o.p. reprint, microform trade stands apart as a separate entity from the subscription business. An exception occurs in the case of those agents who order such material when it is readily available through normal trade channels. One agent, among domestic agents, has an active back-issues division. Maxwell International is, according to a company brochure: "One of the world's largest back issue houses which stocks many millions of back issues. Therefore, we have the best facility for obtaining and supplying back numbers of all leading periodicals, whether the requirements are for single issues or completed years of volumes of journals no longer available from the original publisher." No other domestic subscription agent offers such a service and how long it will continue in this instance remains to be seen.

Most international agents have large back-issues departments. Swets & Zeitlinger, Harrassowitz, and Blackwell's, to name only three, conduct an impressive amount of business in the back-issues area. The average domestic agent, however, finds back-issues work unprofitable; and even those who deal heavily in nonperiodical serials, as, for example, Stechert-Macmillan, do not offer back-issues service.

There is some advantage certainly in dealing with an agent who handles back issues. If, say, the librarian enters in June an order for title X, a monthly that begins in January, the agent may or may not try to get for the librarian the issues of the first part of the year. If not, the librarian is forced to send out other orders or to make other arrangements. Conversely, the agent with a back-orders service which often enough finds the needed issues on a shelf in its own warehouse.

Even though agents who deal in back issues generally offer reprints and microforms as well as hard copy publications, they cannot always meet the needs of the library for out-of-print materials. Normally, in this instance, the librarian resorts to tactics that are familiar in the book trade.

> The acquisition of back-files of serials is as closely related to the purchase of out-of-print books as it is to subscriptions and standing orders.... Librarians can work with dealers through their catalogs or through direct correspondence. Librarians usually send requests for quotations to several dealers, although some libraries place their wants with only one dealer at a time.[2]

The Directory in this guide lists some out-of-print agents who specialize in this area, and elsewhere there are references to guides and bibliographies that help the librarian to locate dealers in reprints and microforms. There are two major sources for back issues that are sometimes overlooked:

The publisher. Agents are so fond of pointing out the dereliction of publishers in not keeping back issues that many librarians tend to ascribe this fault to all publishers, and not just to the mass circulation publisher, the only real offender. Other smaller and specialized publishers generally keep at least a limited supply of back issues.

> The practice of assuming that any periodical set or issue, save those of the last year or so, are out-of-print can be a costly one. Certainly the assumption is correct more often than not, but any doubt can be removed by the simple practice of putting in a request for available back sets (to the publisher, or through the subscription agent.)[3]

More than one librarian has been shocked to find that a back-issues dealer or reprint firm is charging double or three times the price for a set of periodicals that may still be obtained at the original price of publication from the publisher. (As of early 1975, the *minimum* charge for any back issue was $3.50.) Outside the mass circulation area, a safe assumption to make is that the publisher has a run of the journal for at least five years back. Some publishers may even have complete sets running back ten, fifteen or twenty years, but this is rare.

The United States Book Exchange (33354 V Street, N.E., Washington, D.C. 20028). Libraries pay a nominal sum for membership in this nonprofit organization. In return, they may purchase periodicals (and books) from the USBE at prices that, though inevitably rising, remain lower than those offered elsewhere.[4] The USBE has proved a boon to librarians. It has its limitations. For instance, it is usually not the best place to go if one wishes to locate scarce, costly materials. Still, it offers libraries a fairly economical means of securing back issues.

A third source of back issues, one not normally considered by some librarians, is suggested by Isabel Jackson:

> In attempting to fill in issues or sets of the periodical publications of profes-

sional societies, contact with an officer or member of a local branch can be productive. It would be difficult to estimate the number of scientists and engineers whose wives will rejoice at the thought of finally emptying the garage of all the journals and transactions which their husbands can't decide to bind or to throw away.[5]

BLANKET AND CONSOLIDATED ORDERS

Blanket-Order and Approval Plans

(*See* Section VIII C of the Checklist)

A blanket-order plan is one whereby the agent selects serials for the library. Selection is based upon a profile of library needs given the agent by the library. The agent selects an item, keeping in mind the scope, purpose, and audience of the plan. Then, without notifying or querying the library, the agent automatically sends the item, or arranges to have it sent, to the library. Approval plans are precisely the same, but have a built-in "approval" clause, that is, the librarian may reject an item the agent selects.

The chief advantage of the blanket-order plan is that it provides material quickly and sometimes at less cost than is otherwise possible. The plan assures, to a reasonable degree at least, that the library will receive at the time of publication everything its profile specifies. Drawbacks exist, of course, but these will not be dealt with here.

Sometimes agents and librarians confuse the blanket order with the standing order. These differ in that the standing order is for specific titles in a series or continuation. The blanket order is for everything published by X or Y publisher; or, as indicated, everything selected to match a library profile. Most agents who handle serials other than periodicals have standing-order plans; and, if the questionnaire used in this study is an indicator, just as many of these agents confuse the two plans. A number of agents, for example, replied that they had blanket-order plans, only to modify the answer by explaining the plan was really a standing-order plan for a given serial.

No agent, domestic or international, provides blanket-order plans for periodicals, but Harrassowitz and Swets & Zeitlinger do send sample copies of a periodical automatically to a library when that library has indicated an interest in a given subject area or country.

When the blanket order or approval plan is used in ordering serials other than periodicals, and more particularly monographic series, a number of agents step into the breach. Among domestic agents, there are Maxwell and Stechert-Macmillan. Smaller agents such as China Books and Periodicals, have similar limited blanket-order plans.

International agents frequently report blanket-order plans for nonperiodical serials. These include Blackwells, Harrassowitz, Swets & Zeitlinger, and many others.

As appealing as it may be to adopt the blanket-order idea in the supplying of periodicals, no agent has been able to surmount the technical difficulties that this sort implies. The book dealer is able to offer blanket-order plans because there are advance reviews of books, and the dealer may actually examine the book before deciding to send it to the library. Furthermore, the library has the option under an approval plan of returning the book. This chain presupposes that the title is usually sent to the dealer and then to the library, or alternatively, that there is considerable knowledge of the title on the dealer's part. The subscription agent has no way of gathering together new periodicals because of publication vagaries in this field. Nor does he or she even have access to advance descriptions of new periodicals.

The lack of enthusiasm evinced both by the average subscription agency and the librarian for blanket orders for periodicals is summed up by William Huff:

> Blanket orders for serials have not been found as dependable as the straight standing order for a title. The idea is deceptively simple at first glance; however, blanket orders create selection problems, budgeting problems, claiming problems, and most of all, add to a lessening of bibliographical control of serials. . . . Exclusive of publications received on institutionally affiliate memberships in societies, associations etc. twenty-seven libraries (out of 49) said they did not use blanket orders in acquiring serials; eighteen said they did. . . . Of those using blanket orders, ten libraries used them with commercial presses and thirteen with university presses.[6]

At present it is not possible to place a blanket order for periodicals with a subscription agency. Other serials, however, may be obtained through a blanket-order or approval plan.

What blanket orders there are for serials are sent for the most part, directly to the publisher rather than to an agency. Under this arrangement, the publisher sends everything he issues in certain fields, or, in some cases, all of his publications. If a foreign program is considered, it may be limited to materials from certain publishers or areas or to materials on certain subjects or in certain languages, etc.

Although no domestic subscription agent has blanket-order or approval plans for periodicals, several seem interested in setting up an operation. Here are replies from agents: *Ebsco*: We would be glad to make a proposal to any interested library. *Maxwell*: Titles would be automatically sent to a library for one year and billed as per arrangement with the library. Also would be glad to select titles by subject or by geographical area. Interested libraries should inquire. *Read-More*: This appears to be a good idea, but we believe the budget picture would have to improve considerably for many libraries before such a plan could be instituted. *Turner*: If the library thought it feasible, we would establish a blanket order or approval plan.

Apparently this is an area worth exploring, but libraries entertaining it must be prepared to pay for the extra work required on the part of the agent or make an arrangement according to which costs are reduced by encouraging participation in a plan by a group of libraries. There is latitude here for creative thinking by both librarians and agents.

If there is interest in this particular idea, less of it is shown in what looks like a reasonable plan for solving some of the problems periodicals, especially those of other than daily or weekly frequence, give rise to. This is the consolidated-order plan.

Consolidated Orders

(*See* Section VIII D of the Checklist)

Most problems connected with periodicals occur because no one, other than the librarian assumes responsibility for having the periodical reach its proper place on the shelf. Agents help, as they can, but what they do is little enough.

Essentially, under a consolidated-order plan, the agent would take full responsibility for the titles supplied. He or she would, quite literally, consolidate library orders before sending out titles to a library. Such an arrangement might cause some delay in having the titles reach the library, but could be used to good effect in obtaining foreign publications and in dealing with difficult publishers. This plan might be expected to eliminate missing issues, delay in the entering of subscriptions, etc. The agent, in effect, would take over part of the work now done by the librarian. Ideally, the librarian would only have to unpack the order, and place the titles on the shelf. (It must be added, of course, that this is not an ideal world.)

No domestic agent consolidates orders for periodicals. Stechert-Macmillan receives some *nonperiodical* serials directly from the publisher and consolidates orders for such serials for the library. There are, however, some international agents who do the same in the case of periodicals.

Such a service works in the following way: The library orders the periodicals through the agent. The agent receives the periodicals directly from the publisher. Then the periodicals are made shelf-ready as follows: the agent claims periodicals not received; after a given amount of time, the library is notified about the claims; call numbers are affixed to serials; the agent pastes on the periodical's cover a label that gives ISSN or some other identifier, the library's routing instructions, and stamping and dating as requested by the library; the library is provided with a copy of the check-in record; the periodicals are sent to the library; the agent handles customs clearance and ensures delivery; the agent assumes responsibility for exchanges; and the agent sends binding instructions at the proper time.

This outline represents an oversimplification of what is bound to constitute a complex procedural and organizational matter, and is given only to suggest the parameters of a possible consolidated-order plan. It would take another book to explore the complexities that such a scheme would create for agent and librarian alike—to say nothing of the publisher.

A quick check will indicate that a consolidated-order plan of the sort suggested might eliminate library claims, missing issues, faulty substarts, etc. At this point, however, no agent is willing to take over, as would be required, many tasks now performed by serials librarians. Beyond this, the notion appalls some librarians, who regard it as another step in the whittling away of their responsibilities. Objections aside, however, the plan, once activated, might well solve certain perennially aggravating problems.

Among international agents—as, for example, Harrassowitz, Martinius Nijhoff, and Swets & Zeitlinger—it is normal for the agent to collect and ship in a lot periodicals that are likely to cause claiming difficulties. Those titles not likely to present a problem are mailed directly from the publisher's plant.

On the other hand, with the possible exception of Swets & Zeitlinger, which is developing a rather sophisticated consolidated-order plan for the National Agricultural Library, no international agent comes close to meeting the requirements of the consolidated order, as these have been outlined. The reason such a procedure is possible in Europe and throughout much of the rest of the world is that many European publishers make bulk shipments of titles to the agents with whom they deal. The agent in this instance quite literally sells the magazine (from newsstands, to libraries, and to individuals) for the publisher. The agents make their own sales, maintain their own lists of subscribers, and serve as combination fulfillment agents and circulation managers for the publisher.

In the United States no agent serves in this capacity unless, as in the case of Stechert-Macmillan, it is in connection with serials other than periodicals. When agents bothered to comment on what most consider a pie-in-the-sky proposal, the comments were enlightening:

Read-More: The consolidated order plan is not likely in the near future. The cost to the librarians with the limited discount given by publishers would be prohibitive.

Swets & Zeitlinger [Asked about the cost of such total service] : The question is impossible to answer. The added charges would depend on what serial functions we would be asked to take over, the geographical location of the library, and the journal mix of the account.

Maxwell: We would be willing to consider such a plan, but only after consultation with a library.

Moore-Cottrell: The agent might consider for a price. All of this could be performed but the cost would possibly be high or higher as if the library itself were to perform them. Feasible—yes. Advisable—only under special conditions such as air freighting or need to separate operational costs of acquisitions from the rest of the library budget.

Faxon: We provided this service for China Medical Board for some 24 separate medical libraries after World War II for a fee. Additional warehousing, label, crating, customs, shipping, etc. cost approximately six times the basic published rates of the journals. The program was phased out approximately 7 years ago. In order to consider such a program again there would be the necessity to seriously re-evaluate costs.

Martinius Nijhoff [Explaining the normal practice for at least some periodicals when ordered from an international agent] : "We collect and ship periodicals which tend to give problems rather than to have these sent direct." [This is not unusual for many countries, but it should be emphasized it is only for "problem" periodicals.]

MISCELLANEOUS SERVICES AND PROCEDURES

Binding

(*See* Section VIII B of the Checklist)

There are a few domestic and international agents who offer the library some binding services. Among international agents, such as Blackwell's and Swets

& Zeitlinger, the binding is done usually in the case of books, backsets, and nonperiodical serials. Domestic agents offer the same general service, although fewer domestic agents than foreign have binderies on their premises.

What often happens is that the agent provides unbound issues during the course of the year, and a bound set at the end of the year. This arrangement demands two subscriptions (and, of course, an added charge for the binding). Its advantage is that while the unbound issues of more heavily used periodicals may be lost or damaged as the year wears on, the librarian is assured at its end of having a complete bound set at his or her disposal. The arrangement also spares the librarian the time and effort needed to see to the binding himself or herself. Ebsco, Maxwell, and Stechert-Macmillan provide this service here, as does Blackwell's abroad. Swets & Zeitlinger notes that the usual binding service offered by international agents is limited to backsets.

An alternative Maxwell makes available at the end of the year is issuing necessary volumes in microform. Outside of the agency field, a similar service is offered by such firms as University Microfilms, which has standing arrangements with certain publishers to provide microforms of a past run of a given serial, periodical, or newspaper. In this situation, the publisher requires that the library have a standing or until-forbid order for the individual issues of the hard-copy edition of the item in addition to its microform subscription. Several publishers actually provide this sort of service directly to the library. The difficulty here is that most of the microforms do not reach the library until three to six months after the completion of the regular edition.

The advantages and the disadvantages of substituting microforms for binding of hard copies are rife. In general, microforms make a good substitute for newspapers, for little-used journals, and certainly for a vast number of government documents. Nor is there any question of the validity of using microforms in place of out-of-print and difficult-to-locate back issues. Still, the average librarian has yet to be convinced (as does the poor reader) that bound periodicals should be abandoned in favor of microform substitutes. Whenever possible, originals of frequently used journals and serials should be retained by the library.

Sample Copies Geared to Library Interests

(*See* Section VIII A of the Checklist)

Some agents offer to send sample copies to libraries on speculation once the library has submitted an interest profile to the agent. Swets & Zeitlinger and Harrassowitz, for example, send samples automatically if the subject of the sample falls within the library's profile. Most of the medium-sized to large domestic agents will request samples from a publisher for a library, but the library must specify the exact title and indicate whether or not it is willing to pay for the sample. It must be said, however, that normally time and effort are saved when the librarian orders the sample directly from the publisher.

Forms

A major recommendation of the New York Library Association survey of library–agency relations is

The subscription agents develop expeditious ways within the agency through the standardization of forms and procedures for handling correspondence, cancellations, and adjustments.[7]

Larger agents, and more particularly those with automated systems such as Faxon and Ebsco, have standardized forms they offer to libraries. This they do as much out of a desire to serve the library as to meet the needs of their own computer programs. There are forms for use in everything from ordering to claiming and the adjusting of invoices. The smaller agent tends to leave the matter of forms up to individual libraries.

The advantages that preprinted forms bring may be considerable to some libraries and of little value to others. The obvious comparison is the availability of preprinted catalog cards, which, for all sorts of reasons, one library may find useful while another does not. If the library can save time and energy, not to mention printing costs by using agent forms, it might as well use them.

When the agent uses automated records, the forms are compatible with the agency's computer programs. Librarians should be certain that the forms are equally compatible with their library's own procedures, whether automated or not. It should be pointed out, of course, that failure to use the agency forms may delay orders and claims. Whenever doubt exists concerning the sort of form to be used for most efficient service, the librarian should consider how much modification if any, can be made reasonably by the agency in its forms or by the library in its own. A few years ago, such a consideration might have seemed of little consequence, but as agents grow fewer, and as the remaining ones come to depend more and more upon automation, the use of forms poses a real problem. When the agent will not or cannot modify forms (for "forms" read "procedures") to suit individual library needs, the librarian had better look for another agent or else modify his or her own methods somewhat.

The mundane form, then, points up a major potential difficulty between library and agent. Moreover, the difficulty will surely be exacerbated as forms, i.e., computer programs, proliferate. One can only imagine what the future state of agency-library relations will be if compatibility is lacking in wholesale fashion among automated agencies and libraries.

The obvious way out of the difficulty lies in standardization of forms and, beyond that, eventual standardization of routines and procedures. Heretofore, no possibility of the sort existed. It may be, however, that automation in this area, as in so many others, will quite literally force standardization upon libraries and upon agents.

Neither domestic nor international agents have any strong preference as to whether the agency form or the library form should be used in any particular instance. Most agents contacted say that the decision is up to the library.

In general, smaller libraries should use the agent's forms, at least while circumstances permit. The obvious exception occurs in cases in which local law requires use of a preprinted purchase order form. Larger libraries working through agents should use agency forms or consult with the agent about use of the library order and claim forms. This latter step is particularly advisable when the agent is turning to automation. If the agent does not offer forms, the librarian should make certain that information necessary to the agent is included in the library forms.

ISSN and LC Card Numbers

The Library of Congress book numbering system for periodicals and other types of serials, as differentiated from the call number, is the unique number assigned by the LC to differentiate one title from another, and to provide librarians with a handy reference device in the ordering of LC cards. Readers are familiar with the LC number, as it is normally printed on the verso of most title pages in books and nonperiodical serials. It is not usually found in periodicals.

The ISBN (International Standard Book Number) is also becoming familiar. Since the late 1960s, it, too, has been appearing on the verso of the title page. Again, though, it is not usually found in periodicals and nonbook serials. A version of the ISBN for serials is the ISSN (International Standard Serial Number). One or the other is assigned as the book or the first issue of the serial is published.

Today the ISSN is primarily used internally by agents and publishers as a control device. It is also an important element in the National Serials Data Program of the three national libraries (LC, Agriculture, and Medicine) and in the development of the ISSN system as a central machine-readable source of serials cataloging information. No matter what its eventual use in automated systems, the ISSN provides a long sought for means of describing serials separately and uniquely. Furthermore, the ISSN will probably replace the LC card number, although this is an area of furious debate among cataloging experts, not to mention publishers and other librarians.

No agent, domestic or international, requires a library to put on its orders the LC card number for a periodical or serial. Nor does any agent ask for the ISSN. As a method of rapid identification of serials with similar or identical titles, however, either number is of value to the agent.

Automation and Subscription Agents

(See Section VIII F of the Checklist)

A number of subscription agents have automated office systems, some of which are highly sophisticated. One agent who has done much work in automation is Faxon. This firm now even provides an automated claiming system. Other firms use automation more prosaically in tasks such as invoicing and entering orders with publishers.

In the beginning, a good deal of agent automation resulted in poor service to libraries. By mid-1974, agents who had begun flirting with automated systems in the 1960s had rid themselves of most of the bugs in their systems, and were achieving some genuinely fine advances in the services they provided.

Obviously, the success or failure of the automating of a subscription agency can be measured as a function of improved service to the library. And while there have been significant breakthroughs in efforts to standardize automation procedures and practices among libraries, agents, and publishers, much still remains to be done. The following statement indicates just how much:

> In the rush to automate clerical routines, interaction is again being overlooked, and all three parties will suffer because of a lack of knowledge about what is important to the others. . . . Program inadequacies have occurred through failure to consider points of interaction. . . . Librarians . . . should take the professional responsibility of attempting to discover the parameters of interaction between their routines and those of agents and publishers so at least their efforts to mechanize could conform where necessary.[8]

Failure to consider "points of interaction" do result in delays and confusion. Katherine Smith gives the following examples: an automated library claim system failed to function because the form did not carry sufficient information for the agent or publisher; a publisher using a shared time system could have access to the computer (with its renewal, subscription information) only one day a week; one publisher reporting lack of a discrete number makes it impossible to search the tape-stored computer records, and the number is only available on mailing labels, which often are not submitted by libraries or agents.

There are agencies that are highly automated now that offer to supply machine-readable information concerning the titles they carry. The questions here are what types of data are available, and whether or not they are compatible with the library's system.

> It is growing increasingly apparent that as major academic and research libraries move to computerization, subscription agencies which are not able to integrate their systems with those of their customers will find it difficult to handle those libraries in the years ahead.
>
> The agent should make available his data bases and software capabilities—if not now, then in the next few years. Computer experts say that in a purely rational universe . . . information should be keyboarded only once and data should be stored in only one file. I believe we will soon be at the point where it is no longer necessary to keyboard information in the library's purchasing department, at the subscription agency, at *New Serial Titles*, for the New York State *Union List of Serials*, at the *Union Catalog of Medical Periodicals* and at three or four other places. Information should be keyboarded only once. Likewise, I believe that we will in time reach a point at which the storage of serials data will be centralized and that the subscription agency is a likely candidate for both the keyboarding and the storage of serials data.[9]

In the area of accepting and offering machine-readable information to libraries, Faxon seems to be far in advance of other domestic agents. This firm can accept machine-readable orders, renewals, claims, etc., on IBM cards or on tape. Before the library ships off cards or tapes to Faxon, of course, an arrangement has to be made for converting records in a way that makes them usuable by Faxon's machines. Furthermore, Faxon will send IBM cards or tapes to the library, if this is wanted. Among other domestic agents, only Ebsco says it can do the same, but on a "selected, negotiable basis." Abroad, Swets & Zeitlinger is the only agent that will supply any sort of machine-readable information a library wants, and is one of the few that by 1974 was well on the way to catching up with Faxon in skillful use of the computer.

Plans for accepting and supplying machine-readable information are being made by others, including Maxwell (making great progress, it says); Blackwell's (shooting for 1975 or 1976), and Harrassowitz (no fixed date for operation of such a system). Stechert-Macmillan has an automated system, but does not presently supply machine-readable information or accept such input. And still other agents are using automation in in-house systems for rapid fulfillment of orders.

Moore-Cottrell, possibly more candid than some of the other agents that commented on automation, indicates what the agent contemplating automation must expect: "Although we have explored the possibility of automating an entry system, no one has been able to recommend a system acceptable for all types of orders. We do use modern business machines and methods to expedite processing."

Finally, Clasquin, commenting on the future of automation in libraries and agents, raises some important points regarding standardization:

> Libraries with advanced automated systems for serials control can and should be prepared to write interface programs which will pick up and use machine readable output offered in any form by any agent. This will prevent a locked in situation with any one agent. Systems design vary as much from one library to another as they would from one agent to another. Standardization, I feel, is secondary to the quality and quantity of services needed by the library and which can be provided by the agent. Automation standardization suggests a static situation in serials and we all agree that the serials field is too dynamic to have this happen.[10]

REFERENCE NOTES

1. Ernest R. Perez, "Acquisition of Out-of-Print Materials," *Library Resources and Technical Services*, Winter 1973, pp. 42-59. This article deals primarily with books, but has considerable interest for the serials librarian. There are numerous articles in this field and anyone seriously involved with back issues should carefully check out the latest research.
2. Stephen Ford, *The Acquisition of Library Materials* (Chicago: American Library Association, 1973), pp. 125-126.
3. Isabel Jackson, *Acquisition of Special Materials* (San Francisco: Special Libraries Association, 1966), p. 45.
4. Edmund G. Hamann, "Out of Print Periodicals: The U.S. Book Exchange as a Source of Supply," *Library Resources and Technical Services*, Winter 1972, p. 1925. This gives a short history of the USBE and basic data necessary for the librarian planning to use the USBE for back issues.
5. Jackson, *op. cit.*, p. 52.
6. William Huff, "The Acquisition of Serial Publications," *Library Trends*, January 1970, pp. 307-308. See also in the same issue: Norman Dudley, "The Blanket Order," pp. 318ff. While many libraries question the blanket-

order plan for serials, the plan, in general, is common enough for other types of materials. Dudley notes that fourty-four out of fifty-two academic libraries questioned have such plans.

7. "Report on a Survey of Subscription Agents Used by Libraries in New York State" (New York: New York Library Association, 1970), p. 12.
8. Katherine R. Smith, "Serials Agents/Serials Librarians," *Library Resources and Technical Services*, Winter 1970, pp. 17-18.
9. Stanley Greenfield, "The Librarian . . . and the Subscription Agent," *Special Libraries*, July 1972, p. 303.
10. Frank Clasquin, letter to author, June 23, 1974.

5.
SELECTING AN AGENT

The purpose of this chapter is to assist in the intelligent selection of an agent. There are a number of steps a librarian should take in this process: first, determine that materials and services required by the library; next, ascertain which agent or agents offer these most fully and advantageously (see the Checklist and the Directory); then match library needs against the fulfillment promises of the agent as these appear in a written statement from the agent; and, finally, where deemed necessary or advisable, request from the agent price quotes and service charges on the library list of serials.

Following the first three steps is advisable for all libraries. The last may only be necessary or practical for libraries that have relatively large lists, although it has importance certainly for all libraries.

Money is often the most persuasive reason for selecting or rejecting an agent. There are, agent protests not withstanding, enough reliable agents about to offer competitive prices. Few librarians are ever given carte blanche in the ordering of serials. Often they inherit from their predecessors an existing relationship with one or more agents. More commonly, perhaps, the librarian may use an agent for several years, all along harboring the suspicion that somewhere is a better one waiting to come forward with a bagful of unheard-of goodies. In any case, evaluation and selection of an agent are two separate things, although it follows that if the evaluation proves negative, the selection process must begin again.

The old informal method of evaluation is to compare one agent with another. The librarian who is either restless or suspects that the agent services he or she is receiving might be improved upon asks other librarians about the luck they are having with their agents. Answers must be treated with a certain skepticism or, at best, with awareness that total objectivity is unlikely in such matter.

The comparative method is valid only when the librarian is dealing with particulars, has evidence in effect that agent X is performing or not performing certain functions as capably as he or she might. Katherine Smith points out that this introduces another factor into the evaluation:

> Theoretically, all libraries using the same agent should receive the same service from that agent. However, the profit motive will frequently render the

agent more amenable to services requested by larger accounts. Awareness of these favors may also make them available to the smaller account.[1]

Interestingly enough, when the library questionnaire was broken down in terms of size of library and relative satisfaction with agents (see Chapter 14), there was little or no correlation evident between these factors. Apparently both small libraries and large ones receive equal treatment, whether bad or good, at the hands of the agent. This is not to say that favoritism—or its opposite—is always absent in library-agent dealings, but simply that it is probably not as rampant as once supposed.

SELECTION FACTORS
Selecting an Agent Based on Size

Why do so many librarians use the large to medium-sized agencies? Primarily, it is because these offer services not available from small firms. A cursory glance at the Checklist, however, will indicate that a number of small agents offer many of the same services. Thus, when discussing number of services, what the librarian must really consider is the particular services needed by his or her library *and* how efficient the agent actually is in delivering promised services.

Good-sized agents offer extensive lists of serials—sometimes as many as 70,000. Size can, in fact, be a decisive factor in choosing an agent. Knowing that either Ebsco or Faxon, for instance, can deliver just about any domestic periodical and many foreign ones is quite enough to convince librarians to employ one or the other of these agents, or even both. Some librarians do use both for the reason that while overlap occurs in the titles offered, each offers some titles that the other does not.

No matter what its size, no general agent can deliver certain titles or continuations as quickly and as efficiently as agents in specialized areas of service. Furthermore there are libraries that cannot profitably employ an agent of any sort. This is true of many special libraries, those in particular that subscribe for the most part to low circulation, less known periodicals. One librarian puts the matter succinctly: "Our problem is that not many agents deal with our type of esoteric magazine, i.e., motion pictures, video and television." In these cases the librarian has little choice but to buy directly from the publisher.

> The longer one works with dealers, the more puzzling it becomes as to where to place the out-of-the-ordinary subscriptions. None of the dealers are really interested in titles that are difficult to locate, or difficult to keep current, like those that are published in a different [association] secretary. Irregular publications, university publications, international congresses, symposia, foreign publications each create new and different problems and do not lend themselves easily to the current computer approach of regular titles. Yet what is one going to do? Give the cream of the crop to the dealer, and where does that leave one? There is one dealer [name not mentioned] that takes exactly the opposite view. He wants nothing but the difficult foreign titles and does not want to bother with the ordinary regular domestic ones.[2]

Speaking for agents, Frank Clasquin observes: "It is also true that an agent in these situations usually will give poor service or no service. The reason: only the librarian, not the agent, has knowledge of what has been or has not been received."[3]

How does the library know that X title is available from Y agent?—if the title is a general trade title (for example, most of those listed in the *Reader's Guide to Periodical Literature,* as well as in other basic indexes and abstracting services); if the title is listed in the agent catalog, newsletter, etc.; if it is a specialized title in an area where the agent has a specialization; if the agent says so in a letter, phone call, etc.

Except in the second and fourth cases, the librarian can never be sure that a title is available. Even when the agency lists the item, it is not totally unlikely that the item may have become unavailable since publication of the agent's catalog. As vagaries of this sort do occur from time to time, candor on the agent's part regarding titles it can or cannot supply is no more than the librarian's due. What can happen is described below:

> Most agencies say that they accept orders for all serial publications, but it is clear that the average agency prefers not to bother with publications not listed in its own catalog. As for unlisted items, the old, established firms (and, to be sure, some of the newer ones anxious to create a good image) are willing enough to accept orders for them, whether or not delivery is possible. Such firms generally announce that they will do any bibliographic research that an order requires; and, while this is in a measure true, the offer is not attractive to libraries, since few are in a position to forego their own bibliographic work in favor of that done by the agencies. Some orders do require more than an ordinary expenditure of effort on the agency's part; for instance, when the publisher is unknown or when the issuing source varies from time to time (as so often in the case of international meetings), a conscientious agency will go to some lengths to service the order.[4]

Clasquin concedes, incidentally, this statement has point, but adds: "The real problem is time, i.e., getting enough information from the publisher which will permit the agency to order properly and to assure continuing service."

The Smaller Agency

Despite the advantages of working through a larger subscription agency, many librarians prefer small agencies. Why?

The small agent can save the library money. This is as much a matter of low agent overhead as it is the sort of title sold by the agent. Most small agents deal in relatively popular titles, those that, by and large, have substantial discounts. Larger agents deal in a variety of titles, most of which bring limited discounts and in some cases none at all.

There is more to the matter, of course, than simply the price of this or that title. The librarian must consider carefully, for instance, whether or not a saving gained at expense of service is worthwhile. Both the small and medium-sized agents tend to have closer, personal contact with the librarian than do their larger counterparts. An exception occurs in that occasionally considerable attention is shown really big libraries by the giant agents. Somehow, though, the smaller the account, the less attention it usually gets—or so it is believed by librarians. There can be problems. Here, for example, are just two comments by librarians on this subject:

State Library: We work through a small outfit, which may have some advantages, as well as possible disadvantages—they just asked for the addresses of our publishers. *Public Library*: I tried to use a local magazine distributor. The results were very bad—wrong number of copies, billed for magazines not requested and failure to receive those I wished.

Selecting an Agent Based on Cost

The small library with less than one hundred titles, or under $1,000 a year to spend on periodicals, requires only basic agency services, and so would be wise to use a small agent or simply place its orders for mass circulation items with a publisher's agent (e.g., Educational Subscription Service), an arrangement that assures the library of a 30 to 50 percent discount on many of the items it orders. Others wanted by the library could be placed directly with the publisher.

Small to medium-sized libraries, those requiring few services other than placing of orders and attending to claims, should deal with a small agent. Medium-sized to large libraries, depending again upon list size and service requirements, should select one of the medium-sized to large agents.

Special considerations apply in the case of large libraries. When an agent is employed, the large library is literally forced to select a large agent or a medium-sized one that offers a special list of titles. Given this lack of real choice, as the present study has found, the large library is likely to find itself paying a service charge, no matter which agent it employs.

Medium-sized to large libraries, as well as special libraries, have to consider the cost factor, too, and deal with it as they can.

First and foremost, choice of a medium-sized to large agent or of a specialized agent should be based upon a good record of service on the agent's part. Once the librarian has a clear notion about costs and services, the choice of agent may become more or less mandatory, i.e., if only a certain agent offers the services required that is the agent chosen. And because differences in markups between agents of approximate similar sizes are minimal, the choice of agent X is not only necessary but wise in every good business sense. Daniel Melcher sums up:

> The question of whether the agent takes a markup of 10 percent on the money he handles, or perhaps 12 percent, is not a matter of no concern, but is distinctly secondary to making sure that full value is received for the rest of the money. Favoring the agent willing to work on 10 percent over another agent asking 12 percent, on that ground alone, is a bit like buying lunches or dentistry on price alone. There is too strong a possibility that if you pay less, you won't like what you get.[5]

When an agent employed by the library raises the point of a service charge, the librarian should ask for an explanation. Inevitably, in view of publisher and agent costs, such service charges are likely to increase in the years ahead. It could be wrong, of course, to drop an agent because of an increase in his or her charges, as there is every likelihood that other agents will follow suit in instituting increases of their own. A library might have an ordinarily acceptable agent, but find the agent's service charge exorbitant and not satisfactorily explained by the agent. Librarians then would do well to drop that agent for another or to divide the list between the first agent and another with lower prices—at least until enough time has gone by to allow the librarian to determine whether or not the new agent is supporting his or her promise of good services at low cost.

Changing Agents

If in assessing an agent's services and procedures, these are found inadequate, a change becomes essential. So drastic a step should, of course, be judiciously considered. In almost no case should a switch to a second agent be made until the librarian has outlined needed changes and improvements to his or her present agent. The basic problem may be more one of communication between library and agent than anything else, and so resolved easily enough. Once the agent undertakes to improve matters, it is sensible for the librarian to be as businesslike as possible. He or she should require that the needed improvements be outlined in a letter of agreement and a time limit set for their institution.

If a change is in fact, decided upon, careful planning must take place before the change is affected. A good way to proceed is to set the change in motion at renewal time. It is easier to switch agents at such a time than somewhere during the term of existing orders. Depending upon the sort of arrangements made with the new agent and the time needed for the switchover, the librarian may find it necessary to write to the publisher about the impending change. Such correspondence should indicate the name of both the new and old agents in order to help the publisher update his or her records appropriately.

Difficulties in changing agents increase with the number of serials involved. No matter what precautions are taken, no matter how cooperative the agents, both old and new, problems are unavoidable.

> Many subscriptions will appear to have been duplicated, and for several months those titles not specifically recognized as renewals may not be received. Particularly annoying can be the volumes in series for which the previous agent placed orders at the time of publication rather than actually maintaining a standing order with the publisher.[6]

Despite the problems, it is a grave error for the librarian to continue working with an inefficient agent for fear of what may happen when one agent is dropped in favor of another, or, for that matter, when a decision is made to order directly from the publisher. The experience is common enough. Better agents know it well, and give the librarian help and advice in coping with it. Which is another way of saying that in selecting a new agent, there should be a thorough discussion of steps involved in the changeover. If the prospective new agent fails to appreciate the problems inherent in the situation, the librarian is advised to give that one up and go looking for still another.

TO EMPLOY OR NOT TO EMPLOY AN AGENT

If the present survey of 850 libraries is reflective of present attitudes, the majority of libraries consider agents necessary. Nevertheless, the question of how necessary they really are nags every librarian at one time or another. A librarian might actually find himself or herself thinking that he or she should drop all agents because those dealt with have all proved troublesome in one way or another.

Why this should have happened is itself a question worth asking. Some explanations exist. All too often, the librarian fails to use good judgment in choosing an agent. He or she merely accepts the agent who offers the lowest price for the librarian's list. The result may be satisfactory, but it also may be disasterous. In no case—and this is worth repeating many times—should an agent be selected *solely* on the basis of a promised saving to the library.

Moreover, it is easy for the librarian to expect too much of the agent. The librarian may think that the hiring of an agent will eliminate all problems. Were this the case, where there such an agent about, he or she would have a total monopoly on the market—and there certainly would be no need for this book.

And, sadly enough, the librarian can be so inefficient in his own internal operations that no agent, no matter how efficient he or she may be, is able to rescue the library from its self-made straits. Although this situation is common, it is not suggested that all librarians who have dropped an agent are inefficient. In fact, most inefficient librarians retain the agent—and complain constantly without considering that the blame may belong at home. Librarians of this type who drop agents cause the agent no dismay—not until, that is, they return to the agent, having found they are no more able to cope with individual publishers than with individual agents. Finally, it is clear that some librarians do not trust agents to carry out instructions. In a case of the sort, of course, no agent can cope with the librarian and his or her problems.

One point needs emphasizing: the library that has managed to improve service in dropping an agent has made a correct judgment. The real test of a serials plan is not its cost, at least not primarily so, but the success or failure of the plan, whether this plan uses agents or not.

This sort of reasoning may be frustrating for the man or woman who requires definitive, unassailable justification for retaining or for dropping an agent. It ought, in fact, to lend comfort, because as long as any library can operate without an agent, the agent is forced to reappraise his or her costs and services. The agent has got to avoid the day when the few holdouts can prove that the agent really is not needed after all.

Dropping the Agent

Librarians give three basic reasons for dropping agents, and going directly to the publisher for subscriptions. First, the library's list is too small, usually under 1,000 titles. Consequently, the actual expense of processing an order must be absorbed by a staff borrowed from other duties for the purpose. Second, clerks may have to be hired when there is not enough work to keep them busy. Third, when, as is often the case, ordering is done by a person or office not in the library itself, the task is of little interest to the librarian. The agent has a difficult time coping with this line of argument, particularly as the librarian is dealing with numerous variables and not with hard economic facts. Even so it is possible for the librarian to be won over by the counterargument that in using an agent, he or she is likely to save money. In a small public, school, or college library, the agent's presence is necessary, as he or she may receive and pass on a portion of a 30 to 50 percent discount received in the selling of mass circulation, popular titles. Such discounts are not usually available to librarians without the agent's help.

A second reason for dropping an agent is that in cases in which the library's list is heavy in low-discount titles, the agent is *not* likely to save the library enough in subscription costs even to cover the agent's service charge. This situation holds true particularly for special libraries and college and university libraries with relatively narrow curricula. Far from gaining through the use of agents, the library will probably realize a gain in going directly to the publisher. Also some publishers may extend to the library a special multiyear subscription price that is not available through an agency.

There are other variations on the cost theme. These range from added charges for renewals to charges for small orders; and any of them provide some justification for considering the agent a luxury the librarian can do without.

Poor service is a third reason for dropping the agent. The agent's service can in fact be so poor that it costs the library more to cope with the agent than to deal directly with the publishers. Lacking any standard formula applicable to all libraries in all situations for computing the cost of using or not using an agent, most librarians justify the decision to drop an agent on the basis of the agent's inability to perform. It is certainly the most rational argument for such an action and the hardest to refute.

Interestingly enough, the librarian still frequently uses cost as a reason for dropping an agent. Such a justification is grasped easily by even the least budget-conscious of persons.

It is certainly easier to explain why X agent is to be dropped because its services cost too much than to account for the agent's poor handling of claims or failure to obtain certain titles. Usually, when the librarian speaks of cost without producing supporting statistics, he or she is simply using the word as a type of euphemism for poor service on the agent's part or giving vent to a general feeling of dissatisfaction with the agency. Agents tend not to grasp this, and they spend more time in justifying costs than in trying to come to grips with what the librarian is really complaining about.

And yet—and here we are back in an area where solid statistical evidence of costs is lacking—a librarian may rightfully suggest, as one did recently: "Sometimes I wonder if it would not be more realistic to hire another clerk, and drop the agent." One response to such a suggestion is that if the library receives a discount of any size on its list, or is granted the publisher's list price, absolutely nothing is saved in dropping the agent. In fact, if the list costs less than the retail price, or is sold by the agent at retail, the hiring of a clerk simply adds $5,000 to $7,000 a year to the serials' budget. In short, a determination must be made whether the cost of a clerk would be less than the service charge?

Obviously, another factor enters here. The clerk could be doing other things besides processing orders. Not all of his or her salary would be solely charged against the cost of processing serials. Still, even using the minimum estimate of $5 as the cost of processing an order, it would be difficult to justify another salary, unless the agent's service charge were considerably higher than is usual today.

Stripping away subjective opinions about the quality of this or that agent and limiting the discussion solely to costs, it can be said unequivocally that dropping an agent will not save the average library money. In fact, other things being equal, it is likely to boost the cost of serials significantly.

Timothy Sineath tallies the cost of replacing the agent with a clerk:

> Since it is increasingly difficult for the agent to obtain any kind of discount from the publisher, it may well be asked whether a library should still consider using the service of an agent even though there may be an added service charge. Many believe the services provided are worth the cost. Consider the savings in clerical costs alone in placing one order and making one payment to one agent, against placing a separate order with separate payment to each publisher.... The important question to be asked is: Can a library obtain the same goods and services as cheaply in-house as it can from a good subscription agent? The answer to this question is generally "NO."[7]

Serials costs, even by the most skilled performance-budgeting expert, are difficult to ascertain when an agent is used. This is true because the library is not only buying the actual serial but is buying the services of the agency. Or, as Huff puts it: "The question now becomes one of expertise [of the agent] and how much one is willing to pay for it."[8]

Dropping the agent in favor of an extra clerk presupposes that the clerk will be as efficient, if not better than, the agent. One librarian observes: "It is difficult to give a fair evaluation of Read-More since before they were our agent we had nothing but a serials clerk who left the records in a horrible mess.... I suspect that a well trained and conscientious clerk would solve all our problems cheaper than the agent. But agents are easier to get."

Going Directly to the Publisher

When a library is convinced that the agent's help is superfluous, it must take certain steps before it begins dealing directly with the publisher. The most important is to come to an understanding about order procedures with the individual publishers. This is usually accomplished by sending the publisher a questionnaire. (Two samples are reproduced at the end of this chapter.)

When an agent has been employed, sufficient time should be allowed to pass so that subscriptions ordered through the agent lapse, or at least the majority of such subscriptions. In no case, short of a complete breakdown in the library-agency relationship, should the library simply cancel its whole list without waiting for this to happen.

Beyond this simple formula, the library must consider checking procedures, claiming procedures, and any internal operations from accounting to clerical tasks that may be altered by the change from a single agent to, say, 300 to

70 Guide to Magazine and Serial Agents

1,000 or more publishers. No effort will be made here to detail the necessary changes. Suffice it to say they are formidable.

No library should consider dropping an agent without first reviewing the proposal thoroughly. In such a review, it is necessary to know:

1. Precisely what services would be eliminated
2. What eliminated services the library would have to assume itself afterward
3. How much it would cost the library in terms of clerical help, computer costs, office space, etc., to replace these services
4. Whether or not the library can do the job as efficiently as an agent can
5. What the capabilities of the library are in absorbing and rechanneling its efforts in such a way, and what happens to the serials during the change-over period
6. Whether or not the premise of a saving can be justified before a responsible budget group

The term "precisely" must be used throughout, because from time to time libraries do drop agents, deciding to go it alone. Some manage well, others fail dismally; but, whatever the case, there is usually an interruption in serials service. Furthermore, costs and prices are so variable that it is extremely difficult to determine which arrangement is likely to prove more cost effective than the other as time goes by.

The following forms were used by two libraries in clarifying publisher policies and procedures at a time the libraries contemplated ordering directly from the publisher. The forms are reproduced here (without the name of the libraries) not so much to suggest that librarians drop agents as to indicate what sort of information is necessary and useful when the librarian is dealing directly with a publisher.

Form No. 1

Dear Publisher:

We currently subscribe to the periodical listed below through "X" Agency. We have experienced several problems with subscription agencies in the past, and now the proposed change in the agency's ownership portends more headaches for us. Therefore, we have decided to place our subscriptions directly with publishers and give up the services of this agency.

Please change your records and consider this letter as your authorization to *renew our subscription automatically at expiration date as a direct standing order*. This is *not to be considered as a new order, but merely renewal* without the intermediation of a subscription agency. All correspondence, invoices, and publications should be addressed from now on as follows:

Serials Department
X Library
RPQ University
Jonesville, Y State

We have a need to update our records. Please return this letter to the Serials Department with the information requested below. This will serve as acknowledgment of your acceptance of the order. Do you, by the way, offer a savings for multiple-year subscriptions?

Your early attention to this matter would be greatly appreciated. Thank you.

Sincerely yours,

University Librarian

Title: _____

Current Expiration Date: _____

Subscription Account Number (if needed) _____

Cost of Subscription: 1 yr _____ 2 yrs _____ 3 yrs _____ or

over 3 yrs _____

Form No. 2

Dear Publisher:

At present we order and pay for our periodicals through a subscription agent. We are unhappy with the service and are thinking of placing our subscriptions directly with the publishers. Before we take this step, though, we want to find out something about the way you bill and service your subscriptions. We would appreciate it if you would kindly check one box in each category below and return this letter to us in the enclosed stamped, addressed envelope.

Thank you very much.

Very truly yours,

Librarian

_____ We will invoice libraries for subscriptions.
_____ We do not invoice for subscriptions. Checks must accompany orders.
_____ We will start to send issues to libraries when the library is invoiced for the subscription; we do not have to have payment before we renew the subscription.
_____ We send no issues until payment has been received.
_____ We prefer libraries to place their subscriptions directly with us.
_____ We prefer libraries to place their subscriptions through agents.
_____ We don't care whether libraries place their subscriptions directly with us or through agents.

REFERENCE NOTES

1. Katherine R. Smith, "Serials Agents/Serials Librarians," *Library Resources and Technical Services*, Winter 1970, p. 11.
2. Clara D. Brown, *Serials: Acquisitions and Maintenance* (Birmingham, Ala.: Ebsco Industries, 1971), p. 59.
3. Frank Clasquin, letter to author, June 24, 1974.
4. Peter Gellatly, "Libraries and Subscription Agencies," *PNLA Quarterly*, October 1966, pp. 36-37.
5. Daniel Melcher, *Melcher on Acquisitions* (Chicago: American Library Association, 1971), p. 150.
6. Smith, *op. cit.*, p. 12.
7. Timothy W. Sineath, "Libraries and Library Subscription Agencies," *The Library Scene*, Summer 1972, p. 10.
8. William Huff, "The Acquisition of Serial Publications," *Library Trends*, January 1970, pp. 305-306.

III.

MANAGING A SERIALS COLLECTION

6.
LIBRARY SERIALS RECORDS AND ROUTINES

The managing of a serials collection is, as Clara Brown has observed, "maddening and frustrating."[1] There are scores of different approaches to the matter, as it is practiced by librarians, agents, and publishers. The badly needed standardization of routines and records has made it difficult to prescribe rules applicable in each and every situation that may arise. Of more consequence perhaps is the fact that lack of standardization results in unnecessary misunderstandings and frustrations in the relationship of the library with the agent and publisher.

No one is more aware of what is happening than are librarians and agents (and, to a degree, publishers). Efforts to reach some common ground of understanding are evident in the writing on the subject and certainly in the conversation that passes between librarians and agents. The emergence of separate serials divisions, sections, and departments has developed as an effort to cope with the growing complexity of serials recordkeeping. Equally important, the increase in the costs of periodicals has necessitated careful reexamination of heretofore accepted routines and methods of recordkeeping. A push toward standardization is coming in the automating of serials records. Still, Huibert Paul can summarize conditions today as "costly chaos and anarchy." He cites the example of the various records that must be kept concerning a single periodical title:

> A publisher should realize that his title constitutes only one out of some 12,000 to 15,000 serials received by the medium-sized university library in the United States today. He should be aware of the fact that hundreds and in some cases thousands of libraries throughout America and elsewhere in the world have several records of his one title: a check-in card, a payment record, perhaps an edge notched card to keep track of renewal time, several cards in the public record, and perhaps a Linedex strip for quick reference. Furthermore, his title may be listed in the catalogs of subscription agents and second hand dealers, it may be mentioned in the texts and footnotes of many books, and countless invoices may be filed under it."[2]

Paul's statement gives a fair indication of the number of records that must be modified or changed each time a publisher changes a title. Extended to other areas, standardization, in bringing uniformity to routines, reduces staff time needed for correspondence, claiming, checking-in, invoice processing, and modifying records, i.e., it reduces general office costs. Few disagree with the need for such standardization, and a study by an American Library Association committee fairly well indicates that its appeal is merited:

> Librarians have the responsibility . . . for receiving and claiming orders, and for paying invoices properly. The internal operations of the library should be organized to achieve these goals. Regular examination of routines and the maintenance of manual serials operations are essential for this purpose. Librarians also have a responsibility to provide these services at a cost commensurate with the effort necessary to achieve a balance of service and economy.[3]

Given a certain consensus concerning the need for standardization of routines and records, what's the matter? First, and most obviously, the library is not today's child. As an institution it is old and well settled in its ways. And the practices and routines it follows, particularly in recordkeeping, are generally moth-eaten, to say the least. To change these may not be the best thing that can happen; it might, in fact, traumatize everyone concerned. Another aspect of the problem is what D. L. Bosseau calls "the not-invented-here syndrome"; and while he is speaking of automation, the "syndrome" appears when suggestions are made concerning the need for changes in manual procedures. Judith Nientimp says, "It is apparent that in their eagerness to come up with a unique system, many systems librarians do not profit from the systems-design errors of their predecessors. Thus progress to date can be measured more in the proliferation of systems than in improved capacity."[4] Add to this lack of standardized recordkeeping the idiosyncratic nature of serials, and the scope of the problem is evident even to the beginner. Moreover, lack of standardization in the practices of agents and publishers does little to alleviate matters.

In spite of this rather gloomy introduction, let it be said that most agents and librarians operate in a relatively efficient manner. The beginner should be aware that even the best-run system can be modified to its benefit, and, as the ALA committee noted, regular examination of routines is as much a part of the maintenance and operation of a serials department as is the daily keeping of records.

BASIC SERIALS RECORDS

The purpose of any record is to serve as a control device. In the case of serials, the primary point of control is usually the check-in record, the Kardex visible file, or versions thereof. The Kardex may include a variety of information, but it serves first and foremost to tell the librarian what serials holdings there are, what is on order, what has been received, and what has not been received.

The Kardex may be the central source of information on serials, but more than likely holdings will be shown also in the card catalog. The library user at least should be able to tell from the card catalog (or computer-produced book catalog) whether or not the library has X periodical, what volumes of its run, and where they are located.

The Kardex may also include bindery and payment information and such further information as the source and method of acquiring the title, a financial history of the title, claiming data, etc. Depending on the size and organization of the library, the Kardex may or may not include only periodicals; may or may not include other types of serials; may or may not indicate standing orders. "May or may not" is repeated because in small libraries all records may be kept together in one file with relative ease, while the large library can achieve the same end only through automation, that is, through transferring Kardex data into a computer base. (Maintaining parallel manual and automated files, incidentally, is far from unheard-of.) Libraries between the smallest and largest are apt to have a number of separate records, usually manual, and to accord separate handling to periodical and non-periodical serials. The problem is in knowing what to do when one piece of information does not agree with another. For example, how much time must a librarian spend in straightening out the record of a subscription that, according to the agency invoice, starts in December, while in the Kardex the starting point is shown to be September, and in the payment file, January? Which record is the "honest" one?

Considering the various types of records, most serials librarians and administrators advocate use of centralized serials records. They hold, furthermore, that when serials holdings are of any size, one or more librarians are needed to see to serials records maintenance and administration. In smaller and medium-sized libraries, on the other hand, serials records are not usually kept as a separate record, but are integrated in some way with other acquisitions files. In a very small library—one employing no more than a few people and subscribing to fifty to one hundred periodicals—the serials record consists of a simple check-in file. Invoices are likely to be processed by a separate business office, and cataloging, binding, etc., are, for the most part, nonexistent. The librarian in this situation might rightfully ask: "Why bother keeping serials records at all?"

Need for Records

Beyond preparing and sending out the initial order to publisher or agent, small libraries do little more than keep a record of holdings. The rationale is that as the collection is small, the average user can find what he or she wants by looking on the shelf or consulting the librarian. It is usually added that keeping detailed records requires too much time and effort on the part of an already overworked staff and, furthermore, such records provide little, if any, improved service to the user.

A strong argument can be made for keeping reasonably full records in all but the smallest libraries. Such records indicate what is (and is not) in the library, assist the librarian in updating and completing the periodicals file, and provide additional information to those who may want to know more than just the title of a periodical. Records are, of course, also a useful source of budget and cataloging information. Finally, they make it possible for a library to participate in cooperative ventures with other libraries, as, for example, in the preparation of union catalogs.

So far as a library's relationship with a subscription agent (or publisher) is concerned, the library's records are of major importance in that they show accurately the date of receipt (or nonreceipt) of an item. Unless the librarian has information on when to expect a title, he or she may claim the title before it is due. The result is a well-justified complaint of agents and publishers that a good 50 percent of all claims are premature. No sooner is the publisher or agent requested to provide the "missing" item than it appears in the mails. Much premature claiming can be eliminated if the librarian has an accurate check-in record on which notations appear concerning the expected arrival time of an item. If the librarian waits too long before making a claim, of course, he or she risks losing the issue altogether or getting it only at a large cost in the out-of-print market. Timing is always a difficult matter.

Record Information

Efforts to organize and maintain an efficient periodicals service are almost as numerous as there are libraries to provide the service. Then, too, there are literally scores of different sorts of equipment, from files to computer programs, used in the effort. In describing record-management programs, details sometimes appear confusing and contradictory.

Nevertheless, certain generalizations can be made that at least indicate the parameters of the record-management process. There may be no consensus on type of physical record needed for this or that library, or even on the precise sort of information that will be contained in the record, but there is agreement that, in one form or another, periodicals records should include the following basic information:

Current title
Location of title in the library
Holdings statement, i.e., issues held by the library
Frequency
Expiration date
Source of the periodical (publisher, agent, gift, exchange)
Funding and finance information
Data on binding

As the collection grows, more information is likely to be added to the files:

Information on whether to expect to get free or to have to order an index, supplements, or table of contents
Historical information such as changes in title and claiming problems
Holdings of periodicals no longer published, in storage, on microfilm, or in reprint editions
A number for each title in the file (many libraries assign numbers of their own for recordkeeping purposes, but these are now being superseded, at least in part, by the ISSN)
Agents and publisher codes, or separate files of subscriptions by agent or publisher

Arrival cards used in a certain check-in process (these cards are used in some automated check-in systems, variations of the arrangement are occasionally found with manual systems)

The physical form of the file may vary from the simple, yet efficient, check-in record on a 3 X 5 inch card in a file drawer to decks of punched cards used in computer operations. As there is normally more than one set of files, it is essential that all be keyed in a way that allows for easy reference from one to the other. This may be done by arranging a file according to a simple scheme, as under the entry, or by placing the purchase order or invoice number on all files as a means of determining their content.

All of the aforementioned information will appear in the records of a well-organized periodicals collection. This information may be examined in terms of various serials and routines: orders and invoices, agency annual review lists, checking, claiming, binding, cataloging, and correspondence.

Orders and Invoices

Order records include as much bibliographical detail about each item as necessary for placing and tracing orders. Usually this record consists of copies of the original order arranged in some easy to refer to form, e.g., by entry, by purchase order number, by date of order or payment, by fund, or by a combination of any or all of these. As agents do not as a rule return copies of the original order, the library should maintain copies for its own use.

Invoices received from the agent show, among other things, what is supplied, what part of the order cannot be supplied, price, service charges, etc. Invoices are often filed along with the original orders. Payment records usually are incorporated into the invoice record. All such records should show the amount paid, date of payment and, of course, order and invoice numbers. The total record that outlines all payments for a given order, not for a single item, should be filed separately. Librarians vary in their methods of maintaining the invoice payment record. Judith Nientimp argues for a separate invoice record with the check-in record or a record of payment on the check-in card.

> In that way the person authorizing payment can compare the current payment with earlier ones and can check the payment against receipts. Sometimes a subscription is on an agent's records and is renewed automatically, but, when checked against receipts, it is discovered that the publication is two or three years behind schedule. This is happening frequently now with translation journals, and the library has a perfect right to refuse further payment or request credit rather than paying two or three years in advance. If invoices are not entered in the same file as the check-in records, however, this kind of comparison is impossible.[4]

Other librarians argue that this arrangement is too ambitious and that it makes the file too large for comfort.

Claims

Claims may be kept track of in the correspondence file, though this is by no means the only way of proceeding. Claims are notices sent to the agent or publisher regarding nondelivery of an item. The receipt records from which claims are generated normally form part of the check-in apparatus. Claim correspondence may appear in synopsis in the check-in record. In other cases, particularly difficult ones, the correspondence is filed separately. Both arrangements have merit, and both are used in libraries of all sizes.

Checking and Receiving

Most libraries have similar ways of checking in serials. The check in card indicates receipt of the item and its destination (or destinations) in the library. There must be a device indicating when to claim and, equally important, when not to claim a missing issue. The decision to act may come at check-in time (as when one finds upon receipt of the current issue that an earlier one is missing) or at payment time (as when one is asked for a new payment before delivery has been taken of something paid for earlier).

Binding

If the library is going to maintain bound volumes, it must keep a record of decisions about duplicates, microforms, reprints, title pages, indexes, supplements, and anything at all that will help the librarian to determine what is or is not to be bound.

Cataloging

This procedure may include the actual cataloging of the periodical, or simply the provision of the cataloger with information he or she needs to do the job. It also may include consideration of what is to be done concerning withdrawals, discards etc. Each of these steps or decisions represents a basic routine that should be subject to constant examination and appraisal. No plan is ever perfect, and the efficient periodicals librarian must always expect the unexpected. Brown sums up the basic philosophy of anyone planning such routines: "The routines must be so arranged that the title will be reviewed at every collapsible point."[5] And there is no end of "collapsible" points.

The records kept serve as control and processing guides to the librarian. None of the records is static (with the possible exception of those of cancelled and discontinued items) and must be constantly updated. Of particular importance is the holdings statement, which includes, in various forms, not only periodicals in the library but those to be received at a particular time as well as those not received and, therefore, subject to claiming.

Often forgotten in this maze of recordkeeping is the very necessary element of service to the public. No system is truly operative unless it produces information that helps the user. Consequently, from its internal records, the library must produce public records in which the status of current holdings is indicated.

Correspondence File

Correspondence about serials that has not been filed with other records goes here. This correspondence is made up of everything from letters about new orders to claims to lists of renewals. When the correspondence is extensive, it is important that it be keyed to other pertinent records. Standard correspondence forms should be used whenever possible. Forms of this sort are often available free from the agent. The form not only saves everyone time but also requires a direct approach to a problem under consideration.

CHECK-IN RECORDS

The purpose of the check-in record is to show what the library receives and does not receive. With the periodical in hand, the librarian literally checks it into the library on a special check-in form. This form serves other purposes also: it alerts the librarian as to when a volume is complete and ready for binding and it provides information concerning changes in title, frequency, etc.

Not all libraries have a check-in process. Working on the assumption that most titles have arrived in the past and will arrive uninterruptedly in the future, smaller libraries and branches sometimes skip the process. This omission may be reinforced by the library's lack of interest in collecting back issues, by its emphasis on popular reading materials, by a reluctance to engage in other than minimal reference work, and simply by a lack of staff time. Even the largest library may not check in all titles, as, for example, the local newspaper and titles that will be replaced at the end of the year on microform. Given these conditions, the dispensing with check-in records is understandable, possibly even necessary.

Some effort should be made, when the library enters a new subscription, to check the receipt of the title for the first three to six months. If this is not done, the librarian has no way of recognizing nonreceipt of ordered titles (or, for that matter, of all required issues once the order begins arriving). While it may be superfluous to check in titles the library has no intention of keeping for more than a few months or years, it is highly advisable to check in titles that are to be kept and perhaps bound.

In most libraries, as D. L. Bosseau points out, the check-in process is "of the greatest interest to librarians." Why this interest, an interest that is reflected in numerous articles and books?

> Perhaps the check-in, or receiving operation is the focus of attention because it is an ongoing daily operation, and its results are the most critical public service contact which the serials department has with its patrons, especially in providing information on the presence of specific issues in the library or the library system."[6]

Which is another way of saying that order and control are synonymous with librarianship, and nowhere are order and control needed more surely than in a large periodicals collection.

Physical Form of Check-in Records[7]

In the days before mechanization and automation, the normal physical form of the check-in record was the familiar 3 × 5 card. And many libraries, even sizable ones, continue to use such cards, although by now the card has grown in size to 4 × 6 or 5 × 8 to allow space for more information and ease of use. Such cards are placed in a Kardex or a blind file of some sort, such as an ordinary card drawer. Such files are called "blind" because the information in them can be seen only when the card is pulled from the file. The usual arrangement of the cards is alphabetical by title of the magazine (or by catalog entry). As a magazine is received, the card is pulled and its receipt duly noted by a check in the appropriate square on the card. (Sometimes the day of receipt is given.) Once every three months or so, the file is reviewed to see if any issues are missing. If so, the issue is claimed from the agent, publisher, or other source.

This is an extremely simple approach to the check-in process, but it is quite suitable for collections of 50 to 150 titles. If there are more than 150 titles, however, the process becomes tedious and far from efficient. One way of accelerating the search for missing issues is to arrange the cards by frequency, i.e., all cards for monthly magazines in one section, all for bimonthly in another, and so on. As a title is received, the card is moved to the next month's section, the next bimonthly section, or wherever it belongs according to frequency. At the end of the given period, the librarian simply checks to see what cards have not been moved and then claims the missing issues. Still another highly favored approach is to use colored tabs to indicate frequency.

The so-called "visible file" is much preferred for libraries with more than 150 titles. Here the cards are housed in books or in flat sliding trays. The librarian can quickly find the desired title without the necessity of removing cards, which, in other arrangements can be misplaced and misfiled.

While there are numerous forms of the visible file (which is chosen depends as much upon the manufacturer's salesmanship as upon the needs of the library), in general, the file contains trays of single or double cards. The cards are usually combined with attached slips (variously known by serials librarians as "auxiliary sheets," "overriding slips," "flimsies," etc.). Most of the cards are preprinted, as are the attached slips. Osborn fairly well sums up this use:

> The number of kinds of forms should be restricted to approximately four to six.... The most common forms are for weeklies, monthlies, irregular publications, and annuals or numbered series.... By far the most successful device for overcoming the necessity for periodical replacement of entries due to full records is the overriding slip in conjunction with a basic entry card.... Under the system of basic entry cards and overriding slips the cards bear the permanent information: details of entry, call number, checking directions, summarized statement of holdings, billing data, etc. The whole of the card, both front and back, is free for these notations.... The overriding slips are the printed checking forms for weeklies, monthlies, etc.[8]

From Mailroom to Shelf

What is the actual process involved in the transfer of the item from the mailroom to the shelf? When a periodical arrives in the mail the address label should be checked to be certain that the periodical belongs to the library. In a library that has more than a single receiving point, the periodical should be checked to make sure it is reaching its proper destination: The periodical should be unwrapped carefully so as not to mutilate it. If it is not in a wrapper, it should be checked for undue damage created in the mails. If the address label is separate, i.e., on the wrapper, it should be clipped off and slipped inside the magazine's front cover. Obviously, it is not necessary to bother with every mailing label for a single periodical, but in the beginning at least, mailing label information may be useful in the drawing up of one's records. When checking in periodicals, the checker should take account of title, date, and volume and issue number. Care is necessary because the publisher may skip an issue, put out a double number or special issue, or change the title he or she is using. The obvious warning here is to be sure to post the information on the proper card; a distracted clerk might easily confuse *New York* magazine with *The New Yorker*—an error of some proportion as it causes offense everywhere.

The piece is now imprinted with the library's ownership stamp and, depending upon local practice, call numbers, card pockets, and reinforcements are added. Once the periodical is checked in and prepared for use, it is routed to its place in the library. This may be a shelf, a branch, or a periodicals room.

A warning: Even in the largest library, every effort should be made to move the periodical through the serials office and into the service area as quickly as possible (the user is always lining up for the latest issue of his or her publication). If a given title presents a problem, it should be put aside until the problem-free titles are checked in.

The mails should be "cleared" each day. Otherwise disaster threatens. No backlog is harder to dispose of than one occurring in the serials office.

The library should have a system of noting missing issues at the check-in point. This may consist of the checker's filling in a formal claim slip, or simply making an appropriate notation on a slip of paper. Claims for the missing issue(s) are not normally sent out immediately, but at least if this arrangement is followed, the library has a running record of what is missing—a record that can be checked when the missing issues are received or can be used for claiming if they are not received.

Osborn insists: "The two fundamentals of a good checking system are completely reliable records and a vigorous and enlightened follow-up program."[9] Some librarians, and this may be particularly true in smaller and medium-sized libraries, go through the files at intervals to ascertain what has not been received. This should be done at least quarterly. Regular checking, coupled with the checker's notes on missing issues, gives the library a proper record of gaps that need filling.

PUBLIC ACCESS TO SERIALS

Except in the small library, where no list of periodicals is kept and the user must find what he wants by looking on the shelves or by consulting the librarian, there are clearly defined points of public access to the collection.

In large libraries, where in-depth cataloging is used, the catalog card (whether it be a preprinted Library of Congress card or another sort of preprinted card or the library's own card) gives the user much necessary information. The cards may be interfiled in the main collection or separately filed in a periodicals catalog or both arrangements undertaken simultaneously. The separated file is preferable, particularly when it is located in proximity to the collection of periodicals.

A valuable index to the collection is the familiar title-a-line list, an alphabetical list, each line of which gives the title, call number, and location of the item. Using this index, the user can generally find what he needs quickly and easily. The index may be used alone or in conjunction with the public catalog. If the library has more than 500 periodicals but does not catalog them in depth, this index is often all the average user needs. (There should be some easily seen note in the index that refers the user to the librarian when he or she has questions about such things as the length of the run, split location, or missing issues.)

A simple card file usually has the same information as that of a visible reference index. The card file is suitable when the collection is fewer than 500 titles. The file may be a separate entity or, in place of this, a simple title-and-location card may be put in the public catalog. The former alternative is preferable.

At one time, all holdings of a library were listed in alphabetical order in a book. With the use of the computer, the book catalog has returned to prominence as a common library tool. Libraries large enough to use a computer will probably have a separate book catalog for periodicals. Apart from basic title and location information, the book catalog may contain much additional information, depending, of course, on the library's needs and the computer program.

Serials information, then, is made available to the public in visible reference indexes, card catalogs, and book catalogs. And other records are, in many cases, found in serials departments or periodicals rooms. Points of public access in such places may be limited because economy and efficiency dictate the use of only one set of internal records. The user who wants more than location information is encouraged (by signs and experience) to consult the serials librarian. Indeed, in some cases, he or she can obtain information from the librarian not only about holdings on the premises but also about holdings in almost any library in the country, and sometimes in libraries abroad.

REFERENCE NOTES

1. Clara D. Brown, *Serials: Acquisitions and Maintenance* (Birmingham, Ala.: Ebsco Industries, 1971), p. 9.
2. Huibert Paul, "Serials: Chaos and Standardization," *Library Resources and Technical Services*, Winter 1970, p. 20.
3. ALA/RTSD, Acquisitions Section, "Guidelines for Publishers, Agents, and Librarians in Handling Library Orders for Serials and Periodicals" (Chicago: American Library Association, 1973), p. 3.
4. Judith Nientimp, "The Librarian . . . and the Subscription Agent," *Special Libraries*, July 1972, p. 296.
5. Brown, *op. cit.* p. 4.
6. D. L. Bosseau, "The Computer in Serials Processing and Control," in *Advances in Librarianship*, vol. 2 (New York: Seminar Press, 1971), p. 127. This lengthy summary article is one of the best available in that it is an excellent summary of automation and serials but without the unnecessary technical jargon.
7. For examples of such forms, *see* Brown, pp. 23-47 and Andrew Osborn, *Serial Publications*, 2nd ed. (Chicago: American Library Association, 1973), pp. 90-94. Also almost any article dealing with automation of serials includes examples of forms.
8. Osborn, *op. cit.*, pp. 165-171.
9. *Ibid.*, p. 143.

7.
THE PERIODICALS COLLECTION: SIZE AND COST

What percentage of the library's total acquisitions budget should be allocated for periodicals?* The answer: whatever is needed. The problem: no one is quite sure what is needed, or, more precisely, there is far from total agreement among libraries that it is possible to say X library should have X number of periodicals. Agreement is general that the world's total periodicals resources should be available, in one form or another, to all readers. However, the establishment of international, national, and regional lending centers is a problem that defies solution. Librarians who want to pursue either of these questions will find much to mull over in the literature concerning them.[1]

Beginners will discover some help in the various "standards" established by the American Library Association. For example, the *Standards for School Media–Programs* (Chicago: ALA, 1969, pp. 30–33) gives figures representing the minimum number of periodicals that belong in schools of all sorts, from elementary schools through high schools. Knowing the minimum number required, the librarian can estimate cost and then, in examining that cost in terms of the school's total annual acquisitions budget, arrive at an approximate periodicals allocation.

What might also be done is to consider the findings of the present survey. The purpose of the survey was not to ascertain percentages of budget spent on periodicals but to ascertain, keeping ALA standards in mind, the average size of periodicals collections in various types of libraries. The figures given in the survey for average periodicals collections are helpful, although should not be regarded as optimal recommendations. They merely reflect conditions as these existed in late 1973 and early 1974. (For details, see Chapter 13.)

How meaningful are such averages? In this survey they probably are on the

---

*The discussion that follows is directed almost exclusively to a consideration of the cost of periodicals. Whereas serials and periodicals can be dealt with together in considering other aspects of the subscription agent–library relationship, this is hardly so where cost is concerned, as some serials, for example, may be priced much as a book, or it may not.

high side, because librarians who responded to the questionnaire were usually those with bigger than average sized collections—whatever an "average" size may be for academic, school, public, and special libraries. Librarians in charge of smaller collections (as some replies indicated) did not feel it worthwhile to take part in the survey because, as one noted, smallness dictates that "we order directly from the publisher, and have little or nothing to do with agents." (This was a small public library with holdings of about thirty five titles.) One suspects that a majority of those who did not reply had considerably smaller collections than the average cited here.

Despite the statistical qualifications, the averages and ranges (reported in Chapter 13) are at least indicative of periodicals holdings in various types of libraries. A cursory comparison with other studies of this sort indicates that periodicals holdings are increasing in size in all types of libraries. For example, a study of periodicals holdings in public libraries serving more than 10,000 people was made in 1960. It was found at that time that the average number of magazine titles in small public libraries was 61; in medium-sized libraries, 153; and in large libraries, 458.[2] In fifteen or so years, the number in all cases has increased substantially.

PERIODICALS COSTS

Putting aside arguments as to the most desirable number of periodicals a library of one sort or another should have, and putting aside also the various ALA standards (which, except for school and some public libraries are too general to be useful), the librarian may approach the question of size in terms of the percentages of the budgets various sorts of libraries are now (mid-1974) devoting to periodicals. Lacking any national statistical survey, one must fall back upon isolated surveys and studies.[3] Still, these provide a general answer to the original question: What percentage of the library's total acquisitions budget should be allocated for periodicals?[4] (As noted again later, inflation is increasing these basic percentages appreciably.)

Large university, college, and public libraries spend 26 to 30 percent of their materials budgets on periodicals. (If other types of serials are included, the percentage can reach 50 percent or more.) Medium-sized university, college, and public libraries allocate 7 to 10 percent. (Including other types of serials, the percentage would be closer to 10 to 20 percent.) Large school libraries and systems plan on 5 to 8 percent. Medium-sized school libraries and systems drop to about 2 to 5 percent. No figures are given for small public or small school libraries because in the vast majority of such libraries allocation of acquisitions funds is more a fiction than a reality. The librarian simply has to make do with what is available, dividing it up to suit the occasions. Still, beginners might consider the percentages given for medium-sized libraries as desirable percentages for most small libraries.

No figures are given for special libraries because the special library, depending on type and purpose, may allocate as much as 25 to 95 percent of its acquisitions budget for periodicals and other types of serials. In fact, one characteristic of the special library is that emphasis is placed on serials and periodicals to the virtual exclusion of books. The reason for this is that the primary need in such libraries is for current information, which is found largely in periodicals, reports, etc. (An exception occurs if "special" is used to denote a scholarly collection of the sort closed to general use.)

Unlike most other acquisitions allocations, the one for periodicals (and usually other serials) is distinctive. It is normally not for a single item or for a single year. The library's budget is encumbered by this allocation as long as the subscription continues, perhaps for years to come. And even without adding a single new item or a single new subscription, the librarian must consider in his or her calculations built-in increases in subscription costs, as well as increases in agency charges. Add to these costs such growing internal overhead costs as salaries, binding, and shelving, and the ongoing commitment to periodicals, even when a single subscription is entered, tends to loom a little large.

Financial troubles besetting libraries in the 1970s have forced cuts in serials appropriations, and occasionally emergency appropriations have had to be made simply to allow the serials collection to "stay" in place. In cases where budgetary relief is needed but not forthcoming, the result "undoubtedly will be an increased prevalence of broken runs and incomplete files of periodicals. A library will no longer look at a long run of rarely used periodicals as a past investment which must be perpetuated."[5]

Librarians are now wondering whether long-term commitments need always be retained. If budgets continue to be trimmed or not expanded sufficiently to meet increased serials costs, this question becomes more and more important. Unfortunately, the too pragmatic librarian may answer it simply by cutting out a subscription or a standing order without regard for any damage this may create. As Brynteson puts it: "Whether long run or not, subscriptions today are being cancelled for such titles and often without regard to their uniqueness in the collection or even in the geographical area."[6]

Estimating Title Prices

How does the librarian arrive at an estimate of the cost of a periodicals list? The simplest most direct way is to use the publisher's retail price in one's calculations. Retail price may be obtained from the subscription agent's catalogs, by inquiring directly of the publisher, or through consultation of a variety of bibliographical aids such as *Ulrich's International Periodicals Directory*. A necessary warning: be sure the source consulted is current.

If the library is working directly with the publisher, the price quoted will be the approximate cost of the individual title. If the library is working through an agent, the cost may be 5 to 10 percent higher than that quoted by the publisher or possibly (in the case of popular titles) 10 to 20 percent lower. However, here another factor must be considered: the cost to the library of processing an order. This is discussed in the next section.

In even more general terms, the cost of a periodicals list may be estimated simply by multiplying the number of titles by the average price of a periodical title in a given year, e.g., $17.71, the figure given in the 1974 article on serials prices and price indexes in the *Library Journal*; or by accepting an agent's figures by type of library, e.g., "School libraries show an average cost of about

88 Guide to Magazine and Serial Agents

$10 to $15 per title; universities and colleges, $20 to $30 per title."[7] (The agent's estimates here include both periodicals and other types of serials, and so are a bit high.)

The cost of a list may also be found with some accuracy by employing a table designed by Clasquin of F. W. Faxon. Shown in the accompanying table are percentages representing the total number of subscriptions processed by Faxon (approximately one and a quarter million orders) in various price categories and the total amount spent by libraries in each of these categories. Calculations are for the fiscal year July 1973–June 1974.

Subscriptions Processed by Faxon, July 1973–June 1974

Price Range	All Classes of Libraries Percent of Total Subs. Proc.	All Classes of Libraries Percent of Total Expenditure	College and University Libraries Only Percent of Total Subs. Proc.	College and University Libraries Only Percent of Total Expenditure
Less than $3.00	5.2	0.6	3.8	0.4
$3.00–$3.99	5.8	1.1	3.7	0.6
$4.00–$5.99	11.6	2.4	9.8	2.0
$6.00–$9.99	21.7	7.4	21.0	6.5
$10.00–$14.99	17.1	8.8	18.5	8.6
$15.00–$19.99	9.8	7.3	11.0	7.0
$20.00–$29.99	11.7	11.8	13.0	11.9
$30.00–$49.99	7.8	12.2	8.8	12.3
$50.00–$74.99	3.8	9.4	4.6	10.3
$75.00–$99.99	1.5	5.2	1.7	5.5
$100.00–$149.99	1.6	7.8	1.8	8.2
$150.00–$199.99	.9	6.2	1.0	6.5
$200.00+*	1.5	19.8	1.3	20.2
	100%	100%	100%	100%

*Includes *Biological Abstracts, Cumulated Index,* and *Chemical Abstracts.* For instance, on a $50,000.00 budget, these three items account for approximately 7 percent of total purchases.

Another matter that cannot be ignored is inflation. There is some argument as to how much the cost of an average periodical increases in price year by year because of inflation, but a modest estimate is from 10 to 22 percent. The various price indexes for serials and more particularly the annual July figures published in *Library Journal,* indicate that in a ten-year period (1960 to 1970) the price of serials had about doubled. At least until recently, most libraries have been somewhat indifferent to price increases.

There has been a strange silence in our literature concerning the fact that prices are outrunning themselves. The indexes appear regularly with some accompanying comment on percentage gains, but apart from this, one has much searching to do before he turns up with anything else.[8]

Indifference or not, the fact of price increases "has brought us to the point at which our residual serial charges (that is, the amount we must pay in order to maintain our serials file in its present state, leaving aside the need for improving the file with new subscriptions) is climbing at the rate of about 15 percent a year."[9]

In the annual *Library Journal* report on United States periodicals prices for 1973, Norman Brown gives the following data: "The average subscription price of 2,861 titles used in compiling the index: $16.20. The price increase of 1973 over 1972: 22 percent."[10] Librarians should read Brown's summary in full because, as with all statistics, it considers numerous variables that affect these figures in various ways. Disagreement exists among agents concerning the accuracy of Brown's figures. The disagreement, of course, arises from the fact that the data used are not in all cases comparable and from the general impression that accompanies statistical interpretation. It takes no statistician, however, to realize that when a library estimates the gross cost of periodicals subscribed to, it is necessary to add an inflationary factor of 10 to 22 percent to the base figure obtained, and perhaps a still larger one if the 1975 rate of inflation continues unabated.

Recognition that periodicals are going up in price should explain why the librarian receives "bill backs" or added-charge invoices from an agent. The agent may bill the librarian at prices quoted in September only to find a month later that the publisher has raised his price and requires the difference from the agent, i.e., from the subscribing librarian. The agent should not be blamed for such procedures; they are purely and simply beyond his control.

The cumulative effect of inflation, and rising costs for everything from the periodical itself to the cost of processing the title, are economic facts of life. When the librarian is estimating the costs of a subscriptions list from year to year he or she must add a minimum increase of 15 percent to the gross cost or else be prepared to suffer some nasty consequences. There are methods of whittling down costs a bit, such as entering multiple-year subscriptions, as these are offered at lower cost than is a single-year subscription and they may carry a guarantee of no rate hikes for two or three years. Measures such as this are, of course, stopgap measures only. And there is no foreseeable chance that the 10 to 22 percent figure is likely to decrease in the years ahead. If anything, it is likely to increase.

In efforts to cope with inflation, librarians have cut back on the size of their serials expenditures. In 1974, this averaged between 10 and 25 percent in the amount spent on serials. Selection procedures have been strained, but they have also been refined. Nevertheless, librarians have been obliged to increase the proportion of the total acquisitions budget spent on serials. If, as noted earlier, the average university, college, or large public library is now spending 26 to 30 percent of its acquisitions on periodicals—up to 50 percent or more on all serials—this figure is sure to increase proportionately to the library's inability to cut back on dollars spent and the growing rate of inflation. It is not inconceivable that larger universities in the decade ahead may be spending over 90 percent of their acquisitions budget on serials alone, although retrenchment programs are underway even in the serials departments of many such institutions.

Cooperative serials acquisitions made such centers as the Associated Colleges of the Midwest Periodicals Bank models of their kind. Some ten undergraduate liberal arts colleges belong to this center. It offers its members photocopies of both current and back issues of periodicals of all sorts.

More extensive use of regional interlibrary loan, particularly in the case of little-used materials, is not the way out. This will obviously require more cooperation among libraries than now is evident, as well as substantially improved photocopying procedures. Moreover, if accessibility of periodicals on a broad scale is to improve noticeably, regional, state, and even local union lists must multiply.

If inflation has a bright side, then, it is in the fact that it may be forwarding the notion of interlibrary cooperation. So far, however, activity in this area is not markedly high.

LIBRARY COSTS FOR PROCESSING SERIALS

If the librarian calculates the cost at retail of a given list of titles, it is a simple matter to find out how much he or she is paying an agent for the agent's services. This is precisely what many librarians do, and why, when the agent adds a service charge, the librarian may find that the cost of the titles being supplied has gone up an unconscionable 5 to 10 percent. The next mental hop is to figure that the library may save 5 to 10 percent by ordering directly from the publisher. The question remains however: How much will it cost the library to enter individual orders with individual publishers (instead of through one or more agents)? Agents are fond of pointing out that this amount can be large indeed.

What the agent does not ask the librarian to consider is the cost to the library of endless correspondence, claims, missing issues, etc., which may result from poor agency service.

The frustration factor is an important one in an otherwise cold and objective cost analysis. It cannot be measured in dollars and cents, but the librarian who is forced to cope with a less than satisfactory agent is going to consider money saved in working through the agent as inconsequential. How, for example, does a librarian measure the loss to an angry user who can't find a magazine he or she needs because the agent has failed to enter a subscription on time. And the strain on the librarian's mental health may be more than can be compensated for in any saving of dollars. Again, while this matter is not measurable, it is put forward by librarians as an argument to counter the otherwise seemingly rational explanation by the agent that, no matter how high the service charge, he or she is saving the librarian money.

Yet the agent may turn this argument on the librarian by pointing out that publishers can cause the librarian equally bad headaches, or worse ones, than the agent does. However, the probability is that of one hundred publishers, at least half will provide good service, whereas one bad agent can easily undo the work of the fifty good publishers.

What is the actual cost of ordering a title directly from the publisher? Most librarians are too busy or lack the motivation or knowledge to compute such costs. There are as many methods of doing this as there are accountants, consultants, and librarians. In relatively simple terms, the librarian should first ascertain what the approximate costs are for processing a serial. No matter whether or not the librarian uses an agent, a rough estimate of total costs (which includes not only the price of writing an order but of processing the serial, etc.) may be obtained by following a few simple steps:

Take the Total allocation for operation of the serials department, or the sum allotted for ordering serials and periodicals, and divide this figure by the number of serials units processed. For example, the allocations for salaries, materials, overhead, etc., for the serials unit (or for those working with serials) is $10,000 a year. (This figure *does not* include the price of the serials.) If, then, 1,000 titles are on order, divide the $10,000 by 1,000 and the average cost of processing a title is found to be $10.

The average cost of simply ordering a title directly from the publisher (i.e., entering a single order) will range from a low of $5 to a high of $80. The usual figure quoted in mid-1974 was from $10 to $18. Broken down by type of library, the cost of a single order is estimated as follows:

Academic and research libraries. $25. "A major research library in Virginia had a consulting firm come into their automated library for two weeks. The library had been dealing with each publisher on a direct basis. At the end of two weeks, the consulting firm came up with a figure of $24 per title as the cost of requisitioning, ordering and clearing the invoice for a subscription."[11]

University library. $7 to $10. "The cost of a single order for a serial in an average university library is $7 to $10. This would include the clerical processing and the actual writing of the check."[12]

All libraries. $10 to $18. "Perhaps the most important [function of an agent] is simply entering each order through the purchasing and accounting procedures, the costs of which have been estimated at $10 to $18 for each separate purchase."[13]

All of these figures indicate possible costs, but, as Melcher points out: "Every library must make its own determination of the cost of placing 1,000 orders with 1,000 publishers as against placing one order with one agent."[14]

The real problem in generalizing about costs is that the costs vary greatly, depending upon the internal operations of the library. One library's processing may be such that the cost of an agent is minimal, while another—well, here is a quote from a letter received from a college library with 1,600 titles that dropped its agent in favor of working with publishers:

> Our ordering process, no matter whether we work through an agency or go direct, involves an order form for each journal, so there would be no real [savings] there. The time saved would be in stuffing X number of envelopes vs. putting all the purchase orders in one large envelope.
>
> When the invoices arrive, be it from an agency or from a publisher, the processing is much the same, except for a marking of an "Ok for payment" authorization on X number of invoices instead of a single invoice. (Even when

Franklin Square-Mayfair was our agency, we found so many errors and inconsistencies in their invoices that I am sure we spent as much time processing one of their invoices as we would spend processing the same number of invoices for individual journals.) The invoice number, date of invoice, subscription price and term of subscription must be recorded manually on the order information card for each journal. So whether we spend in staff time the funds equal to a service charge of 3 percent is open to debate. We feel that we at least break even. The increased costs for processing of invoices would be felt more severely by the accounting department than by the library. To date, some two years later, we have heard no great or loud protest.

Although satisfied with the library-publisher rather than the traditional library-agent relationship, the library experience quoted here may or may not be applicable in other situations. Also, as the librarian pointed out later, the cost factor was not as important in their situation as the conveniences of dealing directly with the publisher.

Another simplified approach to costs is suggested by a librarian at Simmons College. Here the formula is simplicity itself: Simply divide the agent's service charge by the number of titles ordered and the resulting figure is the cost of at least partially processing an order.

One invoice received by Simmons College, reflecting an order for 534 titles, showed a service charge of $415.97. The simple calculation of dividing the service charge by the number of titles being billed yields an average charge of 78 cents per subscription.[15]

Increasing agency costs will unquestionably push the cost of ordering from an agent to higher levels than they now occupy. At the same time, if only statistically objective computations are employed, it is difficult, if not impossible, to conclude that at any point in the near future the cost of the agent to the library will exceed the cost of the library's entering individual orders with publishers.

The sad fact is that, despite the availability of various estimates and isolated studies, the average librarian does not know what it costs to process an order, or, for that matter, to process a serial from the beginning until it is safely bound and waiting to be used. Estimates galore come from subscription agents. The agents are, for the most part, honest, but they invariably have a built-in bias that makes them show library costs for entering orders to be higher than agent costs. For several generations now, the pleas of people like Helen Welch Tuttle have been heard at countless librarian meetings and have peppered library literature:

The history of libraries in this country over the past hundred years is full of reports of efforts toward more effective use of library staff and discussions of the related topics of statistics, cost accounting, work measurement, performance budgets, and standards. But in spite of both individual and cooperative efforts to find a common statistical language for reporting, we have not yet reached this necessary first goal. . . . Technical services sometimes seem to be the most difficult of areas to justify to those who must produce funds for library operations, whether the chief administrative officers of educational institutions or public library boards. Acquiring, cataloging, and preparing are really the most actual and factual of library operations and should be the easiest to justify and explain. Perhaps it is the pressure of too much to do that keeps technical service librarians from gathering and interpreting the facts which would convince. Instead, they often answer questions about staff needs in vague generalities with a show of defensive impatience if they are pressed for more details. . . . Technical service librarians must be able to show in factual terms what their services cost. They must first be able to prove the figures to themselves, then they can convince those with funding responsibility.[16]

AGENCY CHARGES

(*See* Section IV C-D of the Checklist)

A major obstacle standing in the way of friendly and rational relationships between the library and the agent is the agent's failure to communicate how charges are computed. The advertising brochures that explain such charges appear to be written by lawyers and accountants not familiar with English as it is commonly understood. And a question to agents about cost that was used in the present study was either skipped or, when answered, was done so in language so incoherent and confusing as to rate a readability score of close to zero. Most of the misunderstanding about agency charges can be laid to the domestic agent, who is reluctant to admit that times are changing.

Historically, the library had the best of two worlds when it employed an agent. The agent not only rendered various useful services but gave the library a discount on the publisher's list price of a title. In effect, the library was paying nothing, even less than nothing, for service.

Only ten years ago the National Library of Agriculture reported that the agent discounted most American and Canadian periodicals. The net price to the library was "an average of 14 percent lower than the publishers' price."[17] This was possible because the publisher discount to the agent was large enough to enable the agent to subtract operational costs and a profit and still offer the title at less than full retail price.

The agent made the understandable error of convincing the librarian that the agent was quite literally being paid for his order work by the publisher. And, in the confusion, not many librarians stopped to consider that the agent was, indeed, marking up the price of the periodical or, if you will, adding a service charge. The service charge never came to the surface because a title for which the library would have to pay the publisher $10 was sold to the library by the agent for $9. The agent did not bother to say that the publisher had given him the title for $8, and the extra dollar was his service charge or gross markup. Katherine Smith sums up what happened to this neat arrangement:

> The years following the Second World War, however, saw many changes in this traditional role. Publishers found themselves in a cost squeeze: paper cost more, labor cost more, postage cost more. At the same time, new concepts in office machinery reduced invoicing costs. As a result, discounts to agents are becoming a thing of the past. Most large publishers, though they no longer need the agent, still accept library subscriptions placed through agents. Many

small publishers, and new ones not bound by tradition, are refusing such subscriptions, partly because of postal regulations concerning their mailing privileges. Others are pricing their serials so that subscribing through an agent is prohibitively expensive. Agents, in order to make profits, are instituting service charges against the library.

Traditionally, the librarian placed subscriptions through an agent because the agent offered a discount, thereby lowering costs.[18]

Adding to the confusion is the fact that many small school and public libraries still receive substantial discounts in their lists, up to 20 percent or more. Why? Because while the discounts for other types of periodicals have changed, the mass circulation publishers continue to allow the large discount that other publishers have long since abandoned. For better or worse, it should be noted the average small public or school library has a list heavy in such titles.

When the librarian from a small school moves into a larger school or a public library, it is a shock to find that the discount he or she is used to has either disappeared or has dwindled to almost nothing. Then, too, a serials librarian in a large library may have friends in smaller libraries who boast of this or that agent's discounts, and the librarian in the large library, if he or she has just approved a service charge of 5 or 10 percent, is likely to harbor some unkind thoughts about the agent in the case.

Finally, agents themselves help the situation little by stating loudly that discounts are still a perquisite of the service they offer. Large agencies no longer offer discounts, but smaller ones are somehow reluctant to dispense with what is rapidly becoming a business anacronism. Only the very small one- or two-person agency can still offer discounts successfully. Even so, the rising costs of postage, printing, paper, and editorial work are cutting into the traditional high discounts the mass circulation magazines give. It is a foregone conclusion that sooner or later the large discount itself will dwindle and disappear. Clearly, the discount system is changing. And each change brings with it an increase in the price libraries must pay for their periodicals.

Popular consumer titles, such as those listed in *The Reader's Guide to Periodical Literature*, depend upon advertising for growth and profit. In order to lure advertisers, the magazine must be able to demonstrate that it has a given number of paid subscribers. The more subscribers, the more likely the advertiser's message will reach the desired audience.

In this traditional situation the subscription price is incidental and actually may be lower than the cost of producing the magazine. No matter, cost is covered by advertising. The name of the game, then, is to build up the number of subscribers in order to acquire the advertiser's account. In order to do this, the magazine gives a huge discount to agents, as well as to individuals who participate in advertising stunts designed to build up circulation. However, the discount to the agent is usually larger than to the individual, and certainly this is true in a year-in, year-out way.

The problem: Many publishers of popular magazines now doubt that this traditional formula is still economically feasible. The costs of simply printing and distributing millions of copies of a popular magazine are such that a point is reached at which advertising revenue simply does not meet those costs. Furthermore, advertisers say that they will not pay more than X dollars for an advertisement, regardless of number of subscribers. In this situation, the publisher tries to cut back, not add, subscribers. And in so doing, he cuts back the costs of paper, printing, postage, etc. If a circulation cutback seems in order, it is foolish to continue offers of discounts. Hence, even some popular consumer titles no longer give such discounts, and for those that do, the discounts are lower than in previous years.

Still another development is likely to bring down discounts of 25 to 50 percent on magazines.

> Not so long ago, the magazine Holy Writ had it that subscription sales were the key to publishing success. Advertisers wanted the guarantee of a known audience whose demographic characteristics could be charted. Publishers coveted boxcar circulation figures—the bigger the numbers the better—and regarded long-term subscription income, the "float," as found money for investment. Nowadays, newsstand sales and store sales are considered key circulation because the magazines are unencumbered by postal charges and highly visible to the customer. . . . When a subscription magazine is offered at some ridiculous come-on price, the advertiser is never sure who ordered the magazine or who reads it. . . Many consumer magazines are abandoning both the numbers and the cut-rate subscription game.[19]

The commentator then goes on to explain that several consumer titles (from *Newsweek* to *Good Housekeeping*) are raising subscription rates and cutting discounts to drive out what are termed "marginal" subscribers. This is not to say that most of the consumer titles are going to revert to newsstand sales or going to give less than due value to large circulation figures. For one thing, postal restrictions force them to continue as they have been doing. In order to maintain second-class mailing privileges, a publisher must show that he or she makes at least 50 percent of his or her profit through sale of subscriptions. Hence, even the most persuasive agent cannot promise the library more than a 50 percent discount on any title, and is more likely to offer 30 to 40 percent if he or she is to save a bit for the agency.

Another difficulty with discounts is that most of the 50,000 to 70,000 periodical titles available here are not popular, mass circulation items. Most have only a small circulation. The majority, beyond the mass circulation, the controlled circulation, and business and farm publications, do not depend upon advertisers for support. The publisher looks to an organization, an institution, and, more or less, to subscribers for help in keeping on this side of the red ink. The mass of the 50,000 to 70,000 titles from which a library can choose are not issued by professional publishers at all, but by societies and scholars. It is not stretching the point to say that these "publishers" are apt to know less about publishing than many readers do. Such publishers, moreover, are constitutionally short of money. One result of this is that when approached by an agent, they give him or her the smallest discount possible, 10 percent or none at all.

Why would an agent handle a no-discount title? The agent will not do so if there is little or no library demand for the title. However, if the title is in demand by a number of libraries, the agent will handle it at no charge to the publisher—but, you guessed it, in one way or another pass along the charge to the library. This is entirely reasonable until such time as the agent starts serving as a charity instead of a business.

With the discount remaining in some instances, the rising costs of postage, printing, and distribution foretell its end altogether. Agents may still quote discounts to librarians on popular titles (although, just how long this will last is questionable), but simply cannot give discounts to libraries whose lists are made up of the more typical low-discount or no-discount titles.

ESTIMATING CHARGES

When estimating the probable service charge of this or that agent, there are two major variables to keep in mind:

The size of the agent. Usually the medium-sized to large agents have considerable overhead costs, of which added services constitute one. The necessary gross profit must be higher in this case than in that of the agent with a lower overhead but (usually) offering fewer services. The average gross profit margin (sometimes referred to as "clearance margin") for a large agent is 15 to 20 percent. International agents, with even more items on the list of services they offer, may need as much as 30 percent. The average gross profit margin for a medium-sized to large agent is 12 to 18 percent, and for a small agent, 2 to 5. If these figures are anywhere near accurate, it is obvious that X title ordered from a large, medium-sized, or small agent will vary in price, unless, of course, the small agent aspires to greater profits than does the large agent.

The size of the library. Actually, one is speaking here of the kinds of titles likely to be ordered. The large library is usually dealing with low- or no-discount special titles. The small library is dealing with titles that may be both popular and special. Given these two factors, or variables, it is safe to assume that in 1975 the charges made by agents will be as follows: Large agents depending on the size and wants of the library, will charge anything from zero to 15 percent; medium-sized to large agents will charge from zero to 20 percent; and small agents from 10 to 20 percent.

Added Charges

Either because of accounting practices or because of a desire to keep the service or handling charge at a reasonable level, a number of agents have what they call "added charges." The commonest among international agents is postage for titles delivered by the agent rather than by the publisher. Until a few years ago, among domestic agents, the added charge was the exception rather than the rule. It is now gaining favor.

The most typical added charge—unfortunately not one covered in the extensive questionnaire to agents—concerns the cost of a renewal. The agent levies an additional fixed or added charge of so much per title renewed and a special charge for renewing the list as a whole. Moreover, if fewer than a given number of additions are made to the list during the year, there will be an added charge for processing what orders there are. All librarians should clarify this charge with an agent. In 1975, it is most likely to be common in the dealings a library has with the larger agents. Other added charges, which are not so common, come in fees for ordering fewer than 20 titles, in making claims, in canceling orders, and in rush service. The agent has a considerable amount of money out to publishers, and the librarian who does not pay within thrity to sixty days must also expect to be assessed a one percent or more charge per month on the outstanding balance.

Anyone who has difficulty in understanding the notion of the added charge need only check the advertised price of an automobile and the small print at the bottom of the page that slaps on another $100 to $500 for delivery, preparation, etc.

The Agent Explains

Most agents will explain to a library that the cost of any given library list of periodicals depends upon the "mix" of the list. If any low-discount titles are included, the list will cost the library more; if many high-discount titles are included, the list will cost less.

Roessler, of Maxwell International (in one of the best explanations offered), shows how the agent figures the probable cost of a list to a library:

> The usual procedure, to avoid guesswork, is to price the library's list, forming two columns: the publishers' list price and the remit rate (amount agent must remit to publisher). A necessary gross profit percentage must be established by the agent (in line with his costs, competition and desired net profit). The agent adds that percentage—usually in the neighborhood of 18%—to the total remit column and that becomes the cost to the library (cost plus 18% permits a gross profit). If the list consists of many popular titles or titles with a fair commission to the agency, it would result in a discount to the library. If the list consists of highly scientific, technical or academic titles with little or no commission to the agency, it results in a "handling" or "service" charge to the library.
>
> There are many times an experienced agent can estimate by the nature of the library that the list must command a handling charge of approximately 5 to 7%. He may find that he guess-timated too low, and the following year request an adjustment.
>
> If the library list is very lengthy, the cost of pricing each title (list price and remit rate) may be too expensive and time-consuming, and so the agent must estimate.

Swets & Zeitlinger gives a specific example illustrating the difficulty of simply saying that the agency has a flat service charge of X percentage. The process followed by Swets & Zeitlinger is similar to that followed by almost all agents. The variable is the 15 percent gross profit figure. A representative of Swets & Zeitlinger explains:

> We normally charge publisher's prices for subscriptions. [*Ed. note:* which is to say the publisher's price is not the price charged the agent, but probably represents a 10 to 30 percent or more discount to the agent from the publisher. The discount, of course, constitutes agent's gross profit. And when the discount is large, the agent may not charge the library for services.]

98   Guide to Magazine and Serial Agents

However, some publishers or non-profit making organizations grant us little or no discount. In these cases a moderate service charge is made to cover our costs. We apply no flat rates for service. Each periodical is individually assessed. [*Ed. note:* Swets & Zeitlinger differs here from some agents who simply add up the total list, determine cost, calculate necessary gross profits and then, as illustrated earlier, give the library a discount or, more likely, add a service charge.]   How service charge is computed.   Between 0% and 15% is added by agent to no-discount or little-discount titles to compute charge.

Example A		*Example B*	
Subscription price	$40.	Subscription price	$40.
No agent discount		Agency discount 5%	2.
We add 15%	6.	Net price	$38.
The library pays	$46.	We add 15% of $38.	5.70
		The library pays	$43.70

For high priced periodicals a sliding scale is applicable.

Variations on this theme are employed by all agents.   Here is an explanation from Blackwell's:

We try to charge the prices fixed by the publisher. The exception being journals costing less than £1.50 per annum ($3.75) and those costing more but on which we receive little or no discount. On these we have to make a small handling charge. We also add a handling charge to journals published outside Great Britain costing between £1.50 and £3.00 ($7.50).

Where there is no discount from the publisher the service charge is computed as follows: journal costing up to $45 per annum add 20%; journal costing more than $45 but less than $1,000 add 20%, journal costing $1,000 and up, add 5%.

If the library purchases a substantial number of books and periodicals from us, we do not make any service charge. If their book purchases are low, we may add 3% handling charge to the total on their periodical's invoice.

The List Mix

There are numerous variables in the computing of the price of library lists. Handed a "mixed" list of titles, the agent must consider publisher policy, such as

1. X title allows the agent no discount: in fact, it is sold to the agent at the same price at which it is sold directly to libraries. The agent must make a profit, and it certainly will not be from X title.
2. Y title allows the standard 10 percent discount to the agent, who now has $1 to work with.
3. Z title allows only a 5 percent discount to the agent.
4. P title, a widely distributed, consumer-type magazine, allows the agent a discount of 25 percent or more.
5. Q title, anxious to build circulation to lure advertisers may be a throwaway, i.e., is almost free to the agent.

The lists most libraries prepare are, of course, mixed lists. The agent, as noted, then adds up X, Y, Z, P, and Q (multiplied hundreds or even thousands of times) and sees what the list is going to cost.   Let us say it will cost him $1,000.   The agent then adds up the retail price of the same titles, and finds the figure is $1,100.

If the agent's required gross profit is 20 percent, the result is that the library is billed for the net publisher's price, i.e., $1,100, plus a service charge of $100 more to cover the agent's gross profit target figure.

The agent who is reluctant to express his gross profit needs in percentages may be understandably reluctant to explain in detail how the $1,200 figure was reached. Be that as it may, the confusion seems to disappear to the satisfaction of all concerned with the simple levying of an added or service charge of $100.

Fluctuating Charges

What the average librarian has difficulty in understanding is the need for the gross profit that the agent sets for himself or herself. This is particularly true because the vast majority of domestic agents have a fluctuating gross profit. For example, depending upon the mix of the list being considered, the agent may figure a gross markup of 15 or 20 percent. Why the difference? The risk factor in the case of one list may be higher than of another. In this instance, the nature of the titles matters. Clasquin explains:

> For instance, the risk factor of handling a $10 versus a $200 periodical contributes a variable service cost burden, particularly when publisher order acceptance policies are dissimilar. . . . An order entered in error due to limited information supplied by a client may be cancelable, or the agency, if using mechanical devices for internally processing an order, may err by ordering an incorrect title.[20]

It is worth repeating: The majority of publishers insist that the agent pay in advance for a subscription. In effect, the publisher says: "No money, no publication." Reputable agents pay, as a matter of course, before payment is received from the library. Hence, the agent has considerable amounts of money out and if a high percentage of costly titles is being sought, the amount of money out (with subsequent risk) is such that the agent justifiably covers his risk by raising the markup percentage. In other words, the real loss factor experience determines to an extent the markup that will be used.

The library list may include a number of titles from publishers with whom the agent knows from experience he is apt to have difficulties. Hence, more exppense accrues. For example, when the agent knows that a publisher is likely to generate claims (which requires an added outlay by the agent), the markup on that publisher's titles will be higher than on those of a publisher whose history suggests no such problems.

Price of the titles governs markup. For example, it is one thing to make a markup of, say, 15 percent on an $18 title, but quite another to use the same markup on a title that costs $2,000 or more. The rule of the game: The markup normally drops as the price of the title increases.

So much for the mix of the list, but there are other factors that contribute to fluctuating markups. Although not often expressed by agents, there is a risk factor generated by the library itself. The agent has considerable amounts of money out, and the agent must assume that the library will pay him within the standard thirty days. If the agent knows or suspects that the library will delay payment, the agent must cover the cost of having his money out for an extended period of time. He may do this by raising his markup. Other agents, of course, cover themselves by stipulating that if payment is not received within thirty to sixty days, the agent will add an interest charge to the price of the list. (Some institutions, it might be added, are prohibited by law from paying interest charges incurred beyond the agent's net terms.) Also, if the library is likely to cause undue correspondence, enter unnecessary claims, and generally waste the agent's time, the agent must consider such behavior in determining what his or her markup will be.

The basic condition of the economy may also affect the markup. Clasquin explains:

> Lack of proper financing in a low margin business (i.e., the agency) is a matter which directly affects cost of service. If appropriate sources for operating funds are not available, the services of an agency are affected.... Obviously the total cost of any given list of titles, which cost dictates the principal cash demand on the agency, is a cost of service directly proportional to the cash need to initially place the orders.[21]

If the evaluation of the library list involves so many variables, and if the agent must compensate for these by raising or lowering his service charge, it is inevitable that the markup one library pays will differ from what another library that orders the same titles must pay. Clasquin considers this point:

> It may be argued that such a pricing policy is discriminatory because the net percent return to the agent will fluctuate from client to client depending upon each list of periodicals. A charge for services ... should be logically defined as a variable factor....[22]

The point here is obvious: It is not the mix of the list alone that determines the eventual cost of the list to the library, but that other variables may result in X library's being charged more or less than Y library for pretty much the same list. Given the existence of variables, Clasquin's logic is sound. It would be helpful to libraries, nevertheless, if agents in general were more candid in talking about how they compute their charges.

REFERENCE NOTES

1. Peter Spyers-Duran and Daniel Gore, eds., *Management Problems in Serials Work* (Westport, Conn.: Greenwood Press, 1974). Four of nine papers collected in this work consider national and regional collections and the maximum or minimum size of an individual library's periodicals collection.

    Librarians, as others in our modern culture, have slowly come to abandon the notion that quantity, per se, is the way to meet information needs. As Kochen puts it: "The key problems attendant on the overabundance of literature relative to the fixed information in processing capacities of its consumers have no more to do with the organization and reorganization of knowledge in the sense of deepening understanding and wisdom than in better cataloging or indexing of unassimilated, specialized fragments." (Manfred Kochen, *Integrative Mechanisms in Literature Growth* [Westport, Conn.: Greenwood Press, 1974], p. 11.)

This extended note is by way of recognizing that, when speaking of any optimum number of periodicals for a library, there is considerably more involved in the formula than sheer numbers.

2. "Reference Services in American Public Libraries . . ." (Urbana: University of Illinois Library School, 1961), processed, 22 pp.
3. Statistics quoted here are from the following sources: Leslie W. Dunlap, "National and Lending Libraries," in Spyers-Duran and Gore, *op. cit.*, p. 30. (the result of a survey of members of the Chicago Center for Research Libraries); *The Bowker Annual* (New York: R. R. Bowker, 1969–1974) with various pages relating to library budgets.; William Huff, "Acquisitions of Serial Publications," *Library Trends*, January 1970, p. 296; Gordon Williams, *Library Cost Models: Owning Versus Borrowing Serial Publications* (Bethesda, Md.: Westat Research Inc., 1968); John Kountz, "Library Cost Analysis: A Recipe," *Library Journal*, February 1, 1972, pp. 459+; Ferdinand F. Leimkuhler, "Cost Accounting and Analysis for University Libraries," *College & Research Libraries*, November 1971, pp. 449+; And the survey of libraries included in this guide.
4. Most large and some medium-sized libraries provide for serial payments in a fund that is separate from other acquisitions funds, such as those used for books and audiovisual materials. In addition, larger libraries tend to subdivide the serials fund into two parts: one for periodicals and ongoing subscriptions and the second for serials received as part of a standing order or continuation. Often, too, the larger library will charge serial payments to individual sections or divisions or departments. No matter how the original allocation is subdivided, it is imperative that a library with a substantial outlay for serials have close control over all serials funds. There are numerous articles on this subject, e.g., William E. McGrath, et al., "An Allocation Formula . . ." *College & Research Libraries*, January 1969, pp. 51+.
5. Susan Brynteson, "Serial Acquisitions," in Spyers-Duran and Gore, *op. cit.*, p. 51.
6. *Ibid.*
7. Philip E. Greene, "The Three-Way Responsibility," in Spyers-Duran and Gore, *op. cit.*, pp. 90–91.
8. Peter Gellatly, "The Serials Perplex . . . ," in *Serial Publications in Large Libraries* ed. by Walter C. Allen (Urbana: University of Illinois Graduate School of Library Science, 1970), p. 42.
9. *Ibid.*, p. 44.
10. Norman B. Brown, "Price indexes for 1973," *Library Journal*, July 1973, p. 2052. This is an annual index that the serials librarian should check each July.
11. Greene, *op. cit.*, p. 92.

12. Judith A. Nientimp, "The Librarian and the Subscription Agent," *Special Libraries*, July 1972, p. 296.
13. Frank Clasquin, "The Jobber's Side: Cost of Acquiring Periodicals," *RQ*, Summer 1971, p. 329.
14. Daniel Melcher, *Melcher on Acquisition* (Chicago: American Library Association, 1971), p. 151.
15. Timothy W. Sineath, "Libraries and Library Subscription Agencies," *The Library Scene*, Summer 1972, p. 30.
16. Helen Welch (Tuttle), "Technical Service Costs, Statistics and Standards," *Library Resources and Technical Services*, Fall 1967, pp. 437, 442.
17. Kirby B. Payne, "Procurring Serials by Bid at the USDA Library," *Serial Slants*, April 1965, p. 72.
18. Katherine R. Smith, "Serials Agents/Serials Librarians," *Library Resources and Technical Services*, Winter 1970, pp 5-6.
19. Edwin Diamond, "The Unladylike Battle of the Women's Magazine," *New York*, May 20, 1974, p. 43. This situation is sounded time and again in business publications devoted to periodicals matters, *e.g., Folio* and *Media Industry Newsletter.*
20. Clasquin, *op. cit.*
21. *Ibid.*
22. *Ibid.*

8.
BIDS AND QUOTES

(*See* Section IV E of the Checklist)

When asked whether a library should request agents to submit *bids* on a list of periodicals, the answer is an uncategorical NO. This is not a lone opinion, but one echoed time and again by librarians and agents everywhere. Conversely— and it is important to realize the difference—when a librarian thinks X, Y, and possibly P agents offer similar services, he or she is advised, in order to make a proper comparison, to request *quotes* from the agents.

BIDS

The difference between a quote and a bid is not just a matter of semantics. A bid, by definition, presupposes that the agent who offers the lowest price, other considerations aside, will receive the contract. Obviously, even the most slipshot governmental agency will write into the contract certain qualifiers that will, or at least should, prevent the agent from going West with the money. This side of detailed contracts for large federal libraries, the average bid pays less attention to the qualifications of the agent than to the price the agent quotes.

The rationale used in promoting and defending the bid system is sound enough. This system "protects the taxpayer from collusion between government agents and suppliers, obtains the best use of tax money, guarantees the performance of the supplier, and assures the supplier a flow of business to which he can adjust his operations for maximum benefit to himself and his customer."[1]

The term "catch-bid" means that there is no "guarantee of performance" apart from the mere ordering of the serial. Moreover, as most bids are made on an annual basis, there is no guarantee of a constant "flow of business" back and forth. When dealing with trucks, snow removal, office equipment, etc., there may be sufficient longitude for "collusion between government agents and suppliers," but the opportunities for such collusion between librarians and agents are strictly nonexistent.

Over the years, most librarians have managed to convince their governing bodies that the bid system is poison. The result, according to an ALA survey of the late 1960s, is that the majority of libraries are exempt from the bid process:

Of 31 state libraries, 13 indicate no bid system; of 483 public libraries, 335 mention no bids; and of 296 school libraries, 171 report no bids. . . . Only 5 school librarians and 12 public librarians are voluntarily submitting their purchases to bids. . . . Where librarians are able to avoid the bid system, by and large, they do.[2]

Bidding is sometimes required under the terms of state and federal contracts. In most cases, the size of the contract is so large that the small agent is effectively eliminated for inability to perform the services required. Here, from the start, however, the nature and size of the contract are such that the bid is really a call for a firm quote. Only a handful of domestic agents have the resources to make such bids.

Melcher points out another reason many agents and librarians frown on bids:

There is also the little matter of the cost of entering a bid. Quoting on library subscription needs is expensive and takes time because it must be done with care; a bidder who makes a blind stab without close study of your library's wants and idiosyncrasies can take a real beating.[3]

And, of course, there is no ignoring the expense the library itself is put to in the matter. Describing the library's needs, if done conscientiously, can be a costly and exhausting experience. The red tape alone is fairly well endless.

The routine . . . is considerable. There is the labor of compiling multiple copies of the lists to be submitted to dealers; there is the paperwork that goes with sending out as many as eight lists; almost invariably there is telephone or written follow-up work to secure the necessary number of bids; and eventually there is the task of assembling and comparing the bids, if and when they are received.[4]

An irony of the bid system is that almost all bids contain an escalator clause, i.e., a clause allowing the agent to pass along publisher rate hikes to the library after the bid has been accepted. The irony lies in the fact that, as Ford points out, "the best informed bidder is usually the highest bidder, for in periods of increasing prices he quotes the latest price and is underbid by the less informed and possibly less competent competitor."[5]

Aside from the fact that the low bidder is rarely able to guarantee the library necessary services, another major fault of the bid system is its lack of continuity. Almost without exception, in cases in which libraries must put their serials out to bid, this must be done annually or at least once every two years. The inevitable and frequent changeover from agent to agent is not only traumatic for the librarian but also often fatal to the carrying out of an orderly acquisitions program.

The normal bid runs contiguously with the fiscal year of the library or its purchasing agency. The fiscal year makes no allowance for titles that may follow a different schedule, e.g., January through December, rather than, say, the library's fiscal year of June through May. Nor does it allow for titles that may be irregular, may be added, may be deleted, etc. The bid virtually locks the library into a fixed situation for a given period of time.

Changes in rates and frequencies, added volumes, mergers, etc. all call for additional services which cannot be fulfilled with the lowest bid. Thus, for the library, bids do not always present a simple and clear-cut arrangement, and conducting them costs time and money. Moreover, they breed their own special problems, depending upon such things as the periodicals involved, the manner in which bids are chosen, governmental rules restricting library procedures, the competence of the bidder, etc.[6]

A public librarian describes the sort of debacle the bid system can give rise to:

Beginning in 1972 the library was required to advertise for bids. As a result an agent with a very low bid was our supplier for 1972. Judging from comments of librarians on the staff the agent was guilty of extreme negligence. They underpriced some materials on the original bid, later charging us the correct amount. A number of magazines never received payment from them, or found it difficult to obtain payment. We still have gaps in our holdings from 1972 that we may never be able to fill.

The administration is trying to convince the town officials that compelling a bid procedure to obtain a serial subscription agent is a practice that should be discontinued because the element of service is not given enough attention.[7]

Clasquin puts the bid business in perspective:

We are not suggesting that annual bids for periodicals is purchasing illiteracy, but we wish to stress that the potential of our services will not be fully realized on a one-year contract.... Your library or its procurement authority should, therefore, prudently review the matter of annual bid requests.[8]

When a bid is absolutely necessary, the librarian must demand certain requirements be met. The bid should list not only the titles to be supplied but also all services and procedures expected of the agent. It should be made clear, furthermore, that the arrangement is to continue for a year at least and not under any circumstances for less than a year. Moreover, the bidder should guarantee to supply all of the titles on the library's list or at least 95 percent of them. Those the bidder cannot supply should be designated. Finally, the bidder should give assurance that he or she is handling the order personally and not farming it out to another firm, a practice sometimes followed. All of this should be committed to writing in a letter of agreement or a contract.[9]

It is, of course, in the librarian's best interest that he or she investigate the agent's financial solvency and technical capabilities; and it is the librarian who must signify approval or disapproval of the agent's response to the points listed above, and not simply a purchase officer in an office somewhere nearby.

QUOTES

When a library contemplates hiring or changing an agent, it is wise to ask for quotes. It should be made clear to the agent that the library is asking for a quote, and not a bid. Also, it is perfectly reasonable to inform the agent that the same quote may be requested of one or two other agents, and even to give their names.

When a quote is requested, the librarian should outline, through use of a checklist (the library's own or the agent's) what services are being sought. Sometimes the agent simply cannot offer needed services, and will return the quote request without quoting. At other times, the agent may be less than clear about specific matters, which, when broached, will cause the agent to back away.

In any case, sending a request for a quote to a few agents (no more than two or three) is an acceptable and, for the most part, wise business practice—assuming that one is prepared to change from the chosen agent to another at year's end (a practice not recommended).

The quote request may be either formal or informal, although the latter is preferable if the librarian has reasonable assurance of the agent's reliability. Agents are generally amenable to the quote.

> If a quotation is needed for budgeting, we will cooperate. However, it should be recognized that publishers' prices are subject to change without notice and that price changes will be billed in addition to the original invoice.[10]
>
> Price quotations, which many school and government libraries require before issuing a formal purchase order, are in an entirely different category (than the bid) and we will always be happy to pre-price customers' lists upon request.[11]

All major and most minor domestic agents (those, anyway, both large and small, that engage in general subscription work) submit quotes, but they will not always submit bids. The same holds true in the case of large foreign agents. The exceptions are agents, both domestic and foreign, who supply specialized serials, and are the only reliable source for such materials. In consulting with these agents, the quote request may be framed as a letter of inquiry about the list price of items in which the library is interested and the service charges the agent requires.

In cases when one agent is being compared with other agents, or when a choice must be made between several agents, the quote is an essential part of the evaluation process. Information on general agents who will not provide quotes can be found in the Checklist of this guide.

REFERENCE NOTES

1. Stephen Ford, *The Acquisition of Library Materials* (Chicago: American Library Association, 1973), p. 64.
2. Evelyn Hensel and Peter Veillette, *Purchasing Library Materials in Public School Libraries* (Chicago: American Library Association, 1969), p. 13.
3. Daniel Melcher, *Melcher on Acquisition* (Chicago: American Library Association, 1971,) p. 149.
4. Andrew Osborn, *Serial Publications, 2nd ed.* (Chicago: American Library Association, 1973), p. 103.
5. Ford, *op. cit.*, p. 117.
6. Astha Hirota, "Subscription Agents." *Hawaii Library Association Journal*, December 1966, p. 16.
7. Letter to the author from a public librarian (name withheld), November 1, 1973.

8. Frank Clasquin, "More Than a Low Bid," *Sci-Tech News*, Spring 1965, p. 3.
9. Evelyn Hensel, *op. cit.* The author gives details of bid contracts, although primarily for books. Still there is enough information here to help the librarian contend with the form of a bid, if not its content.
10. Ebsco, advertising brochure, n.d.
11. Maxwell International brochure, n.d.

9.
LIBRARY ORDERS

(*See* Sections II and IX of the Checklist)

Every library has its own individual method of ordering periodicals. Variations depend as much upon the size and the function of the library as upon the objective requirements of the system as seen by the librarian. Attempts to devise satisfactory standardized order procedures for libraries, perhaps especially at the automated level, are difficult. Nevertheless, consensus exists among agents and librarians as to basic procedures.

THE LIBRARY ORDER

The initial order usually takes the form of a consolidated list of titles; it is not usual at this point to issue separate orders for each title. The form on which the list appears may be supplied by the agent or it may be a form worked out by the library itself. The form includes all vital data needed by the agent to fulfill the order, regardless of number of titles. With the initial list in hand, the agent submits to the library an invoice and/or a report on the order. Ordinarily, the invoice is arranged in the same way as is the initial library order.

Under normal circumstances, the initial order is submitted or approved for renewal annually. However, throughout the year, the library may send in individual orders for further titles it finds it needs. And occasionally the library may cancel a title appearing in the initial order. Orders sent throughout the year may again be placed together in the form of a list, if more than one title is wanted; but it is more usual for such orders to go out one at a time, each on an individual form. These separate orders are then incorporated into the total list of orders belonging to the library.

Some libraries issue a requisitions form each time an item is wanted. This may be suitable for the placing of individual orders during the course of the year. It is entirely unsuitable for use in issuing the annual order. In both cases, the librarian should arrange to attach copies of individual orders (or of the annual order) to the requisitions form rather than fill out separate requisitions all along the way.

No matter in what form the order is entered—as a consolidated list, an individual order slip, or a special requisitions form—it is imperative that clear directions be given concerning variant addresses, expiration dates, required forms of billing, etc. Regular procedures should be preprinted on the library forms, or, if preprinted agency forms are used, space should be left for the agent to add information or instructions of his or her own.

Basic Data on the Order

The Checklist indicates the basic data necessary for any type of order, regardless of the form in which the information is sent to the agent or publisher. However, if the agent or publisher has special requirements of any sort, these should be observed, or a mutually satisfactory alternative worked out in advance.

Abbreviations. Many agents ask that the library abbreviate the address and the name of the library. The ordinary mailing label will accommodate only so much information, and it is better to have a clear abbreviation than to have someone at the other end simply "lop off" data to keep the label short. A detailed explanation of the reason for abbreviations is given in a Faxon brochure:

> Our order department uses the following procedure to set up your address. If you follow these guidelines your address will appear on your invoice and be sent to the publisher exactly the way you submit it. You may use as many as four lines for your address. The first line may have up to 24 characters and should contain the name of the library. (A character is defined as a letter, a space, a numeral, or a punctuation mark.) The second line may consist of as many as 19 characters and should clearly indicate the type of library. This is very important as some publishers have more than one rate, depending on the class of the subscriber. If the first line clearly indicates the type of library, you do not have to use the second line.
>
> The third line may have up to 19 characters and should contain the number and name of the street, P.O. box number or R.F.D. number if applicable. The fourth line may contain up to 26 characters and should consist of city, state, and zip code. If you are a foreign customer, place the city and name of the country on this line. If you do not have a four line address information pertains, but you should check to see that the number of characters does not exceed the amount allowed.
>
> Publishers develop their own address techniques to accomplish certain data collection goals hence our address mode, or the library specific address request may not be accepted in its exact form by the publisher.

Other agents with automated systems have similar requirements. The librarian should carefully check this out with the agent. Smith comments:

> Librarians refuse to realize that addressograph plates and computer storage fields are limited spaces. A library having for instance, the name "John H. Ryland Memorial Library, College of Business Arts, University of Southampton, 1114 Southside Street, Southampton, Va. 23239. Attention Serials Librarian" will receive mail addressed to a variety of addresses because the entire name is too long. Furthermore, many librarians themselves use different forms of the library's name depending on what sort of impression they wish to make. It is no wonder that local postal officials cannot locate the correct slot for such mail.[1]

Full title of serial. While some agents find it helpful if the library includes the agent's title number for a periodical, most do not insist that this be done. The ALA *Guidelines* note that Library of Congress numbers are optional, as are International Standard Serial numbers. No agent requests such data. The only required information is the full title.

The full title as printed in the agent's catalog is what should be used. This presupposes, of course, that the agent has a catalog. All large and medium-sized agents issue catalogs or lists of some sort. Smaller agents may not, and in this case the librarian should use the entry found in such sources as *New Serial Titles* and *Ulrich's International Periodical Directory.*

A difficulty is presented by the new title, the elusive title and the fugitive title, as these are not likely to be listed anywhere. Verifying such titles is a challenge to agent and librarian alike, and often requires considerable consultation back and forth between them.

Multiple copies. When the library enters orders for multiple copies of the same title to be mailed to different addresses, care should be exercised in making the instruction as clear as possible. While the ALA *Guidelines* recommend separate orders in these cases, agents do not necessarily require this. Perhaps they are more optimistic than the ALA, or simply confident in their ability to sort things out satisfactorily. In any event, the librarian who uses a single order form requesting copies of a title for various locations would do well to attach a covering letter of explanation.

All duplicate subscriptions to a single title should be ordered from the same agent. Trouble awaits the librarian who orders copies of the same title from a number of agents. If one copy fails to arrive, for instance, it is just about impossible to determine which copy is the missing one. Hence, claiming comes to a standstill.

Subscription starting date. The majority of library orders for periodicals are entered in a way that gives either a complete run of the title or a run beginning with the first issue in a volume. If the title has been underway for a number of years at the time the order goes in, obtaining a full run is possible only by ordering reprints, microforms, or back issues—normally from someone other than the subscription agent. Some libraries, particularly smaller ones where complete runs of a periodical are not necessary, are willing to begin the subscription with the first issue of the current year. This obviates many difficulties about starting dates, if not all.

Consistency in the dating of periodicals is practically nonexistent. The majority of trade publishers tend to begin a new volume with each new year. Others begin in the middle of the year. And to add to the confusion, other publishers begin a volume whenever it pleases them. They may even issue double volumes, i.e., volumes covering more than one year's work; or they may issue two volumes separately within a single year's time. Nor is it unusual to find a volume that covers nine or ten months only.

Most libraries, regardless of the schedule of volumes issued by publishers, enter the initial large subscriptions list at a given time of the year. The time will depend upon when funds are annually made available for purchases. Then, too, the library will enter individual subscriptions throughout the year for other new titles, new or old, requested by users.

The majority of agents do not handle back-issue orders. While this is generally understood by librarians, what is not understood is the meaning of "back issue" to the agent or the publisher. To them, this is quite literally any issue in a current volume that has appeared before the order comes their way, and this may mean only a few days or weeks earlier. Agents handle only current subscriptions, that is to say, usually orders that begin with the current issue. Here, "current" means the first issue supplied by the publisher after the order is received. Anything other than "current" is usually referred to as a "back-start" order.

Given this understanding of how publishers and agents view matters of currency and back issues, the library that enters an order with the instructions to "begin the subscription with the first issue of the current volume" may or may not be satisfied with what it gets. Obviously, if the first issue of the volume is not to be published for sixty days or more, the fulfillment will more than likely be met. But, if an order is submitted in June for a volume that began in January, the likelihood of the library's receiving the first issues is uncertain.

Consequently, when the librarian thinks there is a chance the publisher will not be able to start the subscription with the desired issue, the librarian should give the agent authority to have the order begin with the current issue or any earlier issues in the volume that are still available. This presupposes that the librarian has faith in the agent's ability to take proper action in such a case. In fact, some agents assume the needed authority as a common-sense requirement of their job. Faxon, among all agents questioned, was the only one to report that: "If we know a publisher will not accept a start date earlier than the current issue, the order is entered on that basis without first checking with the library." How many others do this is not known.

As a footnote, it has to be said that some librarians fail to show a desired beginning date for a subscription. In this instance, most agents query the librarian. Others, more particularly Moore-Cottrell, will begin the subscription with the first issue of the calendar year or the first issue of the current volume. The same procedure is followed by such international agents as Blackwell's and Collins. In these cases, the agent acts without prior consultation with the librarian.

Correspondence and conversation with agents and librarians indicate that when the library does not suggest a starting date, the usual procedure among small agents is simply to begin the subscription with the first issue available after the subscription is entered.

Additional materials. Title pages to be used in bound volumes of periodicals are often issued by publishers. The publisher also may publish an annual index to a volume. Some publishers will offer, in addition, a number of regular or irregular supplements to a given title during the year. At one time, all of these "added" items were included in the subscription price of the title. Rising costs have resulted in the levying of an extra amount for indexes (particularly those of the multiple-year sort) and supplements, although title pages still are usually sent "free" with the subscription.

The library should know

1. Whether or not the agent has an up-to-date record of which publishers issue title pages, indexes, and supplements and which do not (or no longer do, if they once did)
2. Whether or not there is an extra charge for such material
3. Whether or not these materials are included automatically in an order

As so often in such matters, the importance of this information increases in proportion to the number of titles ordered by a library.

All agents now request that a library indicate clearly whether or not title pages, indexes, and supplements are wanted if these are billed for separately by the publisher. No agent requires any such word when the added material is automatically included in the order.

How does the librarian know when the added material is sent automatically or when there is a separate charge for it? Two large agents—Ebsco and Faxon—include this information in their catalogs. Others do not. A safe way out is for the librarian to indicate opposite each title in his or her list whether or not added materials are wanted. If the materials are always wanted, a statement to this effect can be made.

Stechert-Macmillan reports that: "Title pages, indexes and supplements are usually supplied without charge by the publisher. Our instructions to the publishers remind them to include such materials as part of each subscription. When these items are not considered by the publisher as part of the subscription, they may be ordered through us separately." Agents, of course, notify the library quickly of added charges, when these come along.

Swets & Zeitlinger, alone among international agents, includes such material "automatically unless the library asks us to exclude." Harrassowitz used to follow the same policy, but now: "Due to the rising prices, we prefer the library's confirmation for the supplements. We contact them if it is not clear to us whether or not supplements are required."

AGENCY PROCESSING OF AN ORDER

(*See* Section II of the Checklist)

Lead-in Time for Subscriptions

Given the potential hazards in the way of the smooth entry of an order, how much lead-in time should the librarian allow in ordering so as to have the first issue arrive in the library when desired? Agents vary in their estimates, as do librarians. In general, however, a library should allow sixty days—and, to be on the safe side, ninety days—for the arrival of a domestic item. Another thirty days should be added to the estimate for international orders.

Agency Reports on the Library Order

The better agents notify the library immediately when a delay is to be expected in receipt of an order. Occasionally an order of many titles will be held up. Generally, however, when a delay occurs, the delay affects only certain titles in the order. When this happens, the agent proceeds to process the rest of the order—as, of course, it should.

All agents listed in this guide that sent out reports on orders say that the reports are sent out "promptly." Translated into days, this usually means no more than thirty days after the order from the library has been received. Exceptions may occur in the case of publications that are issued less often than weekly or monthly, i.e., quarterly, semiannually, annually, etc. In these cases, reports may be delayed another fifteen to thirty days without danger of the library's missing an issue.

Again, the librarian should ascertain the agent's practice in the matter. Why? Because one of the commoner complaints among librarians is the agent's failure to report on titles the agent cannot supply.

> I would greatly prefer that an agent return orders, advising me to place them direct, than for them to remain in the open order file for months on end and not know whether or not they were placed. That kind of lack of response by agents regarding new orders is what leads many librarians to start placing more and more orders direct, an action which may lead to faster response time but which causes many other problems in the future.[2]

Some agents do not issue such reports, or the report is not given until the library receives the invoice. In this case, the report forms part of the invoice, i.e., items the agent is unable to supply are so indicated. Faxon and Ebsco use this form of reporting. Both insist that the invoice is sent as promptly as would be individual reports, i.e., within thirty to sixty days of receipt of the order from the library. The fact is, of course, that reports are issued in this way as a convenience to the agent, as then the work entailed is largely taken care of for it by the firm's computer. Ideally, the agent should send out a report immediately.

Once an agent reports that it cannot supply a given title, the reason for the failure is of value to the library. Simply stating that it does not handle the title leaves the librarian in a bit of a quandary as to where to turn next. If the agent gives specific reasons for not handling the title, then the librarian is in a better position to make a decision about his or her next step. The larger the agent, the more apt it is to give detailed information on why an order is unacceptable. In the case of international agents, size does not matter. Hardly any, large or not, give such information.

The part of the Checklist dealing with agent reports should be studied carefully before an agent is selected. Reports on why an agent refuses an order indicate, at least to some extent, the type of material not handled by that agent. And if the library is likely to require such materials often, the library would be better off doing business with another agent. For example, all domestic agents with the exception of China Books and Periodicals will notify the library that X title is not available through the agent because "it is part of a series where the pricing is too irregular for the agent to handle." Well, not quite all. Ebsco and Stechert-Macmillan do not give this information because they say they handle such titles. Hence, if the library's list includes a number of variously priced series, it would be better for the librarian to contact Ebsco and Stechert-Macmillan than, say, Faxon or Maxwell.

When an agent suggests that no action is being taken on an order because the agent is awaiting word on discounts from the publisher, the librarian should object. What happens is that while the agent negotiates, the issues the librarian requires irretrievably slip by. The ALA *Guidelines* are quite specific and correct in noting:

> Orders should not be delayed while negotiating for special discount. If none are available, the library should be notified [by the agent].[3]

No agent who filled out the questionnaire admitted to holding up an order while awaiting a discount from a publisher. Yet some librarians report that this is a reason small agencies give for delay, and they excuse it on the grounds that if a discount is granted, the library itself benefits. The argument is not very persuasive, however, as missing issues and bookkeeping problems caused by the delay are a source of both anxiety and expense.

Rush Orders

There are occasions when a librarian wants a particular title in a big hurry, usually at some point after the big annual order has gone out. Most medium to large-sized agents will accept rush orders, although a notable exception here is Stechert-Macmillan. Others who do not accept rush orders are Instructor and smaller agents in general. They accept the orders, but they are handled without special attention, as are regular orders. (This latter statement is not supported by questionnaire findings, but rather by statements made by several librarians during the study.)

Two points are worth stressing when the librarian thinks of "rushing" an order: (1) in most cases, a letter or telephone call to the agent will cut the time the agency needs to process the order by one to six days; and (2) when requested to do so, most agents will cut this time even further by telephoning the rush order to the publisher. Some publishers, to be sure, will not accept such orders, as they require cash before they send out their publication. Other publishers will accept rush orders, but treat them more or less as they do regular orders. In other words, "rushing" an order does save time in the exchange that occurs between the library and agent, but does not always galvanize the publisher into action. Trade publishers are, for the most part, insensitive to entreaties to move. Scholarly publishers, which have a more personalized service, may or may not give special treatment to rush orders.

Opportunities for delay and confusion are numerous when the library uses rush orders indiscriminately. The librarian should have a clear understanding with the agent as to how the agent handles such orders. The librarian should understand that even the best of agents with the best of systems for handling rush orders is powerless to do anything when the publisher simply refuses to circumvent its regular routines.

As of this writing, Ebsco was the only agent to make a special charge for rush orders. Other agents indicated that when there are a number of rush orders, they are sometimes forced to levy an added charge. This is another of these matters that the librarian must straighten out with the agent.

AGENCY ORDER PLANS

(*See* Section III A of the Checklist)

Long-Term/Multiyear Subscriptions

Unless libraries are forced by outdated budgetary or statutory procedure to enter a new subscriptions list each year, they tend to retain the same agent as they go along. This is done perhaps less because the agent is satisfactory (which he or she may well be), but rather more from fear of the confusion the transfer to another agent is bound to cause. One particular difficulty is in knowing what to do about long-term subscriptions held by the original agent. Most libraries enter subscriptions to periodicals for two- or three-year periods, not simply for one year alone. The advantages of the long-term subscription are evident to anyone who subscribes personally to a magazine. The subscriber does not have to go to the trouble of entering a new subscription each year. And the longer subscription usually means the publisher is able to give the subscriber a lower rate because renewing expenses are eliminated. Savings average 23 to 30 percent over three years. Which is to say that a $10 annual subscription can be had for about $9 a year.

Even when the publisher does not give a lower rate, the long-term subscription protects the subscriber against a rise in rates during the term of the subscription. Most important, in the case of such orders, there is less chance of interruption in service than in the case of the single-year order. Fewer claims are needed and fewer renewal notices. Errors of any sort are, if not eliminated, at least substantially reduced.

It is estimated that from 12,000 to 20,000 titles are available on multiyear schedules. Faxon's advertising brochure notes: "Of the 50,000 titles in our files, approximately 40% offer three year rates with a savings. The special three year rate is approximately 2.3 times the one year rate." Maxwell agrees that a saving can be effected, but not by any means always: "Of the 75,000 titles in our files, approximately 12,000 offer three year rates with a saving."

Hirota's report on James Barry's "A Study on Long Term Periodical Subscriptions" (*Library Resources and Technical Services*, Winter 1959, pp. 50-54) shows that one agency passes onto libraries a 22.8 percent saving on three-year subscriptions.

> For those libraries who wish to take advantage of long term offers, an analysis of some 23,000 titles shows that 65% of all publishers offer a three year subscription rate. However, only 70% of these publishers offer a three year rate with savings over the one year rate. That is, 30% of these three year rates are simple multiples of the one year rate.[4]

Neither the agent nor the librarian can enter a multiyear subscription when such subscriptions are not offered by the publisher. Some publishers, and more particularly those in the academic and scientific fields, do not offer long-term rates. Many, in fact, refuse to accept a subscription for more than one year at a time. The reason: Rising costs are such that the nonprofit publisher does not want to be tied for a number of years to a subscription price when the regular annual price may go up from 10 to 50 percent during the period. Trade publishers find, on the other hand, that allowing multiyear rates is beneficial in that it saves them the time and effort of securing new subscriptions each year and, more to the point, assures them of a guaranteed number of subscriptions with which to lure the advertiser.

Not all the risk of multiple-year subscriptions is with the publisher. Paul points out drawbacks for both the librarian and the publisher:

> While there is less work for both librarian and publisher, they also assume some risk. The librarian runs the risk of losing money when he has paid for a three year subscription and then sees, to his chagrin, the publisher close shop before the time runs out. On the other hand the publisher may find it necessary to charge more for subscriptions because of unexpected costs, only to come to the unhappy realization that he is stuck with numerous three year subscriptions at the old rate that may still have two years to run.[5]

Multiphase Split Orders

When the library enters an order to a title at a three-year subscription rate, it is necessary to reserve for the purpose about 2.3 to 2.5 times the one-year cost of the title. Multiply this by one hundred, several hundred, or even several thousand titles, and in the year the library enters the order it has a 2.3 to 2.5 times higher expenditure for titles in that year than it will have in the following two years. The disparity in outlay from year to year, then, can be great. It is conceivable that in the first year of a multiyear order, the budget allocation for the order might be $2,000, while in the second year, the amount needed might be only $200. Then, by the third or fourth year the amount jumps back to $2,000 (or, because of inflation, to an even higher figure). The budgetary problems posed by such an arrangement are, of course, enormous.

Information about multiphase plans can be found in the Ebsco and Faxon catalogs. The librarian may confirm with the publisher the figures provided in such plans by the agent, but this requires much time. One thing is certain—the publisher will soon notify the library if the agency's figures turn out to be wrong.

Yet the multiphase plan can be used to good effect. The librarian separates his or her list of subscriptions into three lots—one representing items that must be paid for in the first year; another, items to be paid for in the second year; and the last, items to be paid for in the third year. If this arrangement is carried out successfully, the low three-year rates are obtained without sacrificing budgetary stability.

The trick, of course, is to arrange the lots of subscriptions in such a way as to produce a "fixed" annual expenditure. In their advertising brochures, both Maxwell and Faxon use the following example (the $1,200 per year expenditure was, by mid-1974, closer to $1,500, but the mathematics of the process remains the same). Based upon an average mix of popular and highly academic titles in a library list and assuming a $1,200 per year periodicals expenditure:

First Year Invoicing

40% of first 1/3 renewed for 3 years	$ 368.00
60% of first 1/3 renewed for 1 year only	240.00
Remaining 2/3 renewed for 1 year only	800.00
Total	$1,408.00

Second Year Invoicing

40% of first 1/3 paid thru extended expiration	No Charge
60% of first 1/3 renewed for 1 year only	$ 240.00
40% of middle 1/3 renewed for 3 years	368.00
60% of middle 1/3 renewed for 1 year only	240.00
Remaining 1/3 renewed for 1 year only	400.00
Total	$1,248.00

Third Year Invoicing

40% of first 1/3 paid thru extended expiration	No Charge
60% of first 1/3 renewed for 1 year only	$ 240.00
40% of middle 1/3 paid thru extended expiration	No Charge
60% of middle 1/3 renewed for 1 year only	240.00
40% of final 1/3 renewed for 3 years	368.00
60% of final 1/3 renewed for 1 year only	240.00
Total	$1,088.00

Fourth Year Invoicing

40% of first 1/3 renewed for 3 years	$ 368.00
60% of first 1/3 renewed for 1 year only	240.00
40% of middle 1/3 paid thru extended expiration	No Charge
60% of middle 1/3 renewed for 1 year only	240.00
40% of final 1/3 paid thru extended expiration	No Charge
60% of final 1/3 renewed for 1 year only	240.00
Total	$1,088.00

The academic mix of your selection of titles will result in an annual saving of from 12½%–25% once the plan is in operation. [Faxon, somewhat more modest than Maxwell, quotes possible savings at 9.5% to 23%.] Further you must consider (an additional major saving) that the average annual price increase for periodical literature over the past 10 years has been close to 10%. Thus, the 3 year rate offer becomes even more of a saving in the 2nd and 3rd years as it protects the library from virtually automatic rise in subscription prices due to inflation.

Readers who are interested in learning how an individual school librarian applied this same formula in purchasing titles for a school library system are referred to Sally Mahoney's 1972 article.[6] Whether or not the librarian attempts this program on his or her own (there are always agents willing to lend a hand) will depend upon the librarian's patience and, need it be added, ability to juggle figures. For the most part, and particularly when one's list is long and complicated, it is recommended that such budgeting be worked out with an agent's help. To be sure, as Ms. Mahoney points out, the library may save money by going it alone, but whether or not the saving is worthwhile is another matter.

118 Guide to Magazine and Serial Agents

Renewal Notices

(*See* Section VI G of the Checklist)

The agent often points out that a major service he or she provides is the renewing of subscriptions for the library. Standing agreements with agents should permit the librarian to ignore renewal notices from publishers. Still, this arrangement, as every other, is scarcely foolproof:

> The renewal service provided by subscription agencies, while very useful, is not without its difficulties. It is a little disconcerting, for instance, to find that publishers send out renewal notices to everyone on their mailing list, regardless of whether the subscriptions are obtained directly from them or through an agency. A simple check by the librarian, however, soon establishes the need or not of taking action when such notices come to him. If his subscription is obtained through an agency, the renewal notice can generally be ignored, although in cases in which it appears that the subscription is about to lapse or has, in fact, lapsed, an instruction must be sent to the agency. This can be done simply enough by forwarding the renewal notice to the agency with a request that the subscription be put in order.[7]

Most publishers do not accept "til-forbid" orders, i.e., good-until-canceled or nonstop orders. To overcome this inconvenience, the "til-forbid" orders must be worked out between the library and the agent. Furthermore, the publisher does not maintain a record of what agent placed what order. Consequently, when the publisher notes in his or her records that a subscription is about to lapse, he or she sends a renewal notice to the subscriber, not to the agent. Such notices often go out as early as from three to six months before the subscription lapses. The agent, for his part, likely will not ask the publisher to renew the subscription (which appears, of course, in his til-forbid record) until two to three months before it is due to lapse.

What should the library do when renewal notices begin to appear, even though he knows he has a til-forbid order with the agent? All agents agree routine renewal notices should be ignored by the librarian. There are some obvious exceptions to this rule, Ebsco notes in an advertising brochure that

> While renewal notices should be ignored, there is an exception: When a renewal notice is received after the new subscription term was due to start the library should notify the agent.

And Faxon elaborates upon this matter:

> Renewal notices should be ignored unless they are received after your renewal subscription should have taken effect, or the expiration date differs from that on your invoice. And if a publisher supplies you with an expiration date other than the one that appears on our invoices, please advise us promptly. Also, if the renewal notice is received at the end of the first or second year on a three year order (for which the library was billed) that notice should be sent to Faxon. We will then clarify our order and payment and period with the publisher.

Sometimes, then, the librarian receives renewal notices that he or she thinks can be ignored, as the agent is attending to renewal. Come the time of the new subscription, however, and, alas, none appears. Such an interruption in services has three possible causes: (1) the library did not authorize renewal on time; (2) the agent failed to renew on time; and (3) the publisher did not process on time. Of these errors, Stanley Greenfield, an ex-agent, observes "the last two are most frequent...."[8]

Still, no matter how efficient the agent or publisher, the renewal notices tend to come pouring in. Understandably, the librarian who is inexperienced or tends to be a bit nervous will want to query the agent as to whether or not the renewals actually have been entered. Clara Brown describes the renewal notice process

> The renewal notices themselves tell a graphic picture of advertising and imagination. According to these renewals subscriptions get "killed," "bitten," "come to the end of the line," "challenged," are on their "final performance" and "missed the train." The challenge comes in with the publisher's policy of sending at least 4 to 6 notices blatently announcing on the notices which one you are receiving, when all the time you had taken care of the renewal with a " 'til forbidden" subscription letter and paid the invoice when it came. But the policy is to send out six notices regardless. Try and explain in two minutes to your superiors. There you have a challenge.[9]

Most renewal notices can be ignored safely. However, in larger libraries, where particular attention must be paid to every sign that things may be going askew, renewal notices tend to receive careful attention. In his survey of forty-nine academic libraries, Huff found that the vast majority rely on the til-forbid service offered by agencies, *but* that an equal number (over 60 percent) follow through in the matter themselves "by using first-of-the-month renewal files, notations on calendars, flags, tickler systems, looseleaf books, notations on cards and a variety of other home remedies."[10] And Brown recommends that "the first notice should be reviewed thoroughly with the record."[11]

How renewal notices are dealt with presents a fine example of lack of cooperation between publisher and agent and, to some extent, between librarian and agent. If the agent were totally trustworthy, at least in the mind of the librarian, the librarian in all cases, except those noted, might safely ignore any renewal notices that come along.

Duplicates

(*See* Section VI H of the Checklist)

Agents agree that there is no reason to return duplicates to the publisher unless, of course, the duplicate is expensive. Most periodicals do not fall into this category.

If the librarian finds it necessary to speak to the agent about the duplicates, it is advisable for the librarian to send the agent the mailing labels from the duplicate items. The labels, and particularly their codes, may provide the clue needed to solve the problem.

Clara Brown devotes several paragraphs to the handling of duplicates in a library, and while not all serials librarians may agree with her procedures in this area, she does raise a major point: Continually compare any invoices to see if the library is being charged for them, i.e., the duplicates.

ANNUAL REVIEW LISTS

(*See* Section III C of the Checklist)

One of the big time-saving devices the agent provides is its annual review list. Once a year, the agent sends the library a complete list of its subscriptions, a list that includes newly ordered items along with those previously taken account of. Mention might also appear in the list of items canceled (or otherwise removed from the list, as through cessation) throughout the preceding year. With such a list at his or her disposal, the librarian simply adds new subscriptions, notes those to be canceled, etc. He or she then returns the list to the agent. This eliminates the need of entering a new order every year for the same list, as well as ensuring that subscriptions will always be renewed on time. The catch: Checking a long list is onerous; worse than this, a loss, if the agent ignores the noted changes or gets them too late for use in its renewal invoice.

The lists usually take one of two forms:

1. When the library does not have an automatic renewal program (or til-forbid program) with the agent, the agent normally sends a renewal notice, in the form of the list, approximately three months before he or she has to enter renewals and/or new orders. When the list is returned, with annotations showing additions, deletions, and corrections, the agent uses it as his or her authority to renew the subscriptions.

An example of this is the Faxon "standard service renewal instruction form," which, according to Faxon's advertising brochures, is sent six months prior to the expiration of subscriptions.

> This form allows you to make any changes and to note any new titles you wish to add or to delete from your renewal order. You must sign and return this form to us, even though there are no corrections, additions or deletions. This signed form is our authorization to renew. If we do not receive it, your subscriptions will not be renewed.

Such a list is often too late to do any good; or, if too early, omits the needed changes. A lost situation for many libraries.

2. In most situations the agent has a til-forbid understanding with the library. In this situation, the annual review list is employed as a notification of action already taken or about to be taken by the agent.

The questionnaire to agents revealed that the majority of agents send out such lists automatically, usually three months before expiration of the subscriptions, although the time may vary. Ebsco's list goes out five to six months before expiration of the list, while Faxon sends out such a list six months ahead of time. (In Faxon's case, the list must be requested. Faxon will adjust the date at which it is sent to suit the library's convenience.) French & European Publications sends its list "only at expiration time." And, as the Checklist reveals, the majority of international agents follow this same procedure.

The same time constraints are incumbent upon the library, at least to a degree, in checking and returning the list to the agent as those that apply to entering new orders, i.e., it must be back in the agent's office three or four months before renewal time.

Data on the annual review list vary from agent to agent. Most, but again not all, include the price of the subscription, subject to change, of course, if the publisher raises the price in the new year. Most, too, include the expiration date of the titles.

Once the list is approved by the library, and any additions or deletions noted, the agent submits an invoice for the coming year. Again, though, variations exist in this procedure, depending upon what order plan the library has with the agent.

Smith sums up the importance for librarians of the review lists and other follow-through devices:

> Most annual renewal invoices contain the same titles in the same order year after year, affording the serials librarian the opportunity to develop healthy suspicions about interrupted subscriptions. In fact, no matter how much an agent may brag about his renewal capabilities, many of them lack appropriate back-up procedures. Moreover, the agent cannot guarantee that the publishers' records conform with his, or that the publishers have recorded renewals at all. If, therefore, a title which has appeared regularly on this annual renewal invoice in the past fails to appear on the current one, action should be taken. Some serials librarians create a separate tickler file of these omissions so that they may be checked in February or March. Others append lists of these omissions to the invoice, requesting action or explanation. Only experience with a given agent will indicate the most productive route.[12]

REFERENCE NOTES

1. Katherine Smith, "Serials Agents/Serials Librarians," *Library Resources and Technical Services*, Winter 1970, p. 15.
2. Judith A. Nientimp, "The Librarian . . . and the Subscription Agent," *Special Libraries*, July 1972, p. 295.
3. ALA/RTSD, Acquisitions Section, "Guidelines for Publishers, Agents and Librarians in Handling Library Orders for Serials and Periodicals" (Chicago: American Library Association, 1973), p. 11. A processed 12-page report.
4. Astha Hirota, "Subscription Agents," *Hawaii Library Association Journal*, December 1966, p. 18.
5. Huibert Paul, "The Serials Librarian and the Journal Publisher," *Scholarly Publishing*, January 1972, pp. 178-179.
6. Sally Mahoney, "Can a School Librarian Find Happiness (and Savings) as Her Own Periodicals Jobber," *Wilson Library Bulletin*, September 1972, pp. 56-58. The title is deceptive. Actually the author describes a multiphase budget operation that has been used by agents for many years. However, she does explain how the librarian may set up such an operation without the assistance of an agent.
7. Peter Gellatly, "Libraries and Subscription Agents," *PNLA Quarterly*, October 1966, p. 36.

8. Stanley Greenfield, "The Librarian . . . and the Subscription Agent," *Special Libraries*, July 1972, p. 301.
9. Clara Brown, "57 Ways of Keeping a Serials Librarian Happy," *Stechert-Hafner Book News*, February 1969, p. 3.
10. William H. Huff, "The Acquisition of Serial Publications," *Library Trends*, January 1970, p. 307.
11. Clara D. Brown, *Serials: Acquisition and Maintenance* (Birmingham, Ala.: Ebsco Industries, 1971), p. 137.
12. Smith, *op. cit.*, pp. 15-16.

10.
AGENCY INVOICES

(*See* Section IV of the Checklist)

The agency invoice (sometimes referred to as a statement or bill) for subscriptions is sometimes a bit of a mystery to the librarian, or at least a headache (and as troublesome to the agent, when the librarian misinterprets it). Librarians have two ways of handling problems encountered in dealing with invoices. The first is nicely summed up by Clara Brown:

> The philosophy that some librarians take is that it is not necessary to keep accurate financial records and know exactly what is being paid for each year, saying that it all evens out in the long run. The variation of volumes per year in some publications, along with the changes of accountants in dealers' and publishers' offices, plus the ceased titles that one can go on paying year after year, to mention only a few of the ramifications of serials, make it seem doubtful that this philosophy is legitimate. It was proved that one library saved over a thousand dollars in one year with one publisher just by having accurate records.[1]

The hit-or-miss method of dealing with invoices is simply not recommended, but it does point to another of the advantages in working through an agent. The agent who has a good business sense (most do) and is honest (most are) will usually present invoices that contain enough information to keep the librarian's bookkeeping to a minimum. Such is the case anyway where smaller libraries are concerned.

The second, and preferable, method is to check invoices thoroughly for potential errors. Agents would be the first to concede that this procedure has merit, particularly as it is easier for the agent to correct an error at invoice time than several months afterward, when the library, for example, suddenly finds it is not receiving a desired title or is receiving a wrong one.

The advantage to a library of getting one large invoice each year from an agent, rather than hundreds or even thousands of them from individual publishers, is a major argument in support of the agent. However, as Nientemp observes, "agency invoices are a frequent cause of the annoyance librarians feel toward subscription agents."[2]

Clara Brown, for example, lists some 30 "items to keep in mind when paying an invoice,"[3] any one of which can disrupt the orderly receipt of periodicals and other types of serials.

Given the possibilities of error and other difficulties (these caused as often by a faculty computer as a human hand), it is imperative that the agency invoice give as much information concerning the titles in it as possible. Furthermore, the invoice (and the annual review list) should list certain data year-in and year-out and preferably in the same order. The basic data that agents profess to supply on invoices are found in the checklist.

Desirable data they do not include, or often only in a way unique to their business, are also found in the checklist. When there is any question about such things as the agent's listing or not listing titles in alphabetical order, giving frequency of a title, or defining abbreviations used to indicate renewals, new subscriptions, etc., the librarian should submit these questions to the agent before invoice or annual review list time.

When a librarian is starting an account with a new agent, or switching from one agent to another, it may be helpful to the librarian to request a sample invoice from the agent in question. The librarian may then check to see what data are or are not included and the form in which the data are presented. Such matters are of importance, as they can promote or disrupt recordkeeping in the library. They matter especially when the library is considering an agent with an automated office. Sometimes, the office arrangements are geared to the needs of the computer and not the needs of the library, or, as Clara Brown puts it:

> Some computerized invoices are so long they must be broken into sections to make them manageable. This usually means that new totals must be made for each section. Computerized invoices are apt to use so many abbreviations to the title that it is well nigh impossible to decipher them.... If a title is deducted from an invoice because of some particular problem, the computer is apt not to "recognize" the whole invoice.[4]

SPECIAL INVOICING

Bill Backs

The most common type of supplementary invoice goes by many names. It is described succinctly by Greene of Universal:

> The biggest problem that agencies have in their invoicing procedure is the "bill backs," "due bills," "shortage bills," "debit memos," or whatever you want to call them. This happens when an order is entered in September, and in October, November and December the publisher sends an entire clearing of orders back—not a debit memo, but the whole order, saying it's not $12, it's now $14. So the agency has to bill the library for $2.... Along with this goes the problem of added volumes.... At the end of the year, suddenly another one or two volumes are added. They just suddenly appear in the form of a bill."[5]

Almost without exception, every agency will give some warning about this procedure in advertising brochures. Ebsco, for example, says "... it should be recognized that publishers' prices are subject to change without notice and that price changes will be billed in addition to the original invoice."[6]

Faxon states:
"Prices are subject to publisher rate changes at all times. It may be necessary to bill you for an additional charge or issue a credit, if between the time we invoice you and the publisher accepts our order, the publisher changes his published price or decides to accept orders only on a volume or calendar year basis. If we do not honor the publisher's revisions, he could reject your order or reduce the subscription period to agree with our initial payment, thereby effecting a common expiration date. Occasionally a publisher will release additional material or volumes not included in the original published price. We assume you want all the material published in any publication year and, therefore, we pay the publisher's charges to us and bill you additionally.[7]

As Greene notes, until such time as publishers "establish a universal time for announcing price increases," every agent is caught in the same invoice bind—and particularly so when the library list is made up of more than popular trade titles. Greene continues: "The record shows that, in the past, changes were made in late summer each year. Obviously this is difficult because some publishers now operate on a fiscal year, some on a calendar year, while others price on a volume basis only."[8]

And in years of inflation, this problem is bound to grow rather than to diminish. Consequently, the supplementary invoice, or "bill back," is a widely used device among agents. Harrassowitz is an exception in that, "we normally only charge our customers when we have the publisher's bill and a definite price on record." Other large international agents, however, tend to follow American practice. The library with a question as to how prices are finally determined should request an explanation of the procedure his or her agent follows.

American agents do not wait for the "final" publisher's price, because they must ordinarily pay the publisher for the serials (and particularly periodicals) ordered before payment is obtained from the library. This holds true always when the order the library sends the agent is of the til-forbid sort.

Supplementary Invoices: New Orders

Another common form of supplementary invoices is the one sent monthly, quarterly, or at another interval for titles ordered by the library throughout the year, i.e., titles to be added to those on the initial order. It is, of course, helpful to know when such invoices might be expected. Harrassowitz, for example, sends them quarterly, Ebsco two weeks after receipt of the order, and Faxon sixty to ninety days before payment is required. Other agents, such as Blackwell's, send monthly invoices as occasion demands.

Two notes of warning: "Add ons" during the year of only two or three titles per order can be expensive. The amount of paperwork involved in processing such orders is so extensive that some agents levy an added charge for individual orders or orders containing under twenty titles. The precise procedure used, agent by agent, was not established by the present study. Nevertheless, most librarians agree that orders should not be held but sent to the agent without waiting. If the agency charge for individual orders is minimal or nonexistent—or the need for the order is great—obviously the librarian will take immediate action in the case. However, where it is feasible to wait until an order of twenty or more titles is put together, money will be saved—at least the agents contacted say so.

LIBRARY PAYMENT TO THE AGENT

(*See* Section V of the Checklist)

The majority of domestic and international agents pay the publisher for the subscription before the library pays the agent. Therefore, the agent is understandably anxious to receive payment of his invoice promptly, and usually asks that it be remitted within thirty days. Where laws or budget regulations make prompt payment difficult, the agent will sometimes extend the deadline. In such cases, terms should be worked out in advance between the library and the agent.

Most domestic agents ask for payment within thirty days, although a few are willing on occasion to wait for sixty days or even longer. Ebsco has a carrying charge on bills unpaid after the sixtieth day. International agents will usually extend the payment period to ninety days. Harrassowitz notes that the agent simply relies on the library "remitting as promptly as possible."

While there is general agreement and understanding among librarians and agents as to the grace period allowed in paying the invoice, the handling of errors in billing is a source of much ill-feeling. For their part, most agents request that the library pay the invoice in full even when it contains errors. The agent, of course, undertakes to reimburse the library for overcharges by sending a credit memo (a few agents will, if requested, issue a refund check). The credit is used in paying later bills. Almqvist & Wiksell and Instructor suggest a third alternative: return the invoice with corrections before making any payment.

The majority of agents, then, urge the library to remit the total amount shown in the invoice, point out errors, and then wait for the agent to send a credit memo. ALA *Guidelines* say that three options are available: the issuing of memos; amending the invoices; and the remitting of the corrected total once appropriate deductions have been made from the invoice. Interestingly enough, most agents prefer the first option—an indication surely that the average agent does not regard the other options as of much validity.

A rule that librarians should adhere to firmly in their work with invoices appears in the ALA *Guidelines*: "Specific arrangements should be made with vendors to expedite the payment of long invoices on which there may be one or two errors or problems."[9] This is particularly meaningful advice, as much misunderstanding arises between agents and librarians in the proper handling of this matter.

CANCELED AND DISCONTINUED TITLES

(*See* Section VII of the Checklist)

A situation that angers librarians is the failure of the agent to refund money when the librarian cancels a subscription or an item ceases publication. This is one situation, however, in which about all the agent can do is sympathize with the librarian. How much chance is there of the library's receiving a refund? There is no answer to this question. What happens depends primarily upon how the publisher treats the matter.

The agent is not legally responsible in this situation. He enters the subscription in good faith, and he pays for it. At this point his legal responsibility to the library ceases. Yet the agent may, and usually does, attempt to get a pro rata refund from the publishers. The difficulty is that unless the publisher is willing, or able, to make the refund, the agency may have to take him to court—a procedure that is morally justified but a bit excessive in practical terms, as the refund may amount to no more than a few dollars. And even if it were one of several hundred dollars, the recourse to the law might still be too expensive to endure.

As subscribers to such defunct magazines as *Life*, *Look*, and the *Saturday Evening Post* came to realize, the publisher sometimes attempts to repay subscribers by offering them a subscription to another magazine rather than a literal refund. This may satisfy the individual, but is of little use to the average library, which probably already has a subscription to the proferred substitute. The sudden cessation of an established title constitutes a risk factor that simply must be accepted by librarian and agent alike. Unless the agency sees reason, when a title ceases, to start a class action to regain the lost subscription money, the library is simply out the amount paid.

Often, when a new periodical comes along, the librarian may adopt a wait-and-see attitude, i.e., he or she will wait and see if it lasts past the first few issues. The problem here is that if a subscription is entered afterward, the librarian may find it difficult to secure the necessary first numbers for binding. This is particularly true of mass circulation magazines at one extreme and "little" magazines and underfinanced titles in general at the other. Early issues are always hard to find—the large publisher fails to retain a decent supply and the small publisher fails to print an appreciable run. If the librarian accepts this factor, he or she will opt for taking a chance on the new title. This is the position the librarian should take whenever back issues are important.

Cancellation is resorted to often these days. What does the librarian do who finds that a new periodical, or, for that matter, a well-established older one simply is not needed or can no longer be afforded? The obvious answer: Cancel the subscription.

Most publishers will not refund money when a cancellation is made, at least not in the first year of subscription. When a subscription has a two- or three-year duration, refund is usually made for the second or third year—if cancellation is entered soon enough. Reflecting the general agency policy, Faxon notes that: "One year subscriptions may only be cancelled at expiration; two year subscriptions at the end of the first full year; three year subscriptions may only be cancelled at the end of the first or the second year." The agent adds a thought which may not always occur to librarians: "As a rule the third year is free of cost, and therefore is not subject to cancellation by the publisher."[10]

The most difficult sort of publisher to work with in making cancellations is the publisher of the learned journal. Most will not accept cancellation once the library's money has been received. On the other hand, the publishers of mass circulation magazines and of expensive serials and periodicals will usually refund on a pro rata basis for issues not sent.

Most librarians, however, will agree with Maxwell that "cancelling any but the most expensive journals seldom proves to be in the customer's best interest when the time and the cost involved are examined."[11] The reluctance of most publishers to make refunds is a matter of simple economics. The cost of canceling the subscription and processing the refund often runs to more money than the refund accounts for.

Whereas most cancellations involve only a few titles, there are times when the process may be called "wholesale." This is when the library must cut back substantially on serials purchases because of budgetary problems, or when the librarian decides either to drop the agent relationship in favor of going directly to the publishers or to switch from one agent to another. The crucial element here is time. The agency should be notified well in advance if wholesale cancellations are to take place. Regardless of the number of cancellations, however, the library should consider the length of existing subscriptions. If all or most titles have a common expiration date, no real problem exists. If, on the other hand, no such common date exists, the librarian may elect either to cancel on the spot regardless of money lost in the process (by way of unobtainable refunds) or make cancellations only as expiration dates approach. Wholesale canceling is invariably expensive, and requires more attention than does the canceling of a few titles only.

Ebsco is, so far, about the only domestic agency that charges for cancellation, but others are likely to follow suit here. Generally, an agent who charges for cancellation may justify the charge on a cost basis, but such a charge understandably bothers librarians. Moreover, the practice can be abused, e.g., when the librarian threatens to cancel, the agent announces the institution of a prohibitive cancellation charge.

There is strong sentiment among librarians that the agent should not charge for cancellations and the sentiment assumes the proportions of conviction when it is considered that cancellation generally imposes its own penalties upon the subscriber.

REFERENCE NOTES

1. Clara Brown, *Serials: Acquisition and Maintenance* (Birmingham, Ala.: Ebsco Industries, 1971), p. 137. Not only is the idea of ignoring records not legitimate, it may even be illegal. According to Clasquin: "Financial autonomy delegated to a library includes a clear and complete set of detailed itemized financial records for each title. The laws in each state usually indicate it is the librarian's legal responsibility to maintain such records." Clasquin then goes on to observe that such legal responsibility might rightfully be used by the librarian as an argument against the bid system, as this does not take the individual title into consideration, i.e., the bid requirement may actually be in conflict with the law.

2. Judith A. Nientimp, "The Librarian . . . and the Subscription Agent," *Special Libraries*, July 1972, p. 296.
3. Brown, *op. cit.*, pp. 138–141.
4. *Ibid.*, p. 169.
5. Philip E. Greene, "The Three Way Responsibility . . . ," in *Management Problems in Serial Work*, ed. by Peter Sypers-Duran and Daniel Gore (Westport, Conn.: Greenwood Press, 1974), p. 100.
6. Ebsco, advertising brochure, n.d.
7. Faxon, advertising brochure, n.d.
8. Greene, *op. cit.*, p. 100.
9. ALA/RTSD, Acquisitions Section, "Guidelines for Publishers, Agents and Librarians in Handling Library Orders for Serials and Periodicals" (Chicago: American Library Association, 1973), p. 4. A processed 12-page report.
10. Faxon, *op. cit.*
11. Maxwell, advertising brochure, n.d.

11.
CLAIMS AND CLAIMING

(*See* Section VI of the Checklist)

No single term is heard more often when agents and librarians discuss serials than the term "claim." Claiming is the process of locating and obtaining an item that has failed to reach the library on schedule.

In what may be an understatement, Nientimp observes that: "Claiming is an area of great discord between librarians and subscription agents.[1] Smith seconds this with: "Claiming is frequently the most irritating aspect of the relationship between agents and librarians. Often serials librarians do not claim intelligently."[2]

In graphic terms, Fred Roessler, formerly of Maxwell International Subscription Agency explains what a claim is all about:

"Here it is December and we haven't received the November issue of ———!" This cry and similar cries are heard regularly in libraries and schools throughout the nation. It is a very frustrating lament to librarian and subscription agent alike, neither being able to say confidently: "We'll get it in the next mail or we'll write the publisher and he'll send it to us or we can send for a back issue if it doesn't come."[3]

Claims are generally brought about as a consequence of

Late issues. There are numerous reasons why a library may not receive a given issue at the expected time: the publisher is late in supplying editorial material to the printer, the mails are delayed, or difficulties, such as material shortages and strikes, overtake the printer or fulfillment office.

Missing issues. Not only are some issues late, some never arrive. Again, reasons for the omission vary from a misunderstanding about the initial subscription to a loss in the mails to a breakdown of the labeling machine.

Renewal failure. While the til-forbid process usually prevents a lapse in receipt of a title between subscription periods, interruptions occur when the subscription is entered on an annual basis; when the library fails to return the authorization list of periodicals to be renewed; when either the agent or the publisher fails to process the order on time.

Badly printed or damaged issues. A claim is entered when the item is not properly printed or is mutilated in the mails. The librarian should, of course, use discretion in claiming items that may be only slightly damaged but still legible and usable.

Multiple issues. The publisher who is not careful or has a less than efficient computer sometimes has difficulty in keeping track of multiple-copy subscriptions, particularly when the copies go to closely related addresses or when billing is to a single library. The common result—delayed or missing issues.

Financial snags. Often the records kept by publishers as to who paid for what are confused and difficult to retrieve when a question arises about a subscription. The tracing of the financial transaction may take months, not merely days—again with the result of missing issues.

In a statistical analysis of reasons given for claims by librarians, Clasquin provides the following data:

... compiled from a sampling of claims received at Faxon during four separate three week periods. The claims distributed themselves in the following fashion:

74%	Single missing issues
15%	Interruption at renewal time
2 to 7½%	Claimed more than once
2%	Known delays—suspended or other irregularities
1½%	Multiple copy order—service break—1 or more copies at renewal time
1%	Supplements, indexes, or other miscellaneous parts unknown to agency[4]

Other reasons for claims from "new subscription not started" to "mutilated copies" Clasquin reports as "not measurable." However, the important figures here are the first two. The vast majority of claims are generated by the librarian who realizes that an issue is missing or that a subscription has not been renewed.

LIBRARY RESPONSIBILITY FOR CLAIMING

While it is difficult for the librarian to believe he or she is at fault in such a matter, sometimes a claim is unwarranted. The single biggest error librarians commit in this area is to submit claims prematurely. Without first checking to see if a reason for a delayed or missing issue cannot be readily explained, the librarian shoots off a claim to the publisher or agent. Soon thereafter and before the claim is properly on its way, the missing issue appears. The claim was unwarranted. Clasquin observes that: "It is the opinion of a large number of publishers that premature claims are responsible for at least 50 percent of all missing single issue claims."[5]

Here is the way it looks from the viewpoint of someone who has been both a librarian and a publisher:

As a librarian I have always complained about publishers failing to send all issues due [*PNLA Quarterly*], but as a publisher I have developed second thoughts. The publisher is not always to blame, nor is the mailman. While it is probably true that the majority of claims from libraries are genuine and the issues indeed never were received, there must also be many cases where issues arrived but simply got lost in the library itself. I do not know how otherwise to explain some of the complaints I have received about missing issues.[6]

If the library is to have a rational and workable claims system, the librarian must at minimum

1. Have an accurate record of serials received, and not received. These records may vary from computer printouts to manual notations.[7]

2. Have a record of receipt (and nonreceipt) patterns for specific titles. Libraries with no such records should consult with agents, many of whom have information of this type. These records help, as Nientimp illustrates, "to avoid situations like claiming the May issue in July when it is never published until September or claiming the 1970 volume when the 1968 volume was not received until 1970 and is the last volume published."[8]

When receipt patterns have not been established, some general considerations may govern the issuing of claims:

1. Frequency of publication
2. Delays in the mails, strikes, and other such imponderables
3. Discovery that the issue preceding one just received is outstanding

The annual review lists supplied by most agents are useful, too, in that they can be checked to see whether a subscription has actually been entered, when it was entered, whether or not it has expired, etc. The more information on the list, the more likely the librarian is to enter accurate claims rather than claims based upon inaccurate knowledge or guesswork.

Prompt placing of claims should be the responsibility of the library. Here it should be noted that the automatic claiming of serials without due observance of patterns of delay is counterproductive. Such activity results in more work than necessary for all concerned.

The claim-form—whether it is the agent's or the library's own—should be filled out completely and accurately. In working with international agents, letters instead of standard claim-forms are often employed. These should include all of the information that would normally be given on the claim-form.

The claim-form should be sent to the proper destination, i.e., either to the publisher or to the agent—and possibly to both. The arrangement used should be clearly understood by both librarian and agent.[9]

Automation, of course, considerably modifies the manual procedures described above. For example, the New York State Library system is automated, at least to the extent that a computer is used to account for titles that arrive regularly enough so that some date of receipt can be predicted. The difference between the cover date and the receipt date of the title is arrived at, and the computer then prints out a list of periodicals that should arrive during a given week. The titles appear on the list about a week before they are expected, and a late warning is issued in the week following the predicted date of arrival. The library then waits an average of three weeks before it generates a claims notice—

a notice, which, incidentally, is printed out by the computer. Thus, what was once an entirely manual process has now been, to a large extent, automated. (It must be pointed out that this automated claims system is employed only in taking care of fairly regular titles, i.e., those of more or less predictable frequency. Irregular titles continue to be treated manually.)

Internal Claims Procedures

Once a claim has been sent to the agent or publisher, what records must the library keep while awaiting receipt of the missing item? There are two arrangements that can be followed here. The first, discussed later, has to do with the keeping of a claims diary as a means of evaluating agent performance and/or of establishing a history of the claiming of particular titles. The second concerns the ongoing vetting of the progress of the claim.

Procedures vary, of course, from library to library, but basically they should include a notation on the check-in record that shows the date on which the claim is entered and the date on which it is fulfilled, i.e., the date the missing item is received.

When a claim is entered, a colored tab or some type of "flag" should be affixed to the check-in record to indicate when a second claim should be entered. The flag should be of a sort that the librarian can tell at a glance when further action is needed in the case of items of different frequencies, such as weeklies, monthlies, etc. When the claim is sent out on a claims slip, a copy of the claims slip should be affixed to the record.

There are variations on these arrangements. For example, instead of flagging the check-in record, some libraries prefer to set up a claiming record. The easiest way of doing this is to use copies of the original claims slip in keeping track of the claim's progress. One copy is attached to the check-in record and one or two are filed, usually by date, in a separate claims file. After a given passage of time, one of the duplicates is removed from the claims file and entered as a second claim. At the same time, the remaining slip is refiled under a new date.

Once it is decided to order a replacement for a missing item, all claims slips should be removed from the claims file and/or the check-in file and placed in a missing issues file. Appropriate action should then be taken to purchase a copy of the missing item.

These steps are applicable when the issue belongs to an existing subscription. Other steps are necessary when no response is made upon initial submission of an order or when a total breakdown occurs in an established order, i.e., when a subscription, once arriving regularly, stops completely. In both situations, letters and even telephone calls should go to the agent or publisher in order to get matters put to rights again.

In some school districts, it is the practice of the librarian to have claims dealt with by the school's or district's business office to handle. Insofar as personnel in the office understand and appreciate the claiming system, this may be appropriate. Still, the agent may be working with individuals who have no way of knowing what is required to process the claim efficiently. Where there is a choice, the librarian should handle the claims himself rather than allowing this work to be done elsewhere.

Percentage of Claims

How important are claims in the general scheme of things in a library? One answer is to be found in the number of claims the library will likely have to cope with in a year's time. While variables exist—from the type of publication to the accuracy of library records—some general indicators are available to help in determining this number.

The average library may count on claiming from 5 to 8 percent of its total list of periodicals and serials during a given year. Claims may range from a low of 2 percent to a high of 20 percent, but the 5 to 8 percent figure is average. There are few studies in this area, but those consulted bear out the estimate.

Clasquin notes that in Faxon's case, claims doubled in number in 1972 to 20,000. Faxon circulated 285,000 subscriptions during the year, and it was found that the claims represented 7 percent of the work done. Clasquin reports elsewhere upon the experience of various other publishers in claiming. In general, it appears that the claiming activities of a publisher account for 8 to 10 percent of his or her circulation work.

In a three-month period, Calvin Evans (working with a file of some 4,000 titles) claimed some 4 to 5 percent of his titles.[10] In a study made by Richard Seidel of Newberry Library, it was reported that: "In 1972, 500 new orders for periodicals and other continuations were placed with our various dealers and that after a period of one year, some 50, or 10 percent, required claiming."[11]

A small library with under one hundred popular titles, which come under a til-forbid arrangement, may have little or no claims work to do. A larger library using a similar plan, but with 200 to several thousand titles, will find itself in the position of having to claim, at one time or another, from 5 to 8 percent of its titles.

Translated into work time, Clasquin notes that 18 percent of the Faxon's staff time is spent on claims, and he finds that a similar percentage holds with publishers. All things considered, a serials librarian might do well to emulate the others in their apportioning of time to claims work. Most, however, will find this advice impossible to follow, as staff time is always a commodity in short supply.

Clasquin, as others before him, suggests that the total percentage of claims and the resultant high percentage of staff time needed to handle claims might be reduced if libraries were to accord claims work its proper importance.

> Without demeaning work practices in libraries, it is safe to say the claims staffs have a low priority rating. Part-time help, a high turnover rate, and leftover time are partly responsible for the quality of the work performed on claims. There is no substitute for the professional insight.[12]

Why is "professional insight" necessary for proper claiming? For one thing, claiming is much more than simply recognizing that something is missing. Even in libraries using highly sophisticated automated equipment, someone has to decide when a claim is actually needed, and when it is better to wait or tackle the matter in some other way. More importantly, when a claim is entered, the librarian should know the probable reason that the claim is needed, and explore methods of keeping the need from recurring. Not all elements in the claiming process are within the control of the librarian, but such claim-generating anomalies as entering the subscription under an incorrect title or for an incorrect period he or she ought to be able to control.

DISPOSITION OF CLAIMS

Should the librarian send a claim to the agent or directly to the publisher? In almost all cases, the librarian should send the claim to the agent. The librarian is paying for claims service when the agent is hired to handle the library's subscriptions. Not to use such a service is to waste a valuable resource and one, moreover, that is being paid for.

There are disadvantages in sending the claim to an agent. Time may be saved by eliminating the agent, who takes three days to a week to process it. Agents usually request that the library use agency claims forms. The library with a number of agents finds itself using a variety of forms, each with its own peculiarities and each of which must, of course, be kept in stock along with a multitude of other forms. The librarian is, then, spared some inconvenience by using a claims form he or she devises personally. It is possible that if agents were to accept library claims forms more readily, the tendency of librarians to go directly to the publisher would reduce itself.

A matter of some consequence is that many librarians suspect their agents of dilatoriness in entering claims with publishers. Evans puts it this way: "We did have certain misgivings about claiming through an agent and had a deep dark suspicion that perhaps they were not serving us as promptly and efficiently as they purported to be."[13]

The "deep dark suspicion" may be well founded, at least so far as some agents are concerned. Agents questioned asserted that the time they take to process claims is from 3 days (or less) to 10 days. Whether all agents operate within such limits is a matter of conjecture. Librarians who prefer to send claims directly to the publisher suspect that their claim may sit on the agent's desk for much more than 10 days, perhaps months.

The arguments for using an agent in claiming are mildly convincing. In one of the few studies made of this question, Evans found that a claim entered directly with a publisher or through an agent will usually bring about the same results. The periodicals division chief of a university library with 4,000 periodical titles sent claims for three months only to agents. In the following three months he sent them only to publishers. The results:

    Agent: First claims 157 (second claims 94) Issues received 91
              Success rate 61 percent
  Publisher: First claims 185 (second claims 82) Issues received 114
              Success rate 61 percent

Evans concluded that claims should be sent to the agent rather than to the publisher. The results he achieved were, to be sure, about the same in both cases, but the difficulty of sending individual claims to individual publishers was solved. Furthermore, Evans found that in another three-month period during which all claims were sent to agents: "We had sent 195 first claims (and 176 second claims), and 163 issues had been received. This is for an amazing 84 percent success rate."[14]

There are many variables to be accounted for in an experiment of this sort, but the methodology Evans devised is sound. Librarians who may be considering the advisability of the agency-claims route or the publisher-claims route might do well to conduct a similar test themselves. Otherwise, the issue of whether to make claims to agents or publishers remains academic.

Lack of hard facts in this area continues to plague librarians. One finds the agent's work satisfactory, another has serious doubts about it. Such doubts are expressed in the questionnaries returned by librarians in our survey. A college librarian, for example, said that his library did not use either Faxon or Ebsco for claiming magazines. "We tried and found it very unsatisfactory and frustrating. We feel that direct correspondence with the publisher is more effective." Taking the opposite position, the librarian at a large university noted that "Ebsco was good at following up claims"; and a librarian in a medium-sized public library praised Faxon for "being good with follow ups on claims." Comments concerning other agents were largely of the same nature.

Recognizing the hesitancy of some librarians to enter claims through an agency, Faxon, for one, has special forms for such procedures. "Faxon will supply special direct-claim information which will give you all the necessary data to process a direct claim. A specially designed direct-claim postcard will be supplied to you if you want to use Faxon's form."

There is an advantage to the agent in his or her encouraging the library to work through the publisher in that it saves the agent paperwork and effort. On the other hand, most agents have a special staff (from one to more than a dozen people) who do little other than handle claims. And unless there were to be a general movement away from use of agents in claiming, the average agent saves little when an individual library goes to the publisher instead of the agent.

Automation has had a major effect upon claiming. The New York State Library system, for instance, has an automated procedure whereby claims are generated automatically by the computer. Under such an arrangement, the library finds it advantageous to enter claims directly with the publisher than through the agent. Speed is the important consideration here. Another is that agents are reluctant to accept claims forms generated by a computer. Why? The agent does not usually find on the computer form all the information needed to process the claim readily.

The agency itself, of course, does use the computer in claiming. Faxon, for instance, has an automated claims system that allows the claims sent in by the library to be "entered daily directly into the computer." The advertising brochure goes on to explain that the system automatically adds other information from the date of the agency order to the publisher to the agency check number.

The agent is

> ... then ready to make a claim in a standard usable format which will automatically be collated with similar claims and mailed to the publisher within 3 to 10 days.... One of the most valuable aspects of FACS is a report which will be sent to you quarterly listing all claims made within the previous three months and any responses received by Faxon from the publishers. This report can be used against your check-in records and, if necessary, a follow up claim can be made at any time from the information stored electronically at the time of your original claim.

It is not improbable that in the near future other agents and librarians will use automated methods of claiming much like those now in use at the New York State Library system and Faxon. Whether or not the new arrangement will be any more satisfactory than past procedures remains to be seen, although an obvious benefit computerization will bring is the constructing of a record that can be used over and over until the claim is satisfied.

Time for Claims

When an item is found to be missing, it is imperative to notify the agent immediately. As Ebsco puts it: "Avoid delinquency in claiming. Many publishers will not service a non-receipt claim received 90 days or more from date of issue." Moore-Cottrell, as do most other agents, agrees that the ninety-day limitation must be observed, but adds that "at least one publisher restricts the time to 30 days, so prompt notification is imperative." (And, indeed, quicker action should be the rule in the case of weekly publications and others of similar frequency.)

The ninety-day admonition is a heartfelt one when it is issued by publishers because a good many of these do not keep back issues of their titles. If a claim is not entered quickly enough, the needed issues simply are not available from the publisher. (It is true that some missing issues may be purchased from back-order dealers, but this may take months and reams of correspondence to effect.)

Claims schedules demand two things: First, the library must have some idea of when the item is usually received; and second, the library must know how many days or weeks to wait before entering a claim.

Over the years agents and librarians have worked out schedules that fairly well solve the question of when to claim a missing or lapsed issue. (The basic schedule is given in the Checklist.) The difficulty here is that the schedules of the larger agents differ radically from one another. For example, most agents say to claim a missing daily after ten days; but Faxon says to wait only seven days, and Ebsco says to wait all of twenty-one.

The best advice on missing issues is given in the ALA *Guidelines*: "It is reasonable to assume a claim is valid if the issue following a missing item has been received."[15] However, it seems questionable that a library should wait another ninety days, as the *Guidelines* suggest, before entering a claim for the first issue of a new subscription.[16] If the librarian has already waited the length of time prescribed by the agent for the establishing of a new subscription, and then adds another ninety days to that, the result will inevitably be loss of many needed issues.

Claims for issues missing from new subscriptions should begin within ten days to two weeks after the agent has indicated the subscription is to begin and/or the library's requested beginning date.

The Checklist includes a time schedule for periodicals only. As a rule of thumb, claims for annuals, biennials, etc., should be made about once a year—on a given schedule. Irregular serials should be checked from time to time, according to a schedule prearranged with the agent.

Agent Reports on Publishers

To the uninitiated, the obvious question about time schedules and claiming must be: If many libraries in the country maintain records on arrival times of periodicals, and if all large agents (and many smaller agents) do the same, why is there not somewhere a central pool of such information into which librarian and agent alike may dip to find out such things as X or Y title always arrives two days late, two days early, or in the fall is apt to be three weeks late. Or even including a little information of the sort in, say, such a guide as *Ulrich's International Periodicals Directory* would help everyone keep serials files in good, usable order.

Well, no such help is yet on the way. In the meantime, however, several of the larger agents are at least issuing regular information bulletins on publications that, for one reason or another, are likely to be delayed. There are likely to be more bulletins of this sort, as agents find additional ways of putting the computer to work for them. For example, early in 1974, Faxon began its *Serials Updating Service Quarterly*. This is an alphabetical list of titles carried by Faxon. After each title, such vital information appears as changes in publishing schedule, suspensions, when to expect indexes, what titles are out of print, double issues, etc. Faxon is now issuing also a monthly report on serials. This is sent free of charge to customers.

A more limited yet useful publication is offered by Stechert-Macmillan in its *News*. This quarterly reports on new titles, title changes, order-direct titles, cessations, format changes, etc. However, the *News* does not provide claiming information.

Among international agents, Swets & Zeitlinger offers possibly the most sophisticated reporting service. This firm issues a bimonthly publication, *Swets Info*, which gives information on periodicals and serials such as titles that are behind schedule, ceased titles, title changes, mergers, etc. *Swets Info* also offers reviews of publications lists of dispatch dates used by periodicals publishers.

Libraries, too, acquire along the way titles they order and it would be helpful if this information might be somehow centralized and channeled to other libraries—possibly through the agents involved. At any rate, present information on when to claim, what to claim, and potential and real delays is obviously in need of some centralized processing, if only to avoid tremendous duplication of effort among agents and librarians.

The agent should know which publishers are the ones who account for quantities of claims. Beyond this, he or she should have available a history of the subscription transaction. This information may be necessary to settle a claim.

Typical kinds of data the agent should be able to produce for the publisher or librarian include period paid, amount paid, date ordered, and agency and library order numbers.

Furthermore, the agent should be able to support any question about payment with a photocopy of the check used to pay the publisher. This should be accompanied by a copy of the order sent to the publisher. In fact, the agent should be able, on demand, to produce copies and originals of all items employed in a transaction. One advantage of the agent's having complete information at his or her disposal, particularly when the agency is automated, is that the agent may then fill in necessary pieces of information the librarian has inadvertently omitted from claims forms.

AGENCY ACKNOWLEDGMENT OF CLAIMS

All agents should acknowledge receipt of first claims, and should periodically advise the library of progress being made in the case of unsettled claims. Most domestic agents do neither; most international agents do both. Why is it necessary for the librarian to know about the progress of a claim? Nientimp sums up succinctly:

If the serials librarian has an obligation to be prompt in claiming, the agency has a corresponding obligation to be prompt in forwarding and answering claims. It is very awkward when an irate faculty member comes storming in looking for an issue and the clerk on duty says she sent a claim for it two months ago but has not yet received a reply. The faculty member does not understand why there has not been a reply and the serials librarian cannot explain because she does not understand either. It would be very useful if the agency could at least acknowledge receipt of the claim and provide the date on which it was referred to the publisher or note that they are inquiring about the problem. At least then the library would know that the claim arrived at the agency and a date could be recorded in the serials file for use in subsequent checking.[17]

An exemplary procedure is that of Swets & Zeitlinger. In their advertising brochure, they explain:

Sometimes we may be able to give an answer [to a claim] straight away from the information we have on hand, but often we must pass on the claim to the publisher. Meanwhile, a confirmation of the library is printed out, listing the issue which has been claimed with the publishers . . . . Once the answer to our claim has been received from the publisher, a second report is sent to you. If the missing issue is not received within a reasonable time, then we are willing to repeat the claim, this time by registered post.

The most sophisticated claims-notification process at present is Faxon's FACS (Faxon's Automated Claim System). All claims are acknowledged by way of a quarterly report that feeds back the complete nature of the claim, including a note on the reply or lack of reply from the publisher. The library, according to the agent, is "supplied with a special form to use in reporting surface irregularities." The information received from the library is "entered daily directly into the computer." The claim is then mailed to the publisher. The most important feature of this system, however, is the quarterly report, which lists "all claims made within the previous three months and any responses received." With this available, Faxon has no problem in providing a library with any follow-up information needed.

Why is it that only four domestic agents say they acknowledge first claims? The agent will explain that no report can be made to the library because some two-thirds of the time the publisher does not report back to the agent on claims action. This is true. Still, a report from the agent would at least indicate that the claim had been forwarded to the publisher. Equally important, the information would help to ward off suspicion of the library user that the librarian has done nothing about the missing item.

The Second Claim

How long should a library wait before a second claim is entered? This depends primarily upon how quickly the claim is processed by the agent and forwarded to the publisher. Most agents assert that this is done within three days to a week. How long, then, does it take the publisher to process the claim? Again, as with guesses by agents on how long it takes the publisher to process a new order, there is no real consensus. Guesses, educated or otherwise, range from a low of three weeks to a high of ninety days in the case of domestic publishers. Allowing an additional thirty days for mailing, the time in the case of international agents is about the same. No agent can be any more definite in the matter because publishers tend to follow their own inclinations in answering claims.

Despite the lack of any specific rules as when to enter a second claim, in most cases the librarian should do so within twenty-one days after the first claim has been entered. The librarian should err on the side of too much action if he or she is to err at all. It is better to enter a second claim within the minimum period suggested, i.e., three weeks, than to wait three months. Exceptions are if the agent's advice about claiming time frames has proven correct over the years, or if the librarian's historical record of claims in the case of a particular publisher shows a different schedule.

Third Claim

Again, recognizing the difficulty of a standard time frame for claims, a third claim should be entered twenty-one days after the second claim. However, a sounder rule is to contact the agent by telephone or letter with a request for an explanation as to why the needed item has not arrived. Even the best of agents sometimes cannot get an explanation from the publisher, but the majority will at least try; and an even greater number will be able to make a fairly reasonable guess on the probable arrival time of the item, or the advisability of the library's forgetting the claim and trying to obtain the item from another source.

Rush Claims

All general domestic agents, with the exception of Stechert-Macmillan, accept rush claims. No agent charges for this service except Ebsco. Most international agents also accept the same type of claim. Rush claims may be entered by way of the telephone, TWX, Telex, etc.

When should the librarian enter a rush claim? The answer: When there is truly a rush, i.e., an emergency exists that must be dealt with immediately. Examples are when the librarian cannot obtain the necessary item anywhere else—even through interlibrary loan—or, more likely, when he or she has failed to receive the first issue of a much-needed periodical. Another example is when a volume is held up at the binder for lack of a final number.

Rush claims should only be entered judiciously, and librarians should resist the temptation to consider every inadvertency an emergency.

How quickly will a rush claim expedite matters? It will likely cut back the processing time at the agency by several days, and, if the agent is able to exert necessary pressure on the publisher, it may cut the time needed at the publisher's end by a week or more. However, it is wise to remember that here, too, there are many variables, particularly where the publisher is concerned. Some publishers will not accept rush claims; others will accept them, put them in the hopper along with all the ordinary claims they are dealing with; and still others will dutifully respond, but do nothing. While all agents questioned say they accept such claims, some not questioned may well proceed in the matter exactly in the way the others do.

Claims Forms

All agents (and most publishers, too, for that matter) require specific types of information when a claim is entered, and usually want it to come to them on their own claims form. While the library with only one or two agents may find the agency claims forms useful, they can be a problem. Here are some of the difficulties:

> The use of special forms in making claims is also a matter of some concern. Many agencies, in this country at least, now have claim forms that they urge their customers to use. As a rule, such agencies make the point that using the form they supply is a help both to themselves as they have many claims to deal with every day, and to their customers, who are thus spared the need of a form of their own. There are however, objections to the use of the agent form. The biggest of these is that most libraries have forms of their own, the use of which is a matter of convenience, if not of necessity, to them. Further, it is awkward to have to use a multiplicity of forms where one form alone should do, and to have to keep a supply of each form on hand at all times. Finally there is the additional expense of using the agency forms, which invariably must be put in envelopes and sent out at the maximum rates, whereas libraries are satisfied, in the main, to make their claims on preprinted postcards, which cost little and are easy to use.[18]

Should, then, the library use the agency form? If only one or two agents are involved, the answer is yes. The reason is that this speeds the claim along, as the agency form fits well in every sense into agency files. The library may spend a little longer time in filling out the form, but, in the end, will find use of this form an effective means of acquiring missing items. However, if more than two agents are employed, and the library has its own peculiar records and forms, it is probably desirable to use the library forms. The rule at this stage: Check with the agency to see how much time will be lost if library forms are employed.

EVALUATING AGENCY CLAIMS SERVICE

After the smoke of agency advertising claims has cleared, after the complaints of librarians (real and imaginary) have been heard, how does one evaluate the agency claims service? The single best answer: Has the library received the missing title(s)? No agent can guarantee delivery of all titles missed, but a majority of claims should be satisfactorily resolved. A rough rule, giving due consideration to variables, is that from 70 to 85 percent of all claimed titles should be received if the agent is doing his job properly. Such a return must extend itself over a period of at least one year in order that the test be considered valid.

Other ways of evaluating an agent's claim policies before the agent is employed is to ask the agent to answer the questions in the Checklist.

No librarian is going to be able to check accurately on an agency's claims score unless he or she keeps track personally of what is happening. Smith suggests that a good way of doing this is for the librarian to maintain a claims diary:

> A diary of claiming should be maintained during the agency evaluation period. This can be time consuming, but it is the only way to pull together for analysis those copies of claim slips which are usually filed throughout the check-in records. The diary should consist of titles, dates of claims, dates of follow-ups where necessary, dates of receipt of claimed issues, and notations as to country of publications, since this will affect the speed of receipt.[19]

Thanks to the existence in many larger libraries of automated or partially automated serials systems, information of this sort is a built-in contribution of the system to the librarian's welfare. No claims diary is needed as information about claims is available at the touch of a button. In smaller libraries, the diary serves a useful purpose. In these, of course, the number of serials is not so great as to make the diary process difficult. Smith's warning that this process can be "time consuming" applies certainly in the case of the nonautomated larger library, but it is to be hoped that in this case the library can muster the resources needed for the keeping of the diary.

Evaluation Example

The following evaluation was made by Richard R. Seidel of the Newberry Library in Chicago. Seidel's evaluation is instructive both in particulars and in general. It is also completely fair concerning problems with which library agents must deal. Seidel summarizes the results in a table. Herewith his introductory remarks:

> You will note that in 1972, 500 new orders for periodicals and other continuations (the Serials Department handles all standing orders, monographic as well as serial) were placed with our various dealers and that after a period of one year, some 50, or 10 percent, required claiming.

I need not point out that in some cases, the statistics are really stacked against the dealer. For instance Harrassowitz, to my mind, is one of the best jobbers in the world, yet some 8 percent of our orders required claiming. In many respects, this is highly unusual for Harrassowitz, for they at least supply a report, but I happen to know that most of the titles were rather obscure and very difficult to acquire. One periodical, *Der Globusfreund*, is the publication of a Viennese map collectors circle and apparently Harrassowitz had a very difficult time getting an answer from the organization, but when they did reply, they sent not only the current subscription, but all of the available backfile.

Yet another example is Mrs. Susan Bach, who struggles against increasing obstacles on our behalf in Rio de Janeiro. The study indicates that 40 percent or 4 out of 10 titles required claiming, but God knows the overwhelming difficulties involved in getting materials out of Brazil—and she is one of the best dealers that we have in South America!

In so many cases, our sample is really rather small, but they do give some indication of the scope of the problem here at the Newberry.

Statistics Concerning Claiming/Serials Division, The Newberry Library, Chicago.

New Orders placed in 1972: 500 orders placed. 10 percent required claiming after one year.

Breakdown of the 10 percent.

Dealer	Country	No. of Orders	No. of Claims	Percentage
Martinius Nijhoff	Netherlands	14	3	21
Swets & Zeitlinger	Netherlands	8	0	—
Munskgaard	Denmark	4	1	25
Erasmo	Italy	3	0	—
Libreria Commissionaria	Italy	15	2	13
Seeber	Italy	7	0	—
Blancheteau	France	9	1	11
Livres et Revues	France	4	0	—
Harrassowitz	West Germany	49	4	8
Erasmus	Switzerland	3	0	—
J. Barbazan	Spain	1	0	—
Livraria Portugal	Portugal	3	0	—
Keins	Argentina	3	2	66
Bach	Brazil	10	4	40
Stevens & Brown	England	41	2	5
Dora Hood's Book Room	Canada	5	0	—
Richard Abel[1]	United States	31	2	6
Faxon	United States	59	1	2
Stechert-Hafner[2]	United States/Foreign	27	15	55
Other foreign		39	2	5
Other domestic*	United States	153	12	8

144   Guide to Magazine and Serial Agents

Statistics Concerning Claiming/Serials Division (*Continued*)
Claims for existing standing orders

Dealer	Country	Claims Received†	Time Lapse (Months)
A. Baer		4	4
Baerenreiter	West Germany	3	1
J. Barbazan	Spain	8	3
Blancheteau	France	2	5
Commissionaria Liberia	Italy	3	2
Harrassowitz	West Germany	7	2
Dora Hood's Book Room	Canada	2	1
Herbert Lang	Switzerland	2	2
Livraria Portugal	Portugal	2	3
Messassgeria Italiane	Italy	4	3
Martinius Nijhoff	Netherlands	2	2
Olschki	Italy	2	2
Seeber	Italy	10	2
Stechert-Hafner[2]	United States/Foreign	3	9
Stevens & Brown	England	5	4
Foreign/other	–	20	2
Domestic/other	–	64	3

*Includes university publishers and private publishers (notably genealogy).
†Claims received includes books received in answer to claims, notification that item has not yet been published, notification that item has ceased publication, that item is out of print.
[1] Richard Abel, Inc., became defunct in early 1975. Its resources are now being managed by Blackwell North America, Inc.
[2] Stechert-Hafner (now Stechert-Macmillan). Seidel notes that despite difficulties in 1972 matters have improved since the new owners came onto the scene. He states that Newberry is impressed with the new firm's service: "We now have very prompt replies on queries and claims."

REFERENCE NOTES

1. Judith Nientimp, "The Librarian . . . and the Subscription Agent," *Special Libraries*, July 1972, p. 294.
2. Katherine R. Smith, "Serials Agents/Serials Librarians," *Library Resources and Technical Services*, Winter 1970. p. 14.
3. Fred Roessler, "What Happened to That Issue of . . . ?" mimeographed, n.d., p. 1.
4. Frank Clasquin, "The Claim Enigma for Serials and Journals," in *Management Problems in Serials Work*, ed. by Peter Spyers-Duran and Daniel Gore (Westport, Conn.: Greenwood Press, 1974), p. 76. *See also*, pp. 76–78. Here Clasquin lists thirty-five probable causes of claims with an indication of whether the publisher, agent, or librarian is probably at fault.
4. *Ibid.*, p. 75.

6. Huibert Paul, "The Serials Librarian and the Journal Publisher," *Scholarly Publishing*, January 1972, pp. 178-179.
7. Andrew Osborn, *Serial Publications*, 2nd ed. (Chicago: American Library Association, 1973), pp. 121-192. Osborn gives a thorough, detailed description of several checking systems, manual and automated.
8. Nientimp, *op. cit.*, p. 294.
9. Clasquin, *op. cit.*, pp. 72-75.
10. Calvin D. Evans. "An Experiment in Periodicals Claiming," *Stechert-Hafner Book News*, December 1970, p. 27.
11. Richard Seidel, letter to the author, April 9, 1974.
12. Clasquin, *op. cit.*, p. 75.
13. Evans, *op. cit.*
14. *Ibid.*
15. ALA/RTSD, Acquisitions Section, "Guidelines for Publishers, Agents, and Librarians in Handling Library Orders for Serials and Periodicals" (Chicago: American Library Association, 1973), p. 8. A processed, 12-page report.
16. *Ibid.*
17. Nientimp, *op. cit.*, p. 295.
18. Peter Gellatly, "Libraries and Subscription Agencies," *PNLA Quarterly*, October 1966, p. 39.
19. Smith, *op. cit.*, p. 11.

IV.

DIRECTORIES FOR ANALYZING AND LOCATING SERIALS AGENTS AND SERVICES

12.
CHECKLIST OF AGENCY SERVICES AND PROCEDURES

A recurrent question among librarians who work with subscriptions agents: "What services and procedures should I rightfully expect from X agent?" Put another way: "What services or procedures does X offer that are not offered by Y agent?" And, in still another: "How does X agent compare with Y agent in terms of services and procedures?"

The purposes of this Checklist are to provide the librarian with a list of points and questions that he or she may take to the agent about services, and to give the librarian an idea of what kind of agent provides or does not provide given services; to offer the librarian a basis for comparing agents before deciding which (usually not more than two or three) should be asked for quotes on a library list of titles; and to enumerate for the librarian obliged to use the bid system those items that should be written into the bid contract as a way of ensuring that a low price brings decent service, or at least does not preclude it.

Not all of the checkpoints will be applicable in every instance, but details are included so that nothing that may be useful to the librarian is left out. The list is arranged in such a way that the librarian may easily extract from it matters that, for his or her good, ought to be addressed to the agent, whether verbally or in writing.

The points and questions listed here were sent to twenty-two domestic and international agents in the form of a questionnaire (in some cases, an abbreviated questionnaire was used). The agents were selected on the basis of size, types of service offered, and familiarity to American librarians (as this was made known in citations by librarians consulted during the survey.) The agents who responded range from one with a very limited list of titles to others whose lists contain as many as 70,000 titles. These include:

Domestic Agents: China Books and Periodicals, Ebsco, Faxon, French & European Publications, Instructor, Maxwell, Moore-Cottrell, Read-More, Stechert-Macmillan, and Turner. (After the questionnaire returns had been tabulated the Maxwell International Subscription Agency was purchased by Moore Cottrell. However, as other Maxwell firms offer subscription services comparable to those of the purchased firm, the replies from Maxwell retain their validity, and are referred to from time to time.)

International Agents: Almqvist & Wiksell, Blackwell's, Brockhaus, Chinese Materials, Collet's, Collins Book Depot, Dawson-France, Harrassowitz, Marcel Blancheteau, R. Hill, Stevens & Brown, and Swets & Zeitlinger.

The questionnaire was sent also to a number of agents cited frequently by librarians. Some of these agents chose, for whatever reason, not to participate in the survey or to participate in a minor way only. These were Aquinas, Bernan, Fennell, McGregor, Popular, Universal, and Martinius Nijhoff. Fennell, Popular and Nijhoff, however, did fill out the short questionnaire. After repeated inquiries, McGregor and Universal sent brochures and catalogs, but did not respond to either questionnaire. There was nothing but silence from Aquinas and Bernan.

The replies by the twenty-two agents demonstrate what a librarian may or may not expect of almost any domestic or international agent. Where there is virtual consensus among the agents concerning a service or procedure, it is reasonable to expect that agents not included in the survey offer, in some sort, the same service or procedure. Conversely, where there is no consensus, the librarian is warned that the matter, if important, should be clarified with the agent. The Checklist should be used in conjunction with the Directory of Agents. Although the Directory is less detailed than the Checklist, statements occur in it that occasionally offer further insight into the extent and quality of an agent's services (Chapter 15).

Agents' procedures and services are constantly changing—usually for the better, but sometimes for the worse. The Checklist represents in general the state of things as of late 1973 and early 1974. If an agent's remarks appear to overpraise a service it offers, it is, of course, possible that a change for the better has taken place.

The librarian need not hesitate to question the agent in the matter. Furthermore, if the agent's statement is unclear or equivocal, the librarian should seek an explanation.

Most large and medium-sized agencies issue brochures in which they describe their services. Such brochures should be kept at hand, as the information in them sometimes serves to update what is presented here. The librarian may extract information from the statements made by an agent and ask the agent to expand upon it, however it is felt this should be done.

Given after each statement are the responses of domestic agents. These responses are followed by the responses of international agents. Sometimes the separate responses of each agent are listed, but, more often, when a consensus is found among the agents, a general response, applying in all cases, is set down.

At the bottom of some pages are explanatory notes, prefaced by the term *Guidelines*. This is in reference to the ALA/RTSD Acquisition Section's *Guidelines for Publishers, Agents and Librarians in Handling Library Orders for Serials and Periodicals* (Chicago: ALA, 1973). The *Guidelines* are an effort, as explained by their authors, to formulate "a general guide for librarians, agents, and publishers in their efforts to realize good serial service to the ultimate consumer, the reader." Quotes from the *Guidelines* are given as footnotes to Checklist some statements. These quotes serve to emphasize what is considered a desirable policy or procedure, and to highlight differences of opinion between librarians and the surveyed agents.

The Checklist is primarily concerned with periodicals, although, in almost all cases, the questions and statements are as applicable in discussing serials of other sorts as well.

I. AGENCY-LIBRARY RELATIONSHIPS

A. Agency-Library Contacts

1. *The agent has a representative, account executive, or some specific individual who calls periodically on the librarian.*

Most domestic agents have such representation. The exceptions: China Books and Periodicals, French & European Publications, Instructor, and Turner. Turner will "send representatives, if requested by the library." Only two international agents have American representatives: Blackwell's and Swets & Zeitlinger.

2. *When there is a problem, the librarian may call the agent collect.*

Most domestic agents offer this service. The exceptions: China Books and Periodicals, French & European Publications, and Instructor. The latter "generally will not accept such calls." No international agents accept such calls, although Blackwell's and Swets & Zeitlinger will accept them through their American representatives.

3. *The agent can accept TWX, Telex, and other such messages from the library.*

The following domestic agents can do so: Faxon, Maxwell, Moore Cottrell, and Read-More. Furthermore, Faxon also offers: "WATS lines (long distance direct dial), no charge, coast to coast." International agents offering such service are Blackwell's, Harrassowitz, R. Hill, and Swets & Zeitlinger.

B. Agency-Library Correspondence

4. *The agency will acknowledge all inquiries from the library.*

All domestic agents claim to answer all inquiries. Most international agents make the same claim, except Collins Book Depot and Marcel Blancheteau, although the latter does so sparingly.

5. *The agent will acknowledge all inquiries within an average of _____ days after receipt of the inquiry.*

Domestic agents noted their own versions of average response time: China Books and Periodicals, fourteen days; Maxwell, four days; Read-More, two days; Stechert-Macmillan, fourteen days; Turner, five to ten days.

Two of the largest domestic agents responded with modified answers:

Faxon: The answering time of letters is many times contingent upon obtaining information required from the publisher. We feel no purpose is served with a simple acknowledgment of a complaint letter unless the library so requests. The absence of some vital information in the answering letter only inflates correspondence folders and erodes manpower time which could be spent on solving problems.

Moore-Cottrell: It is impossible to furnish definite information as to answering time of letters. If the publishers do not respond to our inquiries we cannot do more for our customers than the publishers themselves.

The time needed for a reply from international agents ranges from a minimum of five days (Dawson-France) to a maximum of 10 days (Blackwell's and Brockhaus). Two agents added comments:

Blackwell's: We use standard letters for routine correspondence, but specific letters, when they involve problems are dealt with by personal letters from the department manager responsible for the geographic area in which the customer is situated.

Harrassowitz: The time in answering letters depends entirely on the kind and the urgency of the library's communications and types of information required, etc. Usually one to thirty days, depending upon the urgency, is the time of reply.

6. *The agent will acknowledge receipt of all library orders.*

The majority of agents acknowledge. Some only acknowledge when requested to do so. These are Maxwell, Moore-Cottrell, Stechert-Macmillan, and Turner. Instructor will not acknowledge. Most international agents will not acknowledge orders unless requested to do so.

7. *The agent will acknowledge orders (either by request or automatically) within an average of _____ days after receipt of the order.*

There is considerable variation in this matter among domestic agents:

China Books and Periodicals: two to three days
Ebsco: one week
Faxon: 10 days if more than 20 titles
French & European Publications: 30 days
Instructor: Does not acknowledge
Maxwell: 10 days, ordinarily by invoicing
Moore-Cottrell: 48 hours, if requested
Read-More: 30 days
Stechert-Macmillan: 2 weeks, if requested
Turner: 10 days, by invoice

International agents, if requested to acknowledge an order, will do so within an average of one to two weeks.

8. *The agent will notify the librarian promptly when a delay is to be expected in delivery in any part of a library order.*

All domestic and international agents say they make such reports. Ebsco and Faxon, however, make their reports only on invoices, as do Almqvist & Wiksell and Chinese Materials.

9. *The agent will automatically acknowledge all first claims entered by the library through the agent.*

Only a few domestic agents acknowledge first claims: Ebsco, Instructor, Stechert-Macmillan, and Turner. Faxon acknowledges all claims by way of a quarterly report, *FACS*. Domestic agents that will not respond to a first claim but will to a second include Maxwell and Read-More. All agents except China Books and Periodicals acknowledge receipt of first claims *when so requested by the library*.

All international agents except Blackwell's, Brockhaus, Collins Book Depot, and Marcel Blancheteau acknowledge a first claim. Blackwell's acknowledges third and later claims. All of these agents will make acknowledgment on request.

C. Preprinted Forms

10. *The agent supplies all basic forms needed by the library for orders, claims, renewals, etc.*

Most domestic agents supply these upon request; China Books and Periodicals and French & European Publications will not. Two agents have modified policies. Maxwell: "All forms are provided, but order forms. The agency prefers the library use its own order forms." Moore-Cottrell: "The agency will supply claim forms and carbon-inserted order forms when purchase orders are not required." Most international agents, such as Blackwell's, R. Hill, and Swets & Zeitlinger, do not supply forms. Dawson-France supplies order forms and so does Stevens & Brown, "but only if requested by the library."

11. *The agent supplies preprinted claim forms.**

Most domestic agents supply preprinted claim forms. China Books and Periodicals, French & European Publications, and Instructor do not. The latter agent prefers to settle claims "by correspondence with the library." Most international agents do not supply claim forms. Blackwell's, R. Hill, Swets & Zeitlinger, and Marcel Blancheteau do supply them upon request.

12. *The agent supplies the library with preprinted and postpaid claim forms.**

Two domestic agents, Moore-Cottrell and Turner, comply; internationally, Swets & Zeitlinger alone does.

D. Record Information

13. *The library purchase order, number, date, and other necessary record information requested by the library is placed by the agent on all correspondence, invoices, etc., sent to the library.*†

All agents agree to this request. The library, however, must be specific in requesting the information it wants.

14. *The agent will provide check numbers and dates, when requested by the publisher or library.*

**Guidelines:* "Ideally claim forms should be preaddressed and postpaid, and should provide space for a reply so as to expedite reports from vendors." Almost without exception, the agency-supplied claims forms are preprinted and do provide adequate space. As noted, few agents offer the prepaid "ideal."

†*Guidelines:* "The library should permanently record original order numbers and refer to them on all future transactions and correspondence. Every effort should be made to refer to serial titles in terms used by the library in its initial order. In any case, library order numbers must appear on all correspondence, invoices and reports."

All agents agree to this request. The majority will furnish photocopies. Where there is any question at all about the agent's financial status or honesty, this point should be made part of any written contract or agreement.

15. *When the library fails to include essential data in an order, a claim, or request of any sort, the agent will search for the data.*

All agents say they do. The result achieved depends, of course, upon *how much* information the agent has available in his or her files. Under no circumstances should the librarian expect the agent to second-guess him or her.

II. AGENCY PROCESSING OF LIBRARY ORDERS

A. Best Time to Place an Order

1. *The agent will accept an order from the library at any time.**
All agents do so.

2. *The best time of the year for a library to place a basic order is_____.*
Domestic agents have various answers:

China Books: Any time
Ebsco: Any time
Faxon: Two months before start of new volume
French & European Publications: Any time
Instructor: Three months prior to starting time
Maxwell: February through August
Moore-Cottrell: 8 to 12 weeks before beginning date of subscription
Read-More: September
Stechert-Macmillan: September
Turner: January starts: July through September
        September starts: March through May

International agents have equally different requirements:

Almqvist & Wiksell: Autumn
Blackwell's: August through September
Brockhaus: Any time
Chinese Materials: November
Collins Book Depot: October
Dawson-France: Before October for next year
Harrassowitz: Any time. Preferably early in the calendar year in order to avoid losing early numbers—a particularly important consideration with East German and East European publications.
Marcel Blancheteau: Early December for a subscription beginning January 1
Stevens & Brown: Periodicals subscriptions in October; standing orders anytime
Swets & Zeitlinger: No later than June

**Guidelines:* "Subscriptions should begin with the first issue of the calendar year or, where this is not appropriate, with the first issue of the current (or next) volume."

B. Orders and the Time Factor

3. *The agent acknowledges receipt of all library orders. See* I. B6.

4. *The agent acknowledges an order (either automatically or when requested) within an average of ____ days after receipt of the order. See* I. B7.

5. *Once the order is received, it takes the agent ____ days to ____ weeks to process the order.* *

Considerable variation exists among responding agents:

China Books and Periodicals: 5 days
Ebsco: One week or less
Faxon: 14 days
French & European Publications: 10 days
Instructor: 2 weeks
Moore-Cottrell: 7 days or less
Stechert-Macmillan: 10 to 14 days

Blackwell's: 10 days
Brockhaus: 2 days
Collet's: No reply
Collins Book Depot: 7 days or less
Dawson-France: 7 days; "though dailies are processed the day order received"
Harrassowitz: 5 days
Marcel Blancheteau: 1 week. "Orders for subscriptions and periodicals are always sent to the publisher on Friday except for rush orders."
Stevens & Brown: 3 days
Swets & Zeitlinger: 7 to 14 days

6. *The agent estimates that once the publisher receives the order from the agent, it will take the publisher an average of ____ days to process the order.*

There is no consensus among agents as to the real time it takes to process an order:

China Books: 2 to 3 months
Ebsco: 21 days
Faxon: 30 to 45 days
French & European Publications: Depends on each publisher
Instructor: 8 to 10 weeks
Maxwell: "Depends on the publisher. This is a meaningless question, e.g., South America or India should take an average of three months, but the U.S. an average of four weeks."

**Guidelines:* "While the actual supply of serial issues is seldom under control of an agent, the promptness with which orders are processed and sent out to the publishers will certainly affect the speed with which the first issue of a new subscription is supplied, and the ease with which renewals are effected. Internal processing of new orders should require not more than a week."

156 Guide to Magazine and Serial Agents

>Moore-Cottrell: 42 to 84 days
>Read-More: 40 to 50 days
>Stechert-Macmillan: 60 days
>Turner: 60 to 90 days

>Almqvist & Wiksell: 1 to 2 weeks
>Brockhaus: 10 days
>Chinese Materials: Depends on publisher
>Collins Book Depot: 30 days
>Dawson-France: 2 weeks
>Harrassowitz: 5 days for German publishers; others 10 to 20 days
>Marcel Blancheteau: 1 month
>R. Hill: "Too long"
>Stevens & Brown: 2 to 6 weeks
>Swets & Zeitlinger: 7 to 150 days

7. *Given the (a) agency time required to process an order and send it to the publisher, plus (b) the time it takes the publisher to process an order, the library should allow____ days lead-in time before the desired date of receipt of the first issue required.* *

Domestic agents estimate one to three months lead-in time necessary for library orders. Great variation appears in the estimates of international agents, primarily because agent may operate in several countries and have to cope with a multiplicity of publisher situations.

>Almqvist & Wiksell: "Depends on time the mails take"
>Chinese Materials: 3 months
>Collet's: 1 month
>Collins Book Depot: 90 days from Australia
>Dawson-France: 6 weeks plus three weeks for shipment from France to U. S.
>Harrassowitz: 30 days plus travel time
>Marcel Blancheteau: 3 months because postal delays occur
>R. Hill: 9 to 12 weeks for overseas titles
>Stevens & Brown: 2 to 3 months
>Swets & Zeitlinger: Impossible to say

8. *The agent will promptly notify the librarian when there is going to be any delay in delivery of any part of the order. Meanwhile, the agent processes the remainder of the order.*

All domestic and international agents process what part of the order they can without waiting for a special instruction about problem titles. Marcel Blancheteau notes that delays can occur, depending upon the sort of publication involved; which is to say that the agent may delay sending the earlier volumes in a long, expensive series. This is not done in the case of an ordinary periodical.

*Guidelines: "Orders should be placed with sufficient lead-in time, generally three months before the date of publication of the first issue required."

9. *The agent notifies the library of a delay in any part of the order* before *the agent's initial invoice is sent to the library.**

The majority of domestic and international agents notify the library of any delay. There are two notable domestic exceptions: Ebsco and Faxon. Neither does any notifying except on the invoice that goes out for the complete order. Among international agents, only Amlqvist & Wiksell and Chinese Materials wait to notify the library on the invoice. Marcel Blancheteau notes that decision in this "depends on the series."

10. *The agent sometimes holds up an order, or part of an order, while negotiating for special discounts from the publisher.*†

No agent, domestic or international, follows this procedure, or at least admits to doing so.

C. Agency Reports on Orders: General‡

Domestic and international agents alike supply the library with two basic types of order report information: (1) The agent is unable to fulfill the order (i.e., either the complete order or the most titles ordered). This is equivalent to a cancellation. (2) The agent is able to fill the order, but there will be a delay in delivery of certain titles.

11. *When a delay is to be expected, the agent notifies the librarian before the invoice is sent for the body of the order.*

All domestic and international agents say they make reports of this kind, *except* Ebsco and Faxon and the international agents Almqvist & Wiksell and Chinese Materials. The report, in the case of these agents, is made on the invoice. Generally speaking, the agent forwards what information it can to assist the librarian in obtaining titles the agent is unable to supply or in making other decisions about the list.

12. *The agency reports when it is unable to supply the order, and gives reasons for this failure.*

Agents all say they report. Sample explanations contained in the report: The title is not available to the agent (i.e., the publisher will not work with the agent or the agent will not work with the publisher). The library must order

---

*Guidelines: "A status report, if in lieu of supply should be submitted on all anticipated issues and order requests delayed more than 30 days. However, this can only be used as a rule of thumb, since frequency of publication will influence reporting schedules. All reports should carry references to the order number and bibliographic details of the item." (IV B1, Agency section): "Invoices should be used for billing purposes only, with status reports always issued separately."

†*Guidelines:* "Orders should not be delayed while negotiating for special discounts. If none are available, the library should be informed."

‡*Guidelines:* "Agreement on definitions is essential to an adequate reporting system." Suggestions as to how agreement might be attained are offered in Sections D, E, and F. It is to be noted in passing that most reports on periodical subscriptions relate to claims and invoice problems rather than to supply. The same holds true in the case of many serials of other sorts.

title through the publisher. The title is material of a sort not handled by the agent, i.e., back issues, reprints, books, series, etc. The title is discontinued.

13. *The agent reports if there will be a delay, and gives reasons. (The delay, of course, may amount finally to the agent's not being able to supply the order.)*

All agents report they give one to three reasons for the delay: (1) unable to locate or verify; (2) no response from the publisher; and (3) not yet published. Any delay may turn out to be a permanent one, and when the agent cannot be specific in the matter (i.e., give the date of expected publication or a reason for lack of response from the publisher), the order should be canceled, and a new order sent out only if some certainty exists that the item is available.

D. Agency Reports on Periodical Orders: Specific

In addition to basic order-report information, almost all agents, both domestic and foreign, provide other information as a help to the librarian. For example, when the agent is unable to fulfill an order for a specific title, the reason may be indicated. (Depending upon the reason given, the librarian will either give up or send the order elsewhere.)

14. *The title is free upon application to the publisher.*

All domestic and international agents so note, except China Books and Periodicals and Brockhaus.

15. *The title is a controlled circulation item (i.e., it is sent only to an audience chosen by the publisher).*

All domestic and international agents so note, except China Books and Periodicals and Brockhaus.

16. *The title is available upon exchange from the publisher.*

All domestic and international agents so note, except China Books and Periodicals, Maxwell, and Brockhaus.

17. *The title is part of a series in which the pricing is too irregular for the agent to handle.*

All domestic agents so note except China Books and Periodicals. Ebsco and Stechert-Macmillan handle this type of material. No international agent so notes. Blackwell's, Harrassowitz, and Swets & Zeitlinger handle such materials. Marcel Blancheteau invoices as the title comes out.

18. *The title is too irregular in its publishing schedule for the agent to handle.*

The following domestic agents do not handle material of this sort: Faxon, Instructor, Read-More. Ebsco and Stechert-Macmillan do. One international agent, Swets & Zeitlinger, refuses to handle such material. Blackwell's, Harrassowitz, and Marcel Blancheteau do.

19. *As the title costs less than $1.00, the agent does not handle.*

Among domestic agents, Faxon, Instructor, and Read-More do not handle. Ebsco, Moore-Cottrell, and Stechert-Macmillan do. No international agent says he or she does not handle. Blackwell's, Collins Book Depot, Dawson-France, Harrassowitz, and Swets & Zeitlinger say specifically that they do. (Swets & Zeitlinger adds: "We handle, but it is advisable that the library order direct as minimum operating costs should be paid, which is about U.S. $3.")

Checklist of Agency Services and Procedures *159*

20. *The title is usually slow to be delivered, and the agent does not handle. (The rationale here is that slow delivery brings a spate of claims, something the agent prefers to avoid.)*

Only the following domestic agents do not handle: Faxon, Instructor, Maxwell, and Read-More. Agents handling this material are Ebsco and Stechert-Macmillan. International agents Almqvist & Wiksell, Blackwell's, Collins Book Depot, Dawson-France, R. Hill, and Swets & Zeitlinger do not handle. Harrassowitz and Marcel Blancheteau do.

21. *As the title is available only in multiple copies, the agent does not accept single-copy subscriptions.*

All domestic agents so note, except China Books and Periodicals and Ebsco. No international agent so notes.

22. *The title is discontinued; the agent gives the volume and number of the last issue published.*

All domestic agents claim to give this information *when* available. All international agents claim to do likewise, except Brockhaus and Swets & Zeitlinger. These two note that they give it "when possible."

23. *For reasons other than those appearing above, the agent finds the publisher too hard to deal with, and advises the library to order directly from the publisher.*

All domestic agents comply, except China Books and Periodicals, Ebsco, Maxwell, and Turner. All international agents comply, except Brockhaus and Marcel Blancheteau.

E. Rush Orders*

24. *The agent accepts rush orders.*

Almost all domestic agents accept rush orders. The exceptions are Stechert-Macmillan and Instructor. The latter will accept, "but we do not encourage." All international agents accept such orders.

25. *The agent will accept rush orders from the library via telephone, TWX, Telex, etc.*

All domestic agents will accept, except Stechert-Macmillan and China Books. Instructor will accept, but does not encourage such orders. Most international agents accept (usually via Telex) but not Almqvist, Collins, and Marcel Blancheteau.

26. *The agent will place the rush order by phone with the publisher.*

Ebsco, French, and Read-More will do so; China Books, Instructor, and Stechert-Macmillan will not. Others modify; Faxon does so, but this is contingent upon the publisher accepting such orders via phone; Turner does so "only when a telephone order can be effective." Three international agents do not place rush orders by telephone: Almqvist & Wiksell, Brockhaus, and Collins Book Depot. Six use the telephone or some other means of rapid communication: Blackwell's, Collet's, Dawson-France (Telex), Marcel Blancheteau, R.

*Guidelines: "RUSH orders must be given special treatment . . . . Develop a RUSH procedure and identify such orders clearly."

Hill (telephone or Telex), and Stevens & Brown. Two qualify their replies—Harrassowitz: "Yes, but this depends upon the publisher"; Swets & Zeitlinger: "Yes, but it depends on the location of the publisher."

27. *The rush order will cut agent processing time of the order by* _____ .

The amount of time saved by a rush order varies with the agent.

> Faxon: 5 days
> Instructor: Only by time saved over mail delivery
> Maxwell: 10 days
> Moore-Cottrell: 1 to 2 days
> Read-More: 6 days—ordered same day received
> Stechert-Macmillan: Does not accept

> Almqvist & Wiksell: Does not accept
> Blackwell's: 5 to 7 days
> Chinese Materials: 5 days
> Collins Book Depot: Does not accept
> Harrassowitz: Depends upon titles
> Stevens & Brown: 2 days

28. *There is an extra charge for rush orders.*

Only one domestic agent makes such a charge—Ebsco. No international agent makes such a charge.

F. Agency Reports on Orders for Serials Other Than Periodicals

The agents queried were not asked specifically about other types of serials and the reports they make on such serials (although, it should be added, many of the agents handle such serials). Nor were publishers contacted to ascertain what type of report information they give.

As a footnote, it seems advisable then, to indicate what appears in the *ALA Guidelines* concerning agent reports on such serials. The following report forms are reproduced from the *Guidelines* (II.1 and II.2, Agency Section).

Dealer Oriented

Not yet received from the publisher (N.Y.R.). This must mean that the order has actually been sent to the publisher.

Claiming. This must mean that the dealer is following up on an existing order or subscription. (The claiming, of course, is an important part of periodicals, but in the context of this section on reports about orders is not likely to be part of the agency report.)

Out of stock, ordering (O.S.). This must mean out of stock at the dealer and a date when new supplies are expected should be given.

Wrong title supplied. Pending receipt of the correct title from the publisher, libraries must be informed immediately since this will explain the delay.

Defective copy, wrong number supplied, etc. A statement of remedial action taken must be included.

Publisher Oriented

Not yet published (N.Y.P.). This should be based on the publisher's advice and the expected date should be reported. (This is as applicable for agents as for publishers, and is so noted as a desired bit of agency report information elsewhere.)

Out of stock, publisher (O.S.) and

Reprinting/binding/on order, should refer to the publisher's own statement and an expected time of delivery should be given.

Out of print (O.P.). Some publishers use this to dealer but not to direct customers below a certain stock level. The dealer should try to ascertain this and advise the librarian accordingly.

Not our publication (N.O.P.). After rechecking and confirming, the library may regard the order as canceled and should restart it with more information.

Permanently out of stock. This means the same thing as out of print.

III. AGENCY ORDER PLANS AND REVIEW LISTS
A. Subscription Plans

1. *The agent orders all subscriptions for one, two, or three years depending upon library preference and patterns of availability.*

All domestic agents accept such orders, except Instructor; all international agents, except Chinese Materials.

2. *The agent accepts til-forbid orders for all titles.*

All domestic agents, except Instructor, accept these; all international agents, except Chinese Materials.

B. Subscription Expiration Dates

3. *The agent automatically seeks a common expiration date for til-forbid titles.*

All domestic agents, except China Books and Periodicals, Ebsco, and Instructor do this, though Turner says: "only if so requested by the library." Only four international agents will do so: Dawson-France, R. Hill, Stevens & Brown, and Swets & Zeitlinger. Harrassowitz notes that, usually, this procedure is "not applicable" in the work of international agents.

4. *Where the publisher does not allow a common expiration date, the agency renews for two years to establish an advanced date.*

Only two domestic agents offer this service: Faxon and Maxwell. And only three international agents: Dawson-France, R. Hill, and Stevens & Brown.

5. *The agent will split the total til-forbid items over a period of years in order to forestall a disproportionate billing in any single year.*

All domestic agents, other than China Books and Periodicals, Instructor, Read-More, and Stechert-Macmillan, provide this arrangement. Only four international agents follow suit: Blackwell's, Dawson-France, R. Hill, and Stevens & Brown.

C. Annual Review Lists

6. *Once a year, the agent sends the library a complete list of its subscriptions (i.e., the original list, to which new items have been added and from which stopped items—canceled, ceased, etc.—have been removed). Such a list is* not an invoice, *but rather the agent's reminder to the library that the time for putting together the coming year's order is at hand.*

All domestic agents automatically send annual review lists, but China Books and Periodicals ("an itemized invoice is sent"); Faxon ("will do so, but the library must request"); and French & European Publications ("sent only at expiration time"). All international agents automatically send such lists, but Almqvist & Wiksell, Brockhaus, Marcel Blancheteau, Collins Book Depot ("Not applicable. Sends an itemized invoice 3 months before the list expires"). Stevens & Brown ("will send only if requested").

7. *The annual review list includes prices known to the agent at the time of the mailing of the list and advance expiration dates of titles that do not have a common expiration date (usually the end of the year).*

Almost all domestic agents using annual review lists include this information in their lists. The exceptions are Ebsco, which does not include prices, but will send a copy of its last annual invoice, if noncurrent price information can be used, and Stechert-Macmillan, which does not give prices or irregular expiration dates (i.e., dates not coinciding with the agreed-upon expiration date). The information is included in the reports of all international agents except Chinese Materials and Harrassowitz.

8. *The annual review list is sent to the library approximately _____ months before confirmation is due from the library.*

There is no consensus among agents as to when the list is sent:

China Books and Periodicals: 3 months (as itemized invoice)
Faxon: 6 months (if a list is requested)
French & European Publications: 2 months
Moore-Cottrell: 3 to 4 months
Read-More: 5 to 6 months
Stechert-Macmillan: 3 months
Turner: 5 to 6 months (or as requested)

Blackwell's: 4 to 5 months
Chinese Materials: 3 to 4 months
Collet's: 2 to 3 months
Collins Book Depot: 3 months (invoice)
Dawson-France: 4 months
R. Hill: 2 months
Swets & Zeitlinger: 5 to 6 months, usually in early July

9. *The library should return the annual review list within approximately _____ months of receipt from the agent.*
   There is no consensus among agents as to when to return the list:

   Ebsco: 4 months
   Faxon: 8 weeks ("The publisher needs an average of 6 weeks to process the renewal order.")
   French & European Publications: 1 month
   Moore-Cottrell: 2 to 3 months
   Read-More: 3 months
   Stechert-Macmillan: 3 months

   Blackwell's: No reply
   Chinese Materials: 1 month
   Collet's: 1 to 2 months
   Dawson-France: 3 months
   Harrassowitz: 3 months
   R. Hill: 1 month
   Stevens & Brown: 2 months
   Swets & Zeitlinger: 3 months

10. *The agent makes requested corrections in the annual review list, and then sends the library an invoice in which the corrections are reflected.*
    All agents who use annual review lists follow this procedure.

IV. AGENCY INVOICES

A. Basic Data That All Agents Should Supply in an Invoice

All domestic and international agents *do furnish* the following basic data in their invoices:

1. The name and address of the agency
2. The name and address of the library*
   (a) The name of the department or division receiving the serial, if this differs from (2)
   (b) The name of the department or division to be billed for the serial, if this differs from (2)
3. The agency invoice number
4. The library purchase order number or other data requested by the library
5. The title of the serial
6. The period for which the subscription is billed
7. The quantity, i.e., the number of subscriptions to a single item.
8. Total price, *plus* specific pricing data. All agents give a total price, but the amount of specific pricing data varies greatly from agent to agent.

Guidelines: Agents should give special attention to different addresses and account numbers at the same institution.

B. Desirable Data Elements not Automatically Supplied in an Invoice

9. *The full, unabbreviated title is supplied.*

All agents claim they supply this, but Faxon makes a point about automation that will raise an eyebrow or two: "The title is unabbreviated, if no more than 54 characters, including spaces."

10. *The titles are arranged alphabetically.*

All domestic agents submit invoices in this fashion, except China Books and Periodicals. Two others qualify their answer—Read-More: "Yes, except for non-standing-order clients where the invoice is sent in the same order as listed to us." Turner: "Invoices are listed in the same manner as the list is sent to us. If there is a change or merger in title, or a difference in the manner of listing, we will show a cross reference." Among international agents, only Chinese Materials gives a categorical "no" to the question of alphabetical arrangement. All others follow it.

11. *In addition to the agency order number for the serial (when the agency has such numbers), the ISSN is given when available.*

Except for China Books and Periodicals and French & European Publications, all domestic agents use title numbers. Not all use, or plan to use, the ISSN. China Books and Periodicals and French & European Publications do not use, or plan to use, the ISSN; nor do Instructor and Read-More. Among international agents, only Dawson-France and Swets & Zeitlinger employ agency order numbers. However, Almqvist & Wiksell, Harrassowitz, Marcel Blancheteau, and Swets & Zeitlinger plan to use the ISSN.

12. *The frequency, i.e., the annual number, of issues is given.*

Among domestic agents, this information is given only by China Books and Periodicals, Ebsco, Faxon, Moore-Cottrell, Stechert-Macmillan, and Turner. Among international agents, no agent gives this information.

13. *The duration of the total subscription is given.*

All domestic agents indicate that they give this information. Among international agents, Harrassowitz fails to give it.

14. *The starting date of the subscription is given.*

All domestic agents indicate this by means of volume and issue number and/or month and year of the item. Among international agents, Harrassowitz does not give such information (except "where applicable").

15. *A clear indication is given as to whether the subscription is a new order or a renewal.*

All domestic agents make the distinction. Among international agents, Blackwell's does not, but specifies which orders are standing orders and tilforbid orders. Others not making the distinction are Chinese Materials, Collet's, Harrassowitz, and Swets & Zeitlinger.

C. Agency Charges

16. *The agent gives the total amount due for both individual titles and the entire list.*

All agents.

17. *The agent gives the amount of the service charge, where one exists.*
    All agents.
18. *The agent gives the amount of added charges.*
    All agents.
19. *The agent gives the publisher's retail list price of each title.*
    All domestic agents, except French & European Publications. All international agents except Blackwell's, China Books and Periodicals, R. Hill, and Swets & Zeitlinger.
20. *The agent indicates the discount the publisher allows the agent on a title.*
    The following domestic agents do so: Ebsco, Instructor, Maxwell, Moore-Cottrell, and Turner. The others do not. Only one international agent gives this information: Stevens & Brown.
21. *The agent shows the exchange rate if foreign currency is involved.*
    No domestic agent does this, although Maxwell does so, when requested. International agents that give this information include Harrassowitz, Marcel Blancheteau, and Stevens & Brown. The majority of the others do not because of rapid fluctuation in the rates.

D. Added Charges

Some agents now use a service or handling charge to take the place of the vanishing trade, or publisher's, discount. The library should not confuse this charge with the added charge, which is levied as a means of recovering the out-of-pocket expenses of managing an account.

21. *The agent charges for postage.*
    No domestic agent so charges. International agents normally respond by saying: "Where the publisher charges the agent, postage is charged." Harrassowitz notes that postage is charged on all periodicals.
23. *The agent charges for cancellation of a subscription.*
    Only one domestic agent so charges. Ebsco notes: "There is a small processing fee necessary for cancellations in significant quantity." International agents do not charge. Dawson-France is an exception; Its charge: 3 francs per cancellation.
24. *The agent charges for a rush order.*
    Only one domestic agent so charges: Ebsco. No international agent makes such a charge.
25. *The agent charges interest on unpaid invoices.*
    Only two agents exact such charges. Ebsco notes that an invoice "unpaid on the sixtieth day is charged a 1 percent carrying charge, and the carrying charge continues at the rate of 1 percent per thirty days thereafter until paid." Faxon charges, too, "but only as a collection device." Faxon gives no indication as to the amount charged.
26. *The agent charges for a performance bond.*
    Only one domestic agent so notes—Ebsco: "If your purchasing authorities require a performance bond, we can provide one at a slight premium charge."

27. *The agent charges for annual renewals.*

No agent replied to this question, although some do make a charge for renewing. The library should inquire.

28. *The agent charges for placing a continuation order (i.e., an order for a serial other than a periodical).*

No agent replied to this question, although some do charge for this. The library should inquire.

29. *The agent has other added charges.*

No agent replied to this question, *but* it is still a good one for a library to ask because added charges have a way of cropping up out of nowhere.

E. Bids

30. *The agent submits a bid for a library order when so requested by the library.*

The majority of domestic agents agree to submit bids, if reluctantly. Faxon, Read-More, and Turner are included here. They say they submit bids "selectively." China Books and Periodicals is an agent that does not bid. ("We are never asked for bids because our services are not competitive.") International agents that will not submit bids include Blackwell's, Collet's, Collins Book Depot, and Swets & Zeitlinger.

31. *Although a domestic agent normally does not submit bids, the agent will do so when the law governing the library so requires.*

Faxon: Yes, but only on selected occasions. If the only purpose is to place an order at the lowest possible price, we will not bid. Read-More: Yes Turner: Yes *None* of the international agents that do not bid will bid even when the law requires it to seek bids as a condition of ordering.

F. Agency Procedures in Submitting Invoices

32. *The agent normally sends_____ copies of the invoice to the library.*
    The number varies greatly:

    1 copy: French & European Publications
    2 copies: China Books and Periodicals, Moore-Cottrell, Turner
    3 copies: Ebsco, Read-More, Maxwell
    4 copies: Stechert-Macmillan
    5 copies: Faxon

    2 copies: Brockhaus, Collins Book Depot
    3 copies: Almqvist & Wiksell, Blackwell's, Dawson-France
    4 copies: Swets & Zeitlinger
    Up to 5 copies: Collet's, Harrassowitz

33. *The agent supplies as many copies of the invoice as requested by the library.*

All agents will so do when requested. The additional invoices are normally zeroxes or photocopies of the original.

34. *Special invoicing instructions are followed by the agent when the library so requests.**

All domestic and international agents agree to "reasonable" special invoicing requests.

35. *Invoices are used for billing purposes only; other types of reports are issued separately.*†

As noted previously, most, but not all, domestic and international agents use invoices only for billing purposes.

36. *The agent automatically uses separate invoices for separate kinds of material.*‡

The following domestic agents follow such a practice: French & European Publications, Maxwell, Read-More, and Stechert-Macmillan; others do not. All agents send separate invoices for separate kinds of material when so requested. All but a few international agents automatically use separate invoices for separate types of materials. Those who do *not*: Almqvist & Wiksell, Collins Book Depot, Collet's, and Harrassowitz.

37. *The agent automatically submits separate invoices when more than a single account is involved.***

Most domestic agents automatically comply. However, Ebsco, Faxon, Moore-Cottrell, and Turner will do so only upon request. The only international agents that automatically comply are Brockhaus, Marcel Blancheteau, R. Hill, Stevens & Brown, and Swets & Zeitlinger.

38. *The agent automatically submits separate invoices for new and for renewal subscriptions.*††

Only French & European Publications and Stechert-Macmillan follow this policy. Among international agents, the only ones who do are Brockhaus, Chinese Materials, R. Hill, and Stevens & Brown.

39. *The agent automatically sends separate invoices to different addresses at the same institution.*‡‡

Only Read-More and Stechert-Macmillan, of all domestic agents, follow this policy. Others will do so when requested to. Among international agents, those

**Guidelines:* "Special invoice requirements, such as an unusual number of copies, should be arranged in advance. It may be necessary to consult with the financial officers of the institution in order to keep such special requirements to a minimum."

†*Guidelines:* "Invoices should be used for billing purposes only, with status reports always issued separately."

‡*Guidelines:* "It is imperative for vendors to avoid mixing different kinds of materials and different accounts on the same invoice." "Continuations and monographs should be billed separately."

***Guidelines:* "Invoices for special (restricted) accounts, grant funds, etc. must be submitted separately."

††*Guidelines:* "It would also be desirable to have separate billing for new and renewal subscriptions."

‡‡*Guidelines:* "Material shipped to different addresses at the same institution should be invoiced separately."

who do so automatically are: Blackwell's, Brockhaus, Chinese Materials, Collet's, Marcel Blancheteau, R. Hill, and Stevens & Brown.

40. *When the agent ships materials to a library (rather than having them come directly from the publisher), invoices are included in the shipment.**

This procedure is rare among domestic agents. The only ones to follow it are China Books and Periodicals, French & European Publications, and Stechert-Macmillan. It is commoner among international agents. All include invoices in the shipment, *except* Almqvist & Wiksell, Chinese Materials, and Swets & Zeitlinger. Collet's and Dawson-France send copies of the invoice separately.

G. Types of Supplementary Invoices

In cases in which the invoice is sent to the library only after the agent has entered and paid for the subscription, supplementary invoices are not usually needed. However, a perennial headache for agents is the changing by a publisher at the last moment of prices or procedures. Such changes oblige the agent to revise the price it charges the library. Hence, a "bill back" or supplementary invoice goes to it.

41. *The agent will send the library a supplementary invoice for changes in initial billing.*

All domestic agents follow this procedure, except China Books and Periodicals and Instructor. Most international agents follow the same procedure, except Harrassowitz, which observes: "This is usually not applicable because we normally only charge our customers when we have the publisher's bill and a definite price on record." Marcel Blancheteau makes a like statement.

A second, more common sort of supplementary invoice is one on which charges are made for new items ordered during the year. All agents that accept such orders submit invoices on them.

42. *The agent sends supplementary invoices for new orders sent in by the library, once the agent pays the publisher.*

All agents follow this procedure, but modifications of it appear: Ebsco sends supplementary invoices within two weeks of receipt of the order. Faxon, for its part, tends to batch the charges for new orders for sixty to ninety days before it bills the library. It is also generally willing to wait a similar length of time for the library's check to reach it. And Maxwell submits invoices in a way that suits the library's convenience. All international agents send out separate invoices for intermittent orders. At least one, however, Harrassowitz, sends out such invoices only on a quarterly basis.

V. LIBRARY PAYMENT TO THE AGENT

A. Payment Procedures

1. *When the invoice is incomplete, the library should make inquiries of the agent immediately.*†

All domestic and international agents agree with this procedure.

**Guidelines:* "Invoices should be included or received concurrently with the shipment. Any delay in invoicing is inconvenient for the library. If the invoice is mailed separately, a clearly marked packing slip must accompany each shipment."

†*Guidelines:* "Incomplete invoices should be inquired about within 30 days and appropriate action taken."

Checklist of Agency Services and Procedures 169

2. *Any departure from the normal in payment procedure (see 3-5 below) should be approved in advance by the agent.*

All domestic and international agents agree.

3. *The library should pay the agent the full amount of the invoice within thirty days of the date of the invoice, or at least of receipt of the invoice.†*

All domestic agents make this request. Maxwell notes: "Not necessarily within thirty days. We allow thirty to sixty days, and up to ninety days in special cases, or a spring entry for a fall billing." International agents follow the same procedure. Up to ninety days are allowed by Blackwell's, Chinese Materials, and Collet's (in the case of overseas orders).

4. *Although the invoice may contain errors, the library is asked to pay it as it stands. The agent then issues a credit memo to compensate the library for overcharges and problematical items (items that may or may not belong on the invoice).‡*

All domestic and international agents like this procedure. A few domestic and several international agents offer alternatives to the credit-memo mechanism. Agents with alternatives are listed after each statement (a) through (c).

(a) Upon request, the agent issues a refund check to compensate for the problem titles and overcharges. Domestic agents: Faxon, Instructor, Moore-Cottrell, and Stechert-Macmillan. International agents: Chinese Materials, Collet's, Dawson-France, R. Hill, and Stevens & Brown.

(b) Upon request, the agent accepts an exception-to-charge form (i.e., deletion notice), whereby the library makes the necessary deductions from the invoice and, in lieu of full payment, sends the agent the corrected amount. Domestic agents: Faxon and Stechert-Macmillan. International agents: Collet's, Dawson-France, Harrassowitz, Marcel Blancheteau, and Stevens & Brown.

(c) The library returns the invoice for correction before making payment (i.e., requests an amended invoice). Domestic agents: Instructor (apparently Instructor does not issue credit memos). International agents: Almqvist & Wiksell.

Guidelines: "Any limitations imposed by the institution which the library is unable to modify should be carefully spelled out to vendors."

†*Guidelines:* "Librarians should follow the wishes of their vendors in so far as this is possible within the limitations imposed by their own procedures or institutional requirements." "Librarians should make every effort to insure the cooperation of their business offices with regard to prompt payment of invoices. Agents and publishers rely on a high rate of cash flow, and libraries can contribute to this by paying their bills as quickly as possible." "In general, delays in payment of 90 days or longer are unacceptable."

‡*Guidelines:* "Specific arrangements should be made with vendors to expedite the payment of long invoices on which there may be one or two errors or problems. Available options include the following: (a) Credit memos—usually require full payment of the invoice with the problems being worked out later. (b) Amended invoices—the most time-consuming approach, resulting in delayed payment. (c) Deletion notices—allows immediate payment of most of the invoice, avoids manipulation of credit memos and provides corrected invoices for the remainder when appropriate."

Note: Domestic agents are ready enough to permit the use by the library of credit memos. But only one accepts amended invoices; and only one accepts deletion notices. International agents tend to be more flexible.

170 Guide to Magazine and Serial Agents

5. *When a credit memo is issued (a device much favored by agents), there is no time restriction on its use.*

All domestic agents agree with the no-time-limit stipulation, except Ebsco, This agent's credit memo is good for 180 days only, but may be extended in special cases. Faxon imposes no time limit, but asks the library to use the credit to defray the outstanding balance, if such exists, of the invoice against which the credit was issued. International agents who issue credit memos have no time restrictions.

VI. CLAIMS AND RELATED SERVICES*

A. Forms

1. *The agent furnishes the library with preprinted claims forms.*
See Section I. C11 and C12.

2. *Either the agent or library claims form should include, at a minimun, data that appear in the reply space below.*

All domestic and international agents ask for name and address of agent (unless these appear on a preprinted form); name and address of library (address where to send claims forms if it differs); full title of claimed items; issues not received identified by volume, issue, month, and year; number of subscriptions not received, when applicable; library purchase order or fund number or other means of identifying the order used in acquiring the original subscription; agency invoice number.

3. *The following claim data are deemed desirable, but not required by all agents:*

All domestic agents but Read-More ask for the agency invoice date. No international agent requests this. No domestic agent other than Read-More (again) requests the agency number for missing titles, when such are brought to notice. And no international agent requires this number. Among domestic agents, Stechert-Macmillan asks for mailing labels (it accepts the code lines on the label, if the label itself cannot be sent). Faxon says of labels: "Only needed when the publisher requests." Read-More notes that they should be sent when a problem occurs with duplicates. No international agent asks for labels, although Stevens & Brown suggests that having them could be a help sometimes.

4. *The agent will do a limited search for vital data missing on a claim the library sends it.*

All domestic and international agents will make such searches, but, if unsuccessful, will return the claim to the library for further work there.

*Guidelines: "Expeditious handling of claims is one of the most important services which dealers can provide to libraries.

 "1. Claims should result from two sources:
   a. The dealer's own record of payment and renewals. If this record indicates a failure on the part of publishers, the dealer should follow up immediately.
   b. Information from libraries.
 "2. The end result of either type of claim should be a report to the library as described above."

B. Disposition of Claims

5. *The library should send claims to the agent or to the publisher.* *

Domestic agents that request the library send all claims to the agent, not to the publisher, are China Books and Periodicals, Instructor, Stechert-Macmillan, and French & European Publications (French & European Publications notes: "The original claim should be sent to the agent, and a copy to the publisher"). Domestic agents that prefer the claim be sent to the agent, *but* leave the decision up to the library as to whether it sends the claim to the agent or to the publisher, are Ebsco, Faxon, Maxwell and Moore-Cottrell. Domestic agents who simply note the decision is up to the library are Read-More and Turner. (French & European Publications notes: "The decision is up to the library, but we suggest non-service claims be sent to the agency. Occasional missing issue claims should be sent to the publisher.") The vast majority of international agents request that the claims be sent to the agent. International agents requesting that claims be sent to the agent, but leave the final decision up to the library, are Blackwell's, Collins Book Depot, Harrassowitz, and Swets & Zeitlinger. No other international agent concedes that the decision is up to the library alone.

6. *The agent has a special department or division to handle claims.*

All domestic and international agents but Brockhaus say they have such service.

7. *The agent acknowledges receipt of claims.*
See Section I B9.

8. *The agent accepts rush claims sent by telephone, TWX, Telex, etc.*

The procedures and policies here are generally the same as for rush orders. All domestic agents accept such claims, except China Books and Periodicals and Stechert-Macmillan. International agents accept Telex claims when Telex is available.

9. *Each claim should be entered on a separate claims form.*†
All domestic and international agents agree with this procedure.

10. *Claims may be batched for one mailing to the agent.*†
All domestic and international agents agree with this procedure.

C. Time Schedules for Claims

11. *As soon as receipt of the first issue of a new subscription is determined to be late, the librarian should contact the agent. This, to be sure, presupposes the library has at least an approximate idea of when the first issue of a new subscription is due to arrive.*

All domestic and international agents agree with this procedure.

---

*Guidelines: "... agents have the role of go-between in passing on library claims to publishers. It is recognized that publishers' activities are beyond the control of the agent, but the agent is in the best position to obtain and forward information in either direction."
†*Guidelines:* "Each claim should be on a separate sheet, but several may be batched in one mailing."

172 Guide to Magazine and Serial Agents

12. *Single issues missing. A library should begin claiming when the expected arrival date of a title has passed. A possible claims schedule follows:* *

Dailies: Claim 10 days after usual arrival date
Weeklies: Claim 2 weeks after usual arrival date
Monthlies: Claim 1 month after usual arrival date
Quarterlies: Claim 2 months after usual arrival date

Most domestic agents agree in full or in part with the above time schedule, but suggest some modifications—China Books and Periodicals: Weeklies: claim after a wait of six weeks; monthlies: claim after three weeks; quarterlies: claim after three weeks; annuals: claim ten days after receipt of our invoice. Turner accepts the survey time schedule, but adds an important note: "Consideration must be given to the historical record of receipt dates of any particular title . . . . " International agents agree in large part with the time schedule, but all, without exception, caution that the library must add to the schedule sufficient additional time for overseas delivery, and consider whether the delivery is to be by surface mail or by airmail.

13. *After submitting the initial claim, the library should wait a minimum of days before entering a second claim.* *

Domestic agents can reach no consensus on the approximate time to wait before entering a second claim:

Ebsco: 90 days
Instructor: 3 weeks
Maxwell: 60 days (European items, 80 days; others, 100 days)
Moore-Cottrell: 45 to 60 days ("It all depends on the individual publisher.")
Read-More: 42 days
Stechert-Macmillan: 30 days

Neither are international agents able to reach a consensus on the approximate time to wait before entering a second claim:

Brockhaus: 60 days
Collet's: 30 days
Collins Book Depot: 90 days
Dawson-France: 45 days for French titles sent to U.S.
Harrassowitz: 60 days (but more appropriate allowance for overseas delivery)

Guidelines: "Dealers must make absolutely clear the time limits within which they feel claims are valid." "Librarians should consult with major dealers and publishers and follow their suggestions with regard to time and frequency of claiming. (a) As a general rule, however, it is reasonable to assume a claim is valid if the issue following a missing item has been received. (b) Before claiming the first issue of a new subscription, allow 90 days or longer depending on the frequency of publication and the vendor's advice."

Guidelines: "Allowing for postal delivery both ways, follow-up claims can normally be sent at 30-day intervals, if required."

Marcel Blancheteau: 2 months for overseas delivery; fourth-class mail around 4 weeks from Paris to New York: more for West Coast
R. Hill: 14 days
Stevens & Brown: 50 days

14. *Automatic claiming, as this presupposes little or no reference to the history of the publisher's delivery schedule or to use of a proper claims schedule, is not encouraged by agents.**

All domestic and international agents agree with this statement.

15. *Claims submitted to the agency are handled and sent to the publisher within _____ after receipt from the library.*

There is no consensus among agents on the time it takes to process a claim:

China Books and Periodicals: 7 days
Ebsco: 3 days or less
Faxon: 3 to 10 days
French & European Publications: 3 days
Instructor: 10 days
Maxwell: 3 days
Moore-Cottrell: 10 days
Read-More: 3 days or less
Stechert-Macmillan: 3 days or less
Turner: 1 to 5 days

Blackwell's: 3 days
Brockhaus: 2 days
Chinese Materials: 5 days
Collet's: 6 days
Collins Book Depot: 7 days
Dawson-France: 8 days
Harrassowitz: 10 days
Marcel Blancheteau: 3 days
R. Hill: 5 days
Stevens & Brown: 5 days
Swets & Zeitlinger: 3 days or less

D. Agent Reports on Publishers

16. *The agent has a record of publishers that are likely to be dilatory in the processing of new orders and whose servicing of ongoing subscriptions is such as to give rise to claims.†*

---

*Guidelines: "Automatic claiming is counter-productive and should be discontinued."
†*Guidelines:* "Information which is known regarding time-lag experienced in initiating subscriptions should be made available to libraries."

Only four domestic agents have such records: Ebsco, Faxon, Moore-Cottrell, and Read-More. Of the international agents, five have such records: Blackwell's, Chinese Materials, Collins Book Depot, Harrassowitz, and Swets & Zeitlinger.

17. *The information on publishers is made available, usually on request, only to individual customers of the agent.*

Ebsco says the information is so available. Collins Book Depot, Harrassowitz, and Chinese Materials say the information is so available (Chinese Materials adds, "but not regularly").

18. *The information on publishers is made available not only to individual customers but also to libraries by way of an information bulletin issued by the agent.*

Faxon, Moore-Cottrell, and Read-More issue such bulletins. Ebsco does not, nor does it plan to do so. Faxon's publication is the *Serials Updating Service Quarterly* (a subscription costs $7 a year). This publication is in the form of an alphabetical list of titles. Information is given on receipt dates and on delays in receipt. Of the international agents, Blackwell's and Swets & Zeitlinger have such bulletins; Harrassowitz and Collins Book Depot do not.

19. *The agent has a means of showing when and for whom individual orders were entered for a title, i.e., the agent has a record of payments (original and renewal) sent to the publisher.* *

All agents say they can produce payment records for the library upon demand. Faxon notes: "A special claims information printout will be supplied upon request. This lists publisher name and address (where payment sent), Faxon check number, date of order and check, period ordered, order number, invoice number, frequency, and name of periodical."

E. Missing Issues

20. *When a claim made by a library through the agent fails to produce the missing issue, the agent will replace the claimed item,* but *only when it gets a replacement copy free of charge from the publisher. If the publisher makes a charge for the copy, the library will be billed by the agent.*

All domestic agents accept this arrangement, although Faxon notes: "We will, but we prefer to deal with each situation separately." All international agents accept the arrangement, but two add a twist to it—Stevens & Brown: "Depends on the amount involved." Swets & Zeitlinger: "Yes, but the library first would be asked if it still wants the missing items."

21. *The agent replaces a claimed, but not received, issue* free of charge *to the library, i.e., when available from the publisher or another source regardless of whether or not the agent has to pay for the missing issue.*

China Books and Periodicals does so, as does also Maxwell, "provided payment was made by the library before October 1 of the preceding year." Three international agents will so do: R. Hill, Marcel Blancheteau ("if claimed within a reasonable time, and never after more than one year"), and Chinese Materials ("after sufficient time has elapsed to confirm non-receipt").

*Guidelines: "Dealers can be expected to provide check numbers and dates when requested by publishers." And, it should be added, when requested by librarians.

F. Back Issues/Reprints, Etc.

22. *When the publisher begins a subscription only with the current issue, and the library wants a limited number of earlier issues, the agent will make an effort to procure these for the library.*

All domestic and international agents offer this service, usually with the modification suggested by Faxon: "We will attempt to acquire back issues from the publisher, but only in conjunction with an order for a current subscription, and only for the same material up to one prior year."

23. *The agent offers back issues, i.e., o.p. periodicals service.*

Only three domestic agents questioned offer this: China Books and Periodicals, Maxwell, and Read-More. Many international agents offer it: Almqvist & Wiksell, Chinese Materials, Dawson-France, Harrassowitz, Marcel Blancheteau, Stevens & Brown, and Swets & Zeitlinger.

24. *The agency offers microforms or reprints of back issues.*

Three domestic agents do so: Faxon, Maxwell, and Read-More. Faxon does not do so directly, but "will order such materials for the library from the publishers." The majority of international agents offer back issues in other than hardcopy: Chinese Materials, Collins Book Depot, Harrassowitz, Marcel Blancheteau, R. Hill, Stevens & Brown, and Swets & Zeitlinger.

25. *Requests for backfiles should be handled on a separate order form:* *

Domestic agents *that give* such service agree, as do most international agents, although one order form for both current and backfile issues is also generally acceptable.

G. Publisher Renewal Notices

26. *Claims should be sent as issues are found to be missing, not just when a renewal notice comes from the publisher.*

All domestic and international agents agree with this procedure.

27. *All renewal notices from publishers should be ignored, unless service has stopped.*

All domestic and international agents agree with this procedure.

H. Duplicate Issues

28. *The agent recommends that the library contact it if duplicates of a title are received two or three times in a row, or continue to arrive for an "appreciable" length of time.*

All domestic agents recommend this practice. Two agents modify the requirement—Ebsco: "Notification of receipt of duplicates is not necessary until duplication is repeated three times." Faxon: "The publisher should be notified immediately if duplicate issues are being received. These may be caused by a discrepancy in expiration records, or an error in the application of our payment.

**Guidelines:* "In most cases, requests for backfiles should be handled on a separate order from the subscription in order to avoid delays in payment, for example, in cases where either the backfile or the subscription is supplied considerably in advance of the other. But requests for quotes on backfiles can be on the same order form."

176   Guide to Magazine and Serial Agents

The subscriber is requested not to handle such matters directly with the publisher."

29. *The library should send the agent mailing labels of a duplicated title.**

In contradistinction to the claims arrangement, all domestic agents request the library to send them the mailing labels when unwanted duplicates are delivered to the library. Among international agents *only* Swets & Zeitlinger requests the labels. Stevens & Brown notes labels should be sent "if possible"; and Marcel Blancheteau says the labels are "useful."

30. *The library should not return the duplicates to the publisher. (This injunction holds in the case of periodicals, but is reversed in the case of serials of other sorts, especially when the duplicated item is expensive.)*†

All international and domestic agents agree with this procedure.

VII. CANCELED AND DISCONTINUED TITLES

A. Individual Cancellations

1. *Libraries are asked to cancel only at the end of a subscription period.* ‡
All agents agree with this procedure.

2. *When the library asks to cancel before the end of a current subscription, the agent cancels only if the publisher accepts the cancellation.*

All domestic and international agents accept this policy, except French & European Publications: "No cancellation is accepted when the subscription has already been entered with the publisher." Faxon modifies this policy to its own needs, as do some other agents (and some publishers likewise prefer other ways of doing). Faxon says: "One-year subscriptions may only be canceled at expiration. Two-year subscriptions at the end of the first full year. Three-year subscriptions may be cancelled only at the end of the first or second year. As a rule the third year is free of cost and, therefore, not subject to cancellation by the publisher. Some publishers of technical journals will not accept cancellations until expiration of the current payment period, and such noncanceled titles are indicated on your invoice."

3. *If a cancellation is made midway along in the subscription period, the library should allow thirty to ninety days for the cancellation to become effective.*

This matter was not referred to the survey agents, but several volunteered information to the effect that the time needed to cancel a subscription is about the same as that needed to enter a subscription.

**Guidelines:* "Particular attention should be given to mailing labels since the problem of duplicates is often due to errors in this area."
†*Guidelines:* "It should be noted, however, that it is seldom necessary to return issues of a trade publication since most publishers are not concerned about getting back a few issues of a periodical."
‡*Guidelines:* "Libraries should make cancellations effective with the end of a current subscription or a current year, rather than in mid-year."

4. *The agent returns money, if any, received from the publisher for the balance of a canceled subscription.* *

All agents follow this practice. However, Ebsco has a cancellation fee, as does Dawson-France, which charges 3 francs per cancellation.

B. Cancellation of Total Library List
(Usually done when the library is changing or dropping an agent)

5. *When the library plans a wholesale cancellation of an order with an agent, the library should: (a) Itemize all titles ordered through the agent; (b) Submit the itemized list to the agent at least 90 days before the cancellation is to take effect.*†

All agents agree with this procedure, except Faxon: "All we require is a letter simply stating the library no longer wishes to use our service. All prior commitments or requests for service from publishers must be honored unless the publishers will accept cancellation of those requests." And Turner: "We recommend the library immediately telephone the agency and find out the status of the order. The library should do everything possible to avoid mass cancellations of a list."

C. Publisher Discontinued Titles

6. *The agent notifies the library when a publisher discontinues a title mid-way in a library subscription.*

This question was not asked on the questionnaire, but agents contacted since indicate that such notification is normal.

7. *The agent will return money for the discontinued publication, when the publisher has made restitution for the money owed for the unfulfilled subscriptions.*

All agents agree with this policy.

VIII. ADDED AGENCY SERVICES

A. Sample Copies of Periodicals

1. *When the library asks for a sample copy of a periodical, the agent will request the publisher send the sample—if it is free.*

All domestic and international agents will ask for sample copies when so re-

---

Guidelines: "Libraries can expect refunds on cancellations in the case of consumer type publications. But in the trade, technical, professional or learned journal field, no refunds can be anticipated on single year orders once service has started or payment is accepted for the new year. On multi-year orders, the first year is charged at the full rate, and only succeeding years are refunded."

†*Guidelines:* Few guidelines can be enumerated with respect to cancellations since libraries reserve the option to cancel at any time and for any good reason. When wholesale cancellation with a particular vendor is contemplated because of unacceptable service, every effort should be made to solve the problems before subscriptions are assigned to a different vendor. Since a breakdown in communications is often the source of the problem, librarians should state their requirements and expectations as clearly as possible; and vendors should indicate the extent to which they are able to comply, and the steps which libraries can take to expedite service. Unless this is done, it is not possible to evaluate the situation reasonably.

quested by the library. However, Faxon makes an important point about its procedures: "We recommend libraries ask for sample copies directly from the publisher rather than through the agent. Publishers react more promptly upon direct requests from the library."

2. *If the sample copy is not free, the agent will purchase the sample copy and bill the library.*

All domestic and international agents will comply with this procedure.

3. *The agent automatically will send sample copies of new periodicals which are within the library's profile of interests.*

No domestic agent offers this service. Two international agents do. Harrassowitz will automatically send sample issues of new periodicals which are within the library's profile of interests. Swets & Zeitlinger adjusts the arrangement a little by writing to the library about new periodicals when these fall within the library's area of interest. Indication is given as to whether a sample is free or must be paid for.

B. Binding

4. *The agent offers partial or complete binding service.*

Three domestic agents offer some service: Ebsco, Maxwell, and Stechert-Macmillan. Six international agents offer some service: Chinese Materials, Harrassowitz, Marcel Blancheteau, R. Hill, Stevens & Brown, Swets & Zeitlinger.

5. *The agent provides unbound issues during the year and a bound set at the end of the year, i.e., it provides two subscriptions, one bound and the other unbound. The agent holds the unbound issues of the second subscription until the volume is complete, and then sends them, bound according to specification to the library. (If unbounds are not needed in the meantime, one of the subscriptions is dispensed with.)*

Three domestic agents provide such service: Ebsco, Maxwell, and Stechert-Macmillan. Among international agents providing such service are Chinese Materials, Harrassowitz, and R. Hill. Swets & Zeitlinger offers back sets, when available, but does not bind current items in the prescribed way.

C. Blanket-Order and Approval Plans

6. *The agent has a blanket-order plan and/or an approval plan for the supplying of periodicals in the library's area of interest.*

No domestic or international agent presently offers such plans. Many, of course, use either or both of these plans in supplying books and regular serials. Ebsco, alone among domestic agents, expresses interest in the idea: "We would make a proposal to any interested library." Several international agents appreciate its possibilities—Almqvist & Wiksell: Apparently uses both plans on a reduced scale, and offers to make them available "according to a special arrangement." Blackwell's: "We would be interested to hear from any library wishing to operate a plan for periodicals." Brockhaus: "Presently does not offer such a plan for serials, but would consider, if approached by the library." Stevens & Brown: Is willing to create some sort of plan "by arrangement with the library."

Checklist of Agency Services and Procedures *179*

D. Consolidated Orders

7. *The agent accepts responsibility for consolidating titles before shipment to the library (i.e., the agent receives all items from the publisher, makes what claims are necessary, and then, when everything is in order, sends the items along to the library).*

No domestic agent offers such service, although China Books and Periodicals may do so later. Maxwell will consider offering it "at a price." This agent says that consolidated orders are "feasible," but to be used "only under special conditions." Stechert-Macmillan offers a partial consolidated-order service. It sends out *continuations* in this way, but not *periodicals*. A number of international agents offer modified versions of this service, although it is not always clear from replies if periodicals are included among the serials sent. Agents that say they offer some service of the sort include Chinese Materials, Collet's, Marcel Blancheteau, Stevens & Brown, and Brockhaus. Swets & Zeitlinger is the only agent queried that now offers consolidated orders that include all types of serials, including periodicals in its shipments.

E. Returning Purchased Serials

8. *The agent gives a credit against future purchases when the library returns serials to the agent.*

The only domestic agent with such a plan is Maxwell. The plan may be used only in the case of selected scientific serials. Among international agents, Almqvist & Wiksell and Marcel Blancheteau offer credit for returned serials, "but only by arrangement."

F. Automation

The agent uses automated methods of operation.

As of the start of 1974, three domestic agents report that they do: Ebsco, Faxon, and Read-More. Two, Instructor and Maxwell, say that their automation plans are "in development." Six international agents report that they use the computer: Almqvist & Wiksell, Blackwell's, Harrassowitz, Marcel Blancheteau, R. Hill, and Swets & Zeitlinger. Collins Book Depot reports that it has a machine system in development.

9. *The agent accepts machine-readable orders, renewals, claims, etc.*

One domestic agent does: Faxon. One international agent does: Almqvist & Wiksell. Blackwell's, Harrassowitz, and Swets & Zeitlinger report plans to accept such material later.

10. *The agent can supply machine-readable information to the library.*

Two domestic agents can supply this: Faxon and Ebsco (but the latter notes: "Only on a selected negotiable basis.") One international agent can supply it: Almqvist & Wiksell. Blackwell's, Harrassowitz, and Swets & Zeitlinger expect to be able to do so soon.

IX. LIBRARY ORDERS

This is not properly part of the Checklist because the information described is of the kind the library itself must supply. In this last section, an attempt is made to let the librarian know whether or not the orders he or she sends out contain the sort of information the agent really needs.

A. Basic Library Procedures

1. *The library should follow certain basic procedures in submitting orders.*

All agents feel that the procedures merit close attention on the librarian's part. What follows—(a) through (e)—are procedures recommended in the ALA *Guidelines.*

(a) Library-oriented information should be clearly set off from vendor-oriented information.

(b) Items similar in appearance should be separated, as, for example, order numbers and Library of Congress card numbers.

(c) All orders should contain clear instructions concerning any unique requirements the library may have, as in the case of variant addresses, expiration dates, and number of copies of invoices to be sent. These instructions can appear on the order form itself; they can be taken care of in a covering letter.

(d) Single orders sent throughout the year may be batch processes.*

(e) Orders for titles may appear together in a consolidated list.†

B. Minimal Order Data

2. *Certain basic data are required by agents on the order forms used by libraries.*

All domestic and international agents agree that the data mentioned below must be included.

(a) The name and the address of the agent (these are preprinted, of course, on order forms provided by the agent).

(b) The name and address, including zip code, of the library. Personal names are to be avoided whenever possible.

(1) The name and address to which the serial is to be sent if different from (b).‡

(2) The names and address to which the serial is to be billed if different from (b).‡

(3) If the name and address of the library are abbreviated, the abbreviations should be clear. (It may be necessary to abbreviate in order to allow the publisher to fit everything into the allotted space on the mailing label.)

(c) The full title of the serial. This should not be abbreviated. (The correct title is the only basic information required by the agent.)

(d) The number of copies, if more than one, of a title**

Guidelines: "Orders may be batch-processed where this is acceptable to the vendor, but otherwise should be sent regularly and as rapidly as they can be prepared."

†*Guidelines:* "Unless the vendor specifically prefers orders in list form, clarity in ordering is best achieved by means of individual order forms for each title." Agents accept individual order forms or several titles on one form. A single order form is optional with the library, particularly for periodicals.

‡*Guidelines:* "Agents should give special attention to different addresses and account numbers at the same institution."

**Guidelines:* "Specify number of copies to be supplied. If these are for separate addresses, separate orders for each address are recommended. Orders for second or third (etc.) subscriptions should be identified, to indicate intention duplication."

(1) Orders for second or third subscriptions of the same title should be clearly marked so as to avoid questions about unwanted duplication and misapplication of payments.

(2) Separate addresses for multiple copies of a single title should be clearly listed.

(e) The duration of the subscription.*

(1) State whether the order is a new order or a renewal order. Faxon: "If the title is a renewal, please indicate "R" and include the expiration date. If an expiration date is unknown, a mailing label from a current issue will help us determine the expiration date."

(2) State whether a til-forbid or standing order or other type of order, as applicable.

(3) State the common expiration date sought, bearing in mind that agency procedures regarding expiration dates vary (e.g., some agents do not provide a common expiration date; others do it automatically).

(f) Give the requested starting date (month and year) and/or the volume and issue numbers with which the order is to begin.†

(g) Specify whether supplements, indexes, title pages, etc., are to be included in the order for a given title.

(h) Give the library purchase order number (or numbers) and date, as well as other information the library wishes the agent to use in sending the library correspondence, including invoices, that has to do with the order.

Guidelines: "The library's requirements with regard to number of copies and to renewals, whether annual or till forbidden, must be clearly stated."
†*Guidelines:* "Subscriptions should begin with the first issue of the calendar year or, where this is not appropriate, with the first issue of the current (or next) volume."

13.
AGENCY SURVEY SUMMARY

I. NUMBER OF LIBRARIES AND AGENTS SURVEYED

The present study results from a survey of the practices followed by 850 libraries of all types and in all parts of the United States in ordering and maintaining serials subscriptions. A random sampling of 1,245 libraries was constructed, and questionnaires were mailed to them. Eight hundred and fifty replies were received; it is fair to say that these provide a balanced look at what is happening in this country (no questionnaires were sent to Canadian libraries). The one type of library underrepresented in the survey is the school library.

A. Types and numbers of libraries responding:
   University: 150 replies
   College: 199
   Junior college: 71
   Large public: 39
   Small to medium-sized public: 158
   School systems: 32
   Special: 85
   Anonymous (type or name omitted): 116

B. The mean of total periodical collections (including retrospective titles as well as current, and irrespective of source of supply) by type of library:
   University: 2,000 to 3,999
   College: 700 to 799
   Junior College: 400 to 499
   Large public: 1,000 to 1,999
   Small to medium-sized public: 300 to 399
      Under 199 titles: 40 libraries
      Over 900 titles: 2 libraries
   School systems: 200 to 300
   Special: 500 to 599

C. Approximately 95 percent of all libraries responding use one or more agents. Special libraries are the exception, only 70 percent of them using agents. Only forty of the 850 libraries report that they do not use agents at the present time.

And of these forty, twenty-four are special libraries. The other sixteen are distributed fairly evenly among the other categories of libraries.

D. When a library uses an agent, it orders approximately 58 percent (special libraries) to 83 percent (school systems and small public libraries) of its titles through the agent.

E. Approximately 120 domestic and international subscription agents are used by the libraries surveyed—seventy-nine domestic and forty-one international. However, only twelve of the two sorts are used by more than twelve libraries. The gross number adds up to more than 850 libraries, as many libraries use more than one agent.

Ebsco: 329 libraries reported using
Faxon: 251
Stechert-Hafner (now Stechert-Macmillan): 97
McGregor: 70
Moore-Cottrell: 68
Blackwell's: 44
Harrassowitz: 37
Swets & Zeitlinger: 29
Bernan: 25
Universal: 21
Stevens & Brown: 21
Fennell: 17
Turner: 15
Popular: 15
Aquinas: 13
Maxwell: 13
Martinius Nijhoff: 13
Franklin Square (now absorbed by Ebsco): 12

II. MOST OFTEN EMPLOYED DOMESTIC AGENTS

In percentages, the eighteen domestic agents most often employed by the 850 libraries may be divided as follows (the percentage adds up to more than 100 because libraries often use several agents):

A. Two are named by 70 percent of all libraries: Ebsco by 39 percent of replying libraries and Faxon by 31 percent.

B. Of the remaining sixteen domestic agents used by libraries, five are named by 33 percent of all libraries:
Stechert-Macmillan: 11.5 percent[1]
McGregor: 8 percent
Moore-Cottrell: 8 percent
Bernan: 3 percent
Universal: 2.5 percent

C. Of the remaining eleven domestic agents, five are *each* named 2 percent of the time by all types of libraries surveyed:
Fennell

184 Guide to Magazine and Serial Agents

    Turner
    Aquinas
    Maxwell
    Popular

D. Of the remaining six domestic agents most often named, each is named 0.5 to 1 percent of the time:
    Abel[2]
    Read-More
    Ben Squire
    West Coast
    Ancorp
    Wilson

E. The following domestic agents are named by:
    Five libraries: Baker & Taylor, Ellsworth
    Four libraries: Four Continent, Mayfair (now absorbed by Ebsco), Raynor, Yerger
    Three libraries: Grand Rapids, Magazine Supply House, Seaboard
    Two libraries: Brodart, Crowley, Mid-South, Olympic Periodicals, Peck, Railsback, Solle's, Southwest Business

F. Of the remaining forty-four domestic agents, each is named by only one library. (Most of these forty-four are listed in the Directory.)

G. Comparative study: In 1970, the New York Library Association, Resources and Technical Services Section, issued a twelve-page report on agents and libraries in New York State[3] (hereafter referred to as NYA). In this study, replies from 660 libraries of all types are tabulated. These libraries name thirty-seven agents with whom they do business in part or in full. The leading agency turns out to be neither Ebsco nor Faxon, but Moore-Cottrell, a firm located in New York State. Below are shown the agents used by libraries in New York State and the percentage of libraries in the study that use them:
    Moore-Cottrell: 40 percent
    Ebsco (including what was then Franklin Square/Mayfair, a separate agency): 32 percent
    Faxon: 16 percent
    Instructor: 8 percent (one library only)
    Stechert-Macmillan: 3 percent
    Turner: 1.5 percent
    Ancorp: 1.5 percent
    McGregor: no figure given, as agent did not answer questionnaire
    Twenty-eight other agents, domestic and international: 1 percent

III. MOST OFTEN EMPLOYED INTERNATIONAL AGENTS

Of the surveyed libraries, 160 report using one or more international subscription agents (as well, in most cases, as a domestic agent).

A. Six international subscription agents are named by 94 percent of all types of surveyed libraries:[4]

Blackwell's: 29 percent
Harrassowitz: 25 percent
Swets & Zeitlinger: 20 percent
Stevens & Brown: 14 percent
Martinius Nijhoff: 9 percent
Dawson of England: 6 percent

B. Four international subscription agents are named by more than one library. The agents and number of libraries that name them:
Hachette: 3
Angus & Robertson: 2
Marcel Blancheteau: 2
Kubon & Sagner: 2

C. Of the remaining thirty-one international agents, each is named by only one library. Most, but not all, of these are listed in the Directory.

IV. RATING OF AGENTS BY LIBRARIANS

The majority of agents are rated as good to excellent by 60 to 70 percent of responding librarians. The survey strongly indicates that, despite complaints, librarians consider agency service acceptably good.

A. Rating of two most often used agents, Faxon and Ebsco, is equally high. Some 79 percent of those replying consider Faxon good to excellent; some 74 percent give Ebsco the same rating.

    1. In terms of type of library using these agents, academic and special libraries accord Faxon a higher rating than Ebsco, while public and school libraries rate Ebsco more highly than the other. Ninety-two percent of libraries in the anonymous category say Faxon's service is good to excellent, and 81 percent say the same of Ebsco's service.

    2. In terms of size of collection, regardless of type of library, *level of satisfaction* with the service of the two agents is approximately the same in libraries with up to 2,000 titles. However, in libraries with more than 2,000 titles, preference is given to Faxon. (It is of interest that Faxon is preferred to Ebsco by large university and academic libraries.)

    3. *Relative satisfaction* with the service the two agents provide is harder to predict. In Faxon's case, 75 percent of libraries with fewer than 400 titles rate its service as good to excellent; and 75 percent of libraries with more than 10,000 titles do the same. Faxon's service is most highly regarded by libraries with between 800 to 999 titles. Here 86 percent of the libraries give it a good to excellent rating.

It becomes apparent that little is achieved in attempting to compare agents in terms of the size of the collections their customers have when the test applied in Faxon's case is applied also in Ebsco's. Seventy-four percent of libraries with fewer than 400 titles rank Ebsco as good to excellent. Those with more than 10,000 report 100 percent satisfaction (which might have significance, although only five libraries are reporting). Ebsco is at its best apparently in serving libraries—other than the giants, of course—with, yes, 800 to 999 titles.

186 Guide to Magazine and Serial Agents

B. Considerable variation exists in the rating by libraries of the major agents, but this may be accounted for statistically as much by differences in the number of reports received as by real differences in service. For example, thirteen libraries reported on both Maxwell and Aquinas. In each case, 92 percent of the libraries rated these agents as good to excellent. These ratings may or may not be meaningful, and yet, even considering the smallness of the sample, the librarian must find such a rating impressive.

C. Ranking of international agents was not a purpose of this survey; but as a number are named, a few comments must be made. The most highly praised agent in this group is Harrassowitz: thirty-seven libraries report on Harrassowitz, and all thirty-seven rate its service as good to excellent. No domestic agent, regardless of size of the test sample, achieves such distinction.

Interestingly enough, while only five international agents are named by more than twelve libraries, each of the five is given a rating of 84 percent in that it provides service considered good to excellent. (Only three of twelve domestic agents fall into a like category.)

REFERENCE NOTES

1. Larger libraries tend to use Stechert-Macmillan as an international agent. Others, however, use it as a domestic agent (and occasionally in both ways). Hence, its inclusion here.
2. Now defunct and replaced by Blackwell North America.
3. Juanita S. Doares, et al., *New York Library Association Report on Survey of Subscription Agents Used by Libraries in New York State Conducted by the Technical Committee in 1970* (U.S. Dept. of Health, Education and Welfare, Office of Education, 1970), 12 pp., processed.
4. Stechert-Macmillan was named most often, actually by 60 percent of the 160 libraries. However, as noted in an earlier section, it is not possible to ascertain precisely how many of these libraries employ Stechert-Macmillan solely as an international subscriptions agent. Consequently, Stechert-Macmillan is included here under domestic agents.

14.
LIBRARY SURVEY SUMMARY

NUMBER OF PERIODICAL TITLES HELD BY AMERICAN LIBRARIES

The following are the reports from various types of libraries on the *periodical* holdings. Other types of serials are not considered.

The report is based on replies from 850 libraries—from which responses were received. There were 116 replies from libraries with no identification as to size or type. However, these replies are used in the agency evaluation found in Table 3.

	Titles Held	Libraries (%)	(No.)
I. ACADEMIC LIBRARIES			
A. Universities (150 replies)	under 999	16	24
	1,000–1,999	19	28
	2,000–3,999	29	43
	4,000–4,999	11	16
	5,000–5,999	7	11
	6,000–9,999	10	15
	over 10,000	8	13
B. Colleges (199 replies)	under 200	3	6
	200–399	13	26
	400–599	23	45
	600–699	8	16
	700–799	9	19
	800–999	12	23
	1,000–1,500	22	43
	over 1,500	10	21
C. Junior Colleges (71 replies)	under 200	8	6
	200–399	38	27
	400–499	21	15
	500–699	19	13
	700–899	8	6
	over 900	6	4

	Titles Held	Libraries (%)	Libraries (No.)
II. PUBLIC LIBRARIES			
A. Large Size (39 replies)	1,000–1,999	51	20
	2,000–2,999	8	3
	3,000–3,999	23	9
	over 4,000	18	7
B. Small to Medium Size (158 replies)	under 99	3	5
	100–199	18	29
	200–299	17	26
	300–399	18	28
	400–599	22	35
	600–799	13	21
	over 800	9	14
III. SCHOOL SYSTEM LIBRARIES			
Various Types and Sizes (32 replies)	under 99	31	10
	100–199	19	6
	200–300	6	2
	over 300	44	14
IV. SPECIAL LIBRARIES			
Various Types and Sizes (85 replies)	under 299	44	37
	300–499	18	15
	500–599	8	7
	600–999	15	13
	over 1,000	15	13
V. ANONYMOUS			
(116 replies)	(no indication as to size or type)		

SOURCES OF PERIODICAL TITLES FOR 850 AMERICAN LIBRARIES

Of the 850 libraries reporting, 810 librarians—some 95%—reported use of an agent. Of the 810, another 9 librarians reported using an agent for less than 10% of the periodical acquisitions.

Librarians that used agents obtained 68% of their titles through an agent, 20% directly from the publisher, and 12% as gifts and exchanges. The average number of agents used was 1.3 domestic, and 0.2 international.

	(%) Titles Obtained Through:			Average No. of Agents Used	
	Agent	Publisher	Gifts/ Exchanges	U.S.	Foreign
I. ACADEMIC LIBRARIES					
A. Universities (150) (all used agents)	67	18	15	1.8	1.0
B. Colleges (199) (all but 6 used agents)	69	19	12	1.4	.2

	(%) Titles Obtained Through:			Average No. of Agents Used	
	Agent	Publisher	Gifts/ Exchanges	U.S.	Foreign
C. Junior Colleges (71) (all but 2 used agents)	76	15	9	1.4	.01
II. PUBLIC LIBRARIES					
A. Large Size (39) (all but 3 used agents)	60	24	16	1.4	.3
B. Small to Medium Size (158) (all but 2 used agents)	62	22	16	1.2	.01
III. SCHOOL SYSTEM LIBRARIES					
Various Types and Sizes (32) (all but 3 used agents)	83	16	1	1.1	0
IV. SPECIAL LIBRARIES					
Various Types and Sizes (85) (all but 24 used agents)	58	26	16	1.1	.1
V. ANONYMOUS					
Type or Size Not Indicated (116)	66	20	14	1.3	.1

AGENCY RATINGS BY 850 AMERICAN LIBRARIES

The figures tabulated here represent the response of 850 librarians to a brief questionnaire mailed out in the latter part of 1973.

The twelve domestic agents most often mentioned are listed, as are the five international agents most often mentioned. Listings are in alphabetical order. The number in parentheses following the name of the agent is the number of libraries reporting on that agent. As some libraries use more than one agent, the figures for each type of library do not usually add up to the total number of libraries reporting. Agents mentioned by fewer than twelve libraries are not ranked here, but ranking is indicated in the Directory of Agents.

Appraisal of the agent through use of such terms as "excellent," "good," "fair," and "poor" is inevitably subjective. However, some validity may be claimed for the ratings when substantial agreement exists concerning them among reporting libraries.

Moreover, some agents may receive short shrift, or more than their due, because of changes that have occurred since the survey was made. For example, Stechert-Macmillan ratings are ratings accorded before a recent takeover (when the firm was called Stechert-Hafner). Confusion during the takeover period brought the firm a less than glowing report from librarians. Subsequent correspondence with librarians and agents indicates, however, that the relatively poor showing put up by this agent then no longer holds.

Similarly, the service of other agents may have improved or deteriorated since the survey was made, and so the ratings of these agents will be found to be higher or lower than is indicated here.

190   Guide to Magazine and Serial Agents

In any case, the librarian should use the survey rating as a rough guide only in assessing agent performance, and should always interview the agent concerned before selecting a new one or dropping an old one.

A final word: Some reputable agents, such as Instructor, are not listed because most of their business is conducted with school libraries, a type of library not adequately represented in the survey. Which is to say, lack of rating by a library (and most particularly a school library) should not be considered as a lack of confidence in the agent's work.

I. Overall Agency Rating

Agent	Excellent	Good	Fair	Poor	Good to Excellent
Aquinas (13)	54%	38%	8%	0%	92%
Bernan (25)	16	64	20	0	80
Ebsco (329)	49	25	16	10	74
Faxon (251)	56	23	16	5	79
Fennell (17)	23	47	23	6	70
McGregor (70)	34	53	9	4	87
Maxwell (13)	46	46	8	0	92
Moore-Cottrell (68)	20	50	27	3	70
Popular (15)	33	33	33	0	66
Stechert-Macmillan (97)	15	30	36	19	45
Turner (15)	36	21	29	14	57
Universal (21)	19	57	19	5	76
Blackwell's (44)	39	50	9	2	89
Harrassowitz (37)	81	19	0	0	100
Martinius Nijhoff (13)	38	46	16	0	84
Stevens & Brown (21)	48	38	4	10	86
Swets & Zeitlinger (29)	21	62	17	0	83

II. Overall Domestic Agency Rating by Type of Library

University

Aquinas (2)	100%	0%	0%	0%	100%
Bernan (2)	0	50	50	0	50
Ebsco (62)	24	42	23	11	66
Faxon (70)	20	60	13	7	80
Fennell (4)	50	50	0	0	100
McGregor (22)	41	41	14	4	82
Maxwell (2)	0	50	50	0	50
Moore-Cottrell (18)	17	55	28	0	72
Popular (3)	33	33	33	0	66
Stechert-Macmillan (50)	12	26	42	20	38
Turner (2)	0	0	50	50	0
Universal (8)	0	88	12	0	88

College

Aquinas (8)	50%	38%	12%	0%	88%
Bernan (9)	11	77	11	0	88

Library Survey Summary   *191*

Agent	Excellent	Good	Fair	Poor	Good to Excellent
Ebsco (62)	19	48	9	23	67
Faxon (83)	30	53	12	5	83
Fennell (5)	0	80	20	0	80
McGregor (16)	13	75	6	6	88
Maxwell (1)	0	100	0	0	100
Moore-Cottrell (19)	26	53	16	5	79
Popular (3)	67	33	0	0	100
Stechert-Macmillan (27)	30	25	40	5	55
Turner (1)	100	0	0	0	100
Universal (5)	40	20	40	0	60
Junior College					
Aquinas (1)	0%	100%	0%	0%	100%
Bernan (4)	25	25	50	0	50
Ebsco (33)	15	52	21	12	67
Faxon (19)	11	63	26	0	74
Fennell (2)	50	0	0	50	50
McGregor (9)	23	66	0	11	89
Maxwell (0)	—	—	—	—	—
Moore-Cottrell (6)	33	0	50	17	33
Popular (1)	0	0	100	0	0
Stechert-Macmillan (1)	100	0	0	0	100
Turner (0)	—	—	—	—	—
Universal (0)	—	—	—	—	—
Large Public					
Aquinas (0)	—	—	—	—	—
Bernan (2)	0%	100%	0%	0%	100%
Ebsco (22)	32	50	18	0	82
Faxon (10)	10	40	30	20	50
Fennell (2)	0	50	50	0	50
McGregor (2)	50	50	0	0	100
Maxwell (2)	50	50	0	0	100
Moore-Cottrell (5)	0	60	40	0	60
Popular (1)	0	100	0	0	100
Stechert-Macmillan (5)	0	40	60	0	40
Turner (1)	0	0	100	0	0
Universal (1)	0	0	100	0	0
Small to Medium-Sized Public					
Aquinas (0)	—	—	—	—	—
Bernan (3)	33%	33%	33%	0%	66%
Ebsco (78)	24	60	12	3	84
Faxon (31)	13	52	32	3	65
Fennell (2)	0	50	50	0	50
McGregor (9)	56	33	11	0	89
Maxwell (2)	50	50	0	0	100
Moore-Cottrell (6)	17	33	50	0	50
Popular (4)	25	50	25	0	75
Stechert-Macmillan (2)	0	0	50	50	0

192   Guide to Magazine and Serial Agents

Agent	Excellent	Good	Fair	Poor	Good to Excellent
Turner (3)	33	33	33	0	66
Universal (3)	33	33	0	33	66
School Systems					
Aquinas (0)	—	—	—	—	—
Bernan (0)	—	—	—	—	—
Ebsco (11)	27%	55%	9%	9%	82%
Faxon (3)	0	67	33	0	67
Fennell (0)	—	—	—	—	—
McGregor (2)	50	50	0	0	100
Maxwell (0)	—	—	—	—	—
Moore-Cottrell (3)	0	100	0	0	100
Popular (1)	100	0	0	0	100
Stechert-Macmillan (0)	—	—	—	—	—
Turner (1)	100	0	0	0	100
Universal (0)	—	—	—	—	—
Special					
Aquinas (2)	50%	50%	0%	0%	100%
Bernan (4)	25	75	0	0	100
Ebsco (29)	35	31	24	10	66
Faxon (10)	50	50	0	0	100
Fennell (0)	—	—	—	—	—
McGregor (5)	80	20	0	0	100
Maxwell (2)	100	0	0	0	100
Moore-Cottrell (8)	37	63	0	0	100
Popular (0)	—	—	—	—	—
Stechert-Macmillan (8)	12	12	38	38	24
Turner (3)	33	0	33	33	33
Universal (2)	50	50	0	0	100
Anonymous					
Aquinas (0)	—	—	—	—	—
Bernan (1)	0%	100%	0%	0%	100%
Ebsco (32)	37	44	16	3	81
Faxon (25)	32	60	8	0	92
Fennell (2)	50	0	50	0	50
McGregor (5)	0	80	20	0	80
Maxwell (4)	50	50	0	0	100
Moore-Cottrell (5)	0	40	60	0	40
Popular (2)	0	0	100	0	0
Stechert-Macmillan (4)	50	0	25	25	50
Turner (3)	33	67	0	0	100
Universal (2)	0	100	0	0	100

III. Overall International Subscription Agency Rating by Type of Library

University					
Blackwell's (27)	44%	48%	4%	4%	92%
Harrassowitz (25)	80	20	0	0	100

Agent	Excellent	Good	Fair	Poor	Good to Excellent
Stevens & Brown (8)	62	25	13	0	87
Swets & Zeitlinger (24)	21	62	17	0	83
College					
Blackwell's (12)	33%	50%	17%	0%	83%
Harrassowitz (6)	83	17	0	0	100
Martinius Nijhoff (2)	0	50	50	0	50
Stevens & Brown (6)	66	17	0	17	66
Swets & Zeitlinger (3)	0	67	33	0	67
Junior College					
Blackwell's (1)	0%	100%	0%	0%	100%
Harrassowitz (0)	—	—	—	—	—
Martinius Nijhoff (0)	—	—	—	—	—
Stevens & Brown (0)	—	—	—	—	—
Swets & Zeitlinger (0)	—	—	—	—	—
Large Public					
Blackwell's (0)	—	—	—	—	—
Harrassowitz (2)	100%	0%	0%	0%	100%
Martinius Nijhoff (1)	0	100	0	0	100
Stevens & Brown (4)	25	75	0	0	100
Swets & Zeitlinger (0)	—	—	—	—	—
Special					
Blackwell's (3)	33%	33%	33%	0%	66%
Harrassowitz (2)	100	0	0	0	100
Martinius Nijhoff (1)	0	100	0	0	100
Stevens & Brown (1)	0	100	0	0	100
Swets & Zeitlinger (1)	100	0	0	0	100
Anonymous					
Blackwell's (1)	0%	100%	0%	0%	100%
Harrassowitz (2)	50	50	0	0	100
Martinius Nijhoff (1)	0	100	0	0	100
Stevens & Brown (2)	100	0	0	0	100
Swets & Zeitlinger (1)	0	100	0	0	100

IV. Overall Domestic Subscription Agency Satisfaction by Extent of Library Holdings Irrespective of Type of Library

Note: Number of titles given is the number of periodical titles held by the library, *not* necessarily the number ordered from the agent.

Under 99 Titles					
Aquinas (0)	—	—	—	—	—
Bernan (0)	—	—	—	—	—
Ebsco (5)	40%	40%	20%	0%	80%
Faxon (3)	33	67	0	0	100
Fennell (0)	—	—	—	—	—
McGregor (0)	—	—	—	—	—

194 Guide to Magazine and Serial Agents

Agent	Excellent	Good	Fair	Poor	Good to Excellent
Maxwell (0)	–	–	–	–	–
Moore-Cottrell (0)	–	–	–	–	–
Popular (0)	–	–	–	–	–
Stechert-Macmillan	–	–	–	–	–
Turner (0)	–	–	–	–	–
Universal (0)	–	–	–	–	–
100–199 Titles					
Aquinas (1)	0%	100%	0%	0%	100%
Bernan (1)	0	100	0	0	100
Ebsco (22)	27	45	14	14	72
Faxon (11)	27	46	27	0	73
Fennell (3)	67	33	0	0	100
McGregor (5)	0	80	20	0	80
Maxwell (1)	100	0	0	0	100
Moore-Cottrell (1)	0	100	0	0	100
Popular (2)	100	0	0	0	100
Stechert-Macmillan (1)	0	0	100	0	0
Turner (1)	0	0	0	100	0
Universal (3)	33	33	0	33	66
200–399 Titles					
Aquinas (3)	33%	33%	33%	0%	66%
Bernan (4)	25	25	50	0	50
Ebsco (55)	25	49	15	11	74
Faxon (36)	22	53	25	0	75
Fennell (2)	50	50	0	0	100
McGregor (14)	64	36	0	0	100
Maxwell (2)	0	100	0	0	100
Moore-Cottrell (9)	33	33	22	11	66
Popular (3)	0	33	67	0	33
Stechert-Macmillan (1)	0	0	0	100	0
Turner (2)	50	50	0	0	100
Universal (1)	0	0	100	0	0
400–599 Titles					
Aquinas (5)	60%	40%	0%	0%	100%
Bernan (7)	29	57	14	0	86
Ebsco (60)	28	47	17	8	75
Faxon (48)	25	54	17	4	79
Fennell (1)	0	100	0	0	100
McGregor (13)	23	54	15	8	77
Maxwell (0)	–	–	–	–	–
Moore-Cottrell (10)	20	40	40	0	60
Popular (1)	100	0	0	0	100
Stechert-Macmillan (5)	20	60	0	20	80
Turner (5)	40	40	20	0	80
Universal (3)	33	67	0	0	100
600–799 Titles					
Aquinas (2)	100%	0%	0%	0%	100%
Bernan (5)	0	80	20	0	80

Agent	Excellent	Good	Fair	Poor	Good to Excellent
Ebsco (44)	23	57	11	9	80
Faxon (19)	26	58	11	5	84
Fennell (1)	0	0	100	0	0
McGregor (8)	13	87	0	0	100
Maxwell (1)	100	0	0	0	100
Moore-Cottrell (9)	33	56	11	0	89
Popular (3)	0	33	67	0	33
Stechert-Macmillan (10)	30	30	20	20	60
Turner (1)	0	0	100	0	0
Universal (0)	—	—	—	—	—
800–999 Titles					
Aquinas (1)	100%	0%	0%	0%	100%
Bernan (1)	0	100	0	0	100
Ebsco (12)	17	66	0	17	84
Faxon (21)	29	57	14	0	86
Fennell (1)	0	0	0	100	0
McGregor (4)	0	75	0	25	75
Maxwell (0)	—	—	—	—	—
Moore-Cottrell (4)	25	0	75	0	25
Popular (0)	—	—	—	—	—
Stechert-Macmillan (6)	33	17	33	17	50
Turner (0)	—	—	—	—	—
Universal (0)	—	—	—	—	—
1,000–1,999 Titles					
Aquinas (1)	100%	0%	0%	0%	100%
Bernan (6)	17	83	0	0	100
Ebsco (55)	25	48	20	7	73
Faxon (44)	25	52	16	7	7
Fennell (5)	0	60	40	0	60
McGregor (10)	60	30	10	0	90
Maxwell (5)	80	20	0	0	100
Moore-Cottrell (19)	11	63	21	5	74
Popular (3)	0	100	0	0	100
Stechert-Macmillan (28)	18	36	28	18	54
Turner (4)	50	0	50	0	50
Universal (3)	0	33	67	0	33
2,000–2,999 Titles					
Aquinas (0)	—	—	—	—	—
Bernan (1)	0%	0%	100%	0%	0%
Ebsco (17)	18	46	18	18	64
Faxon (11)	36	45	9	9	81
Fennel (0)	—	—	—	—	—
McGregor (3)	0	100	0	0	100
Maxwell (0)	—	—	—	—	—
Moore-Cottrell (3)	33	0	67	0	33
Popular (0)	—	—	—	—	—
Stechert-Macmillan (7)	0	43	43	14	43
Turner (0)	—	—	—	—	—
Universal (2)	0	100	0	0	100

196 Guide to Magazine and Serial Agents

Agent	Excellent	Good	Fair	Poor	Good to Excellent
3,000–3,999 Titles					
Aquinas (0)	—	—	—	—	—
Bernan (0)	—	—	—	—	—
Ebsco (13)	15%	62%	23%	0%	77%
Faxon (13)	23	47	15	15	70
Fennell (2)	50	0	50	0	50
McGregor (4)	75	0	0	25	75
Maxwell (0)	—	—	—	—	—
Moore-Cottrell (4)	0	75	25	0	75
Popular (1)	0	0	100	0	0
Stechert-Macmillan (10)	10	10	50	30	20
Turner (0)	—	—	—	—	—
Universal (3)	0	100	0	0	100
4,000–4,999 Titles					
Aquinas (0)	—	—	—	—	—
Bernan (0)	—	—	—	—	—
Ebsco (10)	30%	40%	20%	10%	70%
Faxon (9)	22	78	0	0	100
Fennell (0)	—	—	—	—	—
McGregor (4)	25	50	25	0	75
Maxwell (1)	0	100	0	0	100
Moore-Cottrell (2)	0	100	0	0	100
Popular (1)	100	0	0	0	100
Stechert-Macmillan (10)	0	20	70	10	20
Turner (0)	—	—	—	—	—
Universal (0)	—	—	—	—	—
5,000–9,999 Titles					
Aquinas (0)	—	—	—	—	—
Bernan (1)	0%	100%	0%	0%	100%
Ebsco (21)	24	33	24	19	57
Faxon (25)	12	64	16	8	76
Fennell (1)	0	100	0	0	100
McGregor (4)	25	75	0	0	100
Maxwell (0)	—	—	—	—	—
Moore-Cottrell (4)	25	50	25	0	75
Popular (0)	—	—	—	—	—
Stechert-Macmillan (11)	9	9	55	27	18
Turner (1)	0	0	0	100	0
Universal (2)	0	100	0	0	100
Over 10,000					
Aquinas (0)	—	—	—	—	—
Bernan (0)	—	—	—	—	—
Ebsco (5)	40	60	0	0	100
Faxon (8)	12	63	12	12	75
Fennell (1)	0	100	0	0	100
McGregor (3)	33	33	33	0	66
Maxwell (2)	0	50	50	0	50

Agent	Excellent	Good	Fair	Poor	Good to Excellent
Moore-Cottrell (2)	50	0	50	0	50
Popular (0)	—	—	—	—	—
Stechert-Macmillan (9)	22	44	22	11	66
Turner (0)	—	—	—	—	—
Universal (0)	—	—	—	—	—

V. Overall International Subscription Agency Satisfaction by Extent of Library Holdings Irrespective of Type of Library

Under 500 Titles					
Blackwell's (1)	0%	100%	0%	0%	100%
Harrassowitz (0)	—	—	—	—	—
Martinius Nijhoff (1)	0	100	0	0	100
Stevens & Brown (1)	100	0	0	0	100
Swets & Zeitlinger (0)	—	—	—	—	—
500-999 Titles					
Blackwell's (8)	12%	75%	12%	0%	87%
Harrassowitz (2)	100	0	0	0	100
Martinius Nijhoff (2)	0	100	0	0	100
Stevens & Brown (3)	67	33	0	0	100
Swets & Zeitlinger (2)	0	0	100	0	0
1,000-1,999 Titles					
Blackwell's (15)	53%	27%	20%	0%	80%
Harrassowitz (7)	86	14	0	0	100
Martinius Nijhoff (2)	0	50	50	0	50
Stevens & Brown (6)	66	17	0	17	83
Swets & Zeitlinger (4)	0	100	0	0	100
2,000-2,999 Titles					
Blackwell's (2)	50%	50%	0%	0%	100%
Harrassowitz (2)	100	0	0	0	100
Martinius Nijhoff (0)	—	—	—	—	—
Stevens & Brown (0)	—	—	—	—	—
Swets & Zeitlinger (1)	0	0	100	0	0
3,000-3,999 Titles					
Blackwell's (6)	17%	66%	0%	17%	83%
Harrassowitz (4)	50	50	0	0	100
Martinius Nijhoff (0)	—	—	—	—	—
Stevens & Brown (4)	50	50	0	0	100
Swets & Zeitlinger (6)	50	33	17	0	83
4,000-4,999 Titles					
Blackwell's (4)	25%	75%	0%	0%	100%
Harrassowitz (3)	100	0	0	0	100
Martinius Nijhoff (0)	—	—	—	—	—
Stevens & Brown (2)	50	50	0	0	100
Swets & Zeitlinger (5)	0	100	0	0	100

Agent	Excellent	Good	Fair	Poor	Good to Excellent
5,000–9,999 Titles					
Blackwell's (5)	40%	60%	0%	0%	100%
Harrassowitz (7)	71	29	0	0	100
Martinius Nijhoff (5)	20	60	20	0	80
Stevens & Brown (7)	29	57	0	14	86
Swets & Zeitlinger (6)	17	66	17	0	83
Over 10,000 Titles					
Blackwell's (3)	100%	0%	0%	0%	100%
Harrassowitz (8)	87	13	0	0	100
Martinius Nijhoff (4)	100	0	0	0	100
Stevens & Brown (0)	—	—	—	—	—
Swets & Zeitlinger (5)	20	60	20	0	80

15.
SUBSCRIPTION AGENTS DIRECTORY

This Directory includes domestic agents and representative international agents mentioned by librarians during the present survey. It includes also a number of agents suggested for consideration by other librarians. Names were located in a variety of sources, the most valuable of which was the Audit Bureau of Circulation's *List of Subscription Selling Organizations,* July 1971. A few back-issues dealers and dealers in serials other than periodicals are included.

Unless a rating is given, mention of an agent in no way constitutes approval or disapproval of that agent's performance. Furthermore, ratings in general, are, impressionistic rather than definitive.

The purpose of this Directory is to offer librarians information on enough agents, of various sizes, specialities, and locations, to help the librarian decide which agents to employ. In every case, of course, the librarian is urged to remember that as changes occur constantly in agents' services and procedures, he or she should seek clarification of doubtful points directly from any agent with whom he or she is considering doing business.

HOW TO USE THIS DIRECTORY

The arrangement is alphabetical by the last name of the agent. An asterisk before the name of the agent indicates that mention is made of the agent's services in Chapter 12. The following information is given, when available, for each agent:

Name, address, and telephone number. When the telephone number is followed by the note "Accepts customer calls," the agent generally accepts collect calls. International agents do not accept collect calls. The original survey was conducted in mid-1974, but name, address, and telephone data are up to date as of mid-1975.

Name of the person who replied to the questionnaire and his or her position with the agent.

Type of agency. The term "general" is employed to describe domestic agents who handle titles of their own countries. "Special" is employed to describe domestic agents who handle primarily foreign titles; domestic and international agents who have a special area of interest; and a few dealers whose interest is in serials or periodicals other than reprints or back issues.

Area served by the agent. With some exceptions in the case of special agents, only "U.S." and "foreign" are used here.

Number of titles the agent says it can acquire for a customer. This figure serves only in a most general way to indicate the scope and adequacy of an agent's operation.

Type of materials provided by the agent. Periodicals and other types of serials are listed as mutually exclusive.

Some agents have entries for charges and claims. When this information is absent, the assumption does not necessarily follow that the agent is reluctant to explain charges or claims. The way in which such matters are dealt with by the twenty-two agents who answered the detailed questionnaire is described in the Checklist. In some cases the information is not given because it was not requested of the agent. In any case, the librarian should clarify charges and claim services with any agent in whom he or she is interested.

Rating: When the agent is rated by more than twelve libraries in the survey, the reader is referred to Chapter 12 for details. When fewer than twelve libraries provide a rating, the result is given in the Directory entry. Some agents are not rated because no library mentioned them while the survey was being conducted. Absence of a rating should not be regarded as a reflection, bad or otherwise, on the agent's quality. After all, even a rating provided by twelve or more libraries can hardly be thought of as totally untouchable. Librarians who find the present directory useful will find three others useful also:

American Library Association. *International Subscription Agents.* 3rd ed. (Chicago: A.L.A., 1974). A carefully annotated list of over 200 international subscription agents containing ratings and comments supplied by librarians. The directory is a required item for any library dealing with more than one or two international agents.

F. J. Neverman. *International Directory of Back Issue Vendors.* 2nd ed. (New York: Special Libraries Assn., 1968). An annotated list of over 200 dealers, subdivided by periodicals dealers, newspapers, and newspaper indexes and documents. Although somewhat dated, it remains highly valuable.

Carol A. Nemeyer. *Scholarly Reprint Publishing in the United States* (New York: Bowker, 1972). This is the basic study in this area. Contains an annotated Directory of Reprint Publishers and an Index to Subject Specialties.

DOMESTIC AGENTS

Abel, Richard, & Co.* Box 4245, Portland, Oreg. 97208. (503) 645-3511. Accepts customer calls. Don Chvatal, Marketing Dir.

Special, primarily series. Serves all types of libraries but emphasis is on large university, college, and special. U.S., foreign. 32,000 series and serials; 2,000 subscription titles. Annuals, irregular and less than annual serials, pro-

---

*Defunct as of spring 1975. Its assets have been taken over by Blackwell North America.

ceedings and transactions (domestic and foreign), monographic series, works in parts, international congresses, some periodicals and newspapers. Will make an effort to order hard to locate titles. CATALOGS: *A Series Catalog*, annual listing of some 30,000 series. Free to customers; others, $17.50. COMMENTS: "Our subscription services (to periodicals) are limited to supplying those items specifically requested by our customers. We are not actively marketing subscription services as such, except for books in series, sets, and other monographic serials which, by definition, can be provided as separates as they are individually priced."
RATINGS (Ten Libraries, all U.S.)
  Excellent: 1 large university
  Good: (4) 3 large university, 1 large college
  Fair: (4) 1 small university, 2 medium-sized university, 1 anonymous
          (approximately 2,000 titles)
  Poor: 1 large college

Abrahams Magazine Service, Inc. 56 E. 13 St., New York, N.Y. 10003. (212) 777-4700. Accepts customer calls. Roy Young.
  Back-issues dealer. Some reprints. Serves public, university, college, and special libraries. U.S., foreign. 400,000 titles. Periodicals, annuals, newspapers, irregular and less than annual serials, proceedings and transactions (domestic and foreign), monographic series, government documents, works in parts. Searches for o.p. titles. CATALOGS: *General Catalog*, annual. Subject and stock discount catalogs, regularly. *Periodical Buying List*, annual. CHARGES: Agent will bid for back runs and volumes only. COMMENTS: Will buy duplicates for credit, but only complete volumes. In turn, institution may purchase any book or periodical in print from Abrahams. Wants listed in *Periodical Buying List*.

Adco Subscription Agency, a division of Western Hemisphere Publishers Representatives, Inc. 89-25 130 St., Richmond Hill, N.Y. 11418. L. Corrado.
  General. Serves all types of libraries, except special libraries. U.S. Periodicals, newspapers, annuals, irregular and less than annual serials, proceedings and transactions. Will not search for hard to locate titles. CHARGES: The agent charges the library a flat service charge on all titles purchased. The charge is usually 15 to 20 percent of the cost of the title. Agent does not bid. CLAIMS: Send claims to agent. Agent acknowledges all claims. COMMENTS: Agent supplies some forms.

Adler, Leo. Drawer 867, Baker, Oreg. 97814. (503) 523-3737.
  General. Serves all types of libraries. "All" titles. Periodicals and newspapers. Will make an effort to order hard to locate titles. CLAIMS: Send all claims to agent. Agent acknowledges claims. COMMENTS: Agent supplies some forms.

Alban, C. W. 901 S. Grand Blvd., St. Louis, Mo. 63103.

Alesco (AMERICAN LIBRARY AND EDUCATIONAL SERVICES CO.), a division of Demco Educational Corp. 404 Sette Dr., Paramus, N. J. 07652. (201) 265-5730. James E. Bogues, Dir.

General. Serves elementary, junior high, and high school libraries. U.S. Catalog lists 300 titles; indicates that "all domestic periodicals generally included in school library collections" are handled. Periodicals, newspapers, annuals, irregular and less than annual serials, government serials. Will make an effort to order hard to locate titles. CATALOGS: *Periodicals for the Elementary and Jr.-Sr. High School Library*, annual.

Alspaugh Magazine Agency. 801 Vanosdale Rd., Knoxville, Tenn. 37919.
RATINGS (One library, South)
Good: 1 small public

American Collegiate Marketing Enterprises Corp. P.O. Box 2408, Boulder, Colo. 80302.
A publisher's field agent that sells popular titles at discount through the mails. Its operation is similar to that of Educational Subscription Service, Inc.

American Literary Service, Inc. 633 Admiral, Providence, R. I. 02908.

American Magazine Services, a division of American Bindery, Inc. Formerly Prebound Periodicals. 914 Jefferson St., Topeka, Kans. 66607. (913) 233-8019. Accepts customer calls. Patricia Selvy.
General. Serves primarily school and public libraries. U.S., select foreign. 5,000 titles through trade channels. Periodicals, newspapers, annuals, irregular and less than annual serials, proceedings and transactions, government documents. Will make an effort to order hard to locate titles. CHARGES: Agent adds 10 percent service charge to titles on which it receives no discount; passes on discount to library for titles on which it receives a discount. Agent will bid. CLAIMS: Send claims to agent. Agent acknowledges claims. COMMENTS: Agent supplies some forms. "We are very new and very small and serve only the schools and libraries that our salesmen call on."
RATINGS (Two libraries, Midwest):
Excellent: 1 small- to medium-sized school system
Good: 1 college

American Readers Service. *See* Ebsco Subscription Service.

Ancorp National Services Inc., formerly American News Corp. 131 Varick St., New York, N.Y. 10013. (212) 255-5100.
RATINGS (Seven libraries, Midwest):
Excellent: 1 anonymous (500–599 titles)
Good: 2 small public
Fair: (3) 1 small college, 2 university
Poor: 1 anonymous (1,000–1,999 titles)

***Aquinas Subscription Agency.** 718 Pelham Blvd., St. Paul, Minn. 55114.

Associates, C. W. P.O. Box 34099, Washington, D.C. 20034.
RATINGS (One library, Mid-Atlantic):
Good: 1 university

Austin Subscription Agency. P.O. Box 9812, Savannah, Ga. 31402. (912) 355-6415.

General. Serves all types of libraries, but primarily school and public and "individual business houses" in Georgia and South Carolina. U.S., foreign. Periodicals. Will make an effort to order hard to locate titles.

Baker & Taylor. 50 Kirby Ave., Somerville, N. J. 08876. (201) 722-8000. Bill Boyer.

A book jobber, but handles some series and nonperiodical series; does not handle periodicals.

RATINGS (Four libraries):
Excellent: (2) 1 large university, 1 medium-sized public
Good: 1 large university
Fair: 1 university

Barber's Books. 28 Prospect Ave., Ilion, N.Y. 13357. E. M. Barber

Back-issues dealer. Limited number specialized titles. Periodicals, newspapers. Will make an effort to order hard to locate titles; for o.p. titles. COMMENTS: Barber's is a specialized back-issues dealer. Most purchases and sales are confined to single issues or volumes of a limited number of titles, e.g., *American Heritage, Leslie's, Harper's Bazaar, Vanity Fair, Puck,* illustrated weekly newspapers to 1890.

Bartley Subscription Agency. 1254 Ranchland Dr., Cleveland, Ohio 44124. (216) 449-4254. Accepts calls in Cleveland area. Mrs. R. F. Bartley: "We have been in the magazine subscription business for 30 years."

General. Serves primarily school libraries in Cleveland, Ohio, and suburbs. U.S. "All American magazines and foreign and trade magazines." Periodicals. CATALOGS: 40-page, preprinted, pocket-sized *Magazine Guide*, free to libraries.

***Bernan Associates.** 4701 Willard Ave., Suite 102, Washington, D. C. 20015. Nan Locker, Mgr. (202) 656-0550.

Handles U.S. government documents only. Until early 1974 this agent supplied all items listed in the Superintendent of Documents *Monthly Catalog*, but since then supplies selected high-return items only.

Black Magazine Agency. Box 342, Logansport, Ind. 46947. (219) 753-2429. Will not accept collect calls. Gordon Muenlhauser, Owner/Mgr.

General. Serves primarily school and public libraries in the Middle West. U.S. 15,000 to 20,000 titles. Periodicals, newspapers, government documents. Will make an effort to order hard to locate titles. CATALOGS: *Educational Reading Guide*, annually for school distribution. Lists "approximately 1,000 publications normally ordered by schools and libraries throughout the U.S. Distributed each spring to approximately 13,000 school systems." COMMENTS: Bids on "Many school and library orders in addition to our regular customers that have been acquired over our 35 years in business."

RATINGS (Two libraries, Midwest):
Excellent: 1 medium-sized public
Good: 1 small- to medium-sized college

Bliss, P. and H. Middletown, Conn. 06457. (203) 347-2255. Philip Bliss.

Back-issues dealer. Serves all types of libraries. U.S., some foreign. Approximately 10,000 serials, over 3 million copies. Provides both in print and o.p.

single copies, volumes, sets, and some reprints of periodicals, government documents, and serial "publications of the learned and scientific societies, associations, schools, colleges, churches and business firms." "We are under the impression that we are the only dealer in the country who will supply [single] back issues. One of the four largest, besides ourselves, advertises that he will not even quote on back issues. Another one has limited his total number of titles to 1,400. A third one, for one copy of a magazine over and above the price, charges $1.50 for just postage and handling, which is too much. And we do know that the fourth one has discarded over one million issues of their single copy stock as it is too expensive to process." (Note: Although the agent suggests exclusivity in this field, other agents, including the U.S. Book Exchange do supply single copies of back issues.) Will try to order hard to locate titles. "We require a 90 day firm order when supplying single copies. Will try to locate, if we do not have." CATALOGS: None. "We do not issue catalogs because our stock is constantly changing. We are glad to have want lists." OTHER SERVICES: Buy or will give an exchange credit for library duplicates. Librarian should write first, and "we then explain the type of titles that we do not want because we have adequate stock."

Boley Subscription Agency. 244-85 61 Ave., Douglaston, N.Y. 11362. (212) 631-0683. Accepts customer calls. H. Boley.

Special; medical and health fields. Primarily serves hospital libraries (33) and special libraries (6); also serves five school libraries. U.S. foreign. 10,000 to 15,000 titles. Periodicals in the medical and health fields. Also annuals, proceedings and transactions, government documents. Will make an effort to order hard to locate titles. CATALOGS: None. "Prices, etc., are given to subscribers by mail or phone upon request of subscribers."

Book Home. P.O. Box 825, Colorado Springs, Colo. 80901. Leo Mohl.

General; primarily serves university, college, and special libraries. U.S. 1,500 titles. Periodicals, annuals, irregular and less than annual serials, proceedings and transactions (domestic and international), monographic series, government documents. Will make an effort to order hard to locate titles. CATALOGS: None. Inquiries invited.

Bookmart. P.O. Box 191, Gardiner, N.Y. 12525. Maureen Hauge.

General. Serves all types of libraries, but primarily foreign libraries outside the U.S. U.S., foreign. "All" titles. Periodicals, newspapers, annuals, irregular and less than annual serials, proceedings and transactions (domestic and international), monographic series, government documents, works in parts. Will make an effort to order hard to locate titles; searches for o.p. titles. CATALOGS: None; however, "bibliographies prepared, if requested." COMMENTS: "All of our subscription customers are in foreign libraries. We do not solicit subscriptions from individuals or casual entries. We offer the subscription services as an additional service to our regular book customers. We service several university libraries. Usually these are for subscriptions on a standing-order basis, with automatic entry and billing. These journals are sent direct by the publishers. Several industrial libraries engage our complete subscription service. This consists of receiving all journals in our office, checking receipt and automatic notices to publishers for any missing issues. Journals are packaged in bulk for air-freight shipments. There is an hourly rate for this service. Customers are relieved of all clerical duties involved with journals. (Except of course paying our invoices!)"

The Book Stable. 5119 Sherril Dr., Fort Wayne, Ind. 46806. Paul H. Regenold.

Special. Serves all types of libraries with magazines about horses. U.S. 50 titles. Periodicals. Will not make an effort to order hard to locate titles. CATALOGS: An annual catalog; not named. CHARGES: 100 percent of subscription price. CLAIMS: Agent will not handle claims.

British Book Center, Inc. 996 Lexington Ave., New York, N.Y. 10021.

Special. Serves all types of libraries with British periodicals and serials. United Kingdom. 5,000 titles. Periodicals, newspapers, annuals, irregular and less than annual serials, proceedings and transactions (domestic and international), monographic series, government documents, works in parts. Will make an effort to order hard to locate titles; searches for o.p. titles. CHARGES: "Agency charges in U.S. currency; conversion formula is based on net cost, currency exchange rate and service cost." Agent will bid. CLAIMS: Send claims to agent. Agent answers all claims. COMMENTS: Supplies back issues. Agent is exclusive U.S. distributor for *Writers & Their Work*, *ATLA Abstracts*, etc.

Broadbent, Marv and Capital Documents Service. 4410 Josephine, Beltsville, M. 20705. (301) 937-8845/937-8846. Accepts customer calls. Marv Broadbent and Maria T. M. Broadbent.

Special. U.S. government publications and commercially or federally produced publications of Spain or Latin America. Serves all types of libraries. U.S., Spain, Latin America. "No meaningful approximation possible since so many of the serials we handle are of short duration." Periodicals, newspapers, annuals, irregular and less than annual serials, proceedings and transactions (domestic and international), monographic series, government documents, works in parts. Will make an effort to order hard to locate titles. CATALOGS: "We have in preparation [late 1973] a catalog of U.S. government series and another on Hispanic titles—largely monographic. We cannot project a publication date. The U.S. catalog will provide GPO series titles and numbers. The Hispanic catalog will describe publications according to ISBD recommendations of the IFLA."

Bro-Dart, Inc. 15255 E. Don Julian Rd., City of Industry, Calif. 91749. (213) 968-6411. Accepts customer calls.

Both special and general. Specializes in technical, medical, and scientific titles; nevertheless, supplies general titles to all types of libraries. U.S., foreign. 1,000,000 titles. Periodicals, annuals, irregular and less than annual serials, "some" monographic serials. Will make an effort to order hard to locate titles. CATALOGS: *Off the Press*, monthly list of annotated new titles in the scientific, technical, and medical fields. (Also has a number of catalogs that lists books for school and public libraries, as well as *Listening Post*, a magazine covering current audiovisual materials.)

206   Guide to Magazine and Serial Agents

RATINGS (One library, Pacific Coast):
  Excellent: 1 small- to medium-sized university

Burke Industries. 5530 MacArthur Blvd., N.W., Washington, D.C. 20016. (202) 362-5645. Accepts customer calls. Robert J.E. Burke.
  Special, "but also incorporates all general class titles." Serves about 100 libraries of all types, "including many government and well-known personages." U.S., foreign. 250,000, including 50,000 U.S. and Canada publications. Periodicals, newspapers, annuals, proceedings and transactions, government documents, works in parts, business house organs. Will make an effort to order hard to locate titles, "provided the account volume of sales merits. Otherwise a fee will be assessed." CATALOGS: *Retail Title & Subscription Rate—Partial Listing*, semiannual.

By's Magazine Shop. 32 W. 2 South, Salt Lake City, Utah 84101.

Campus Subscriptions. 382 Channel Dr., Port Washington, N.Y. 11050. Michael Michaelson.
  Although sometimes listed in directories as a subscription agency, Campus does not deal with libraries: "We sell directly to the consumer."

Candelighters Int'l., Inc. 4431 S.E. 64 Ave., Portland, Oreg. 97206. (503) 775-1516. Accepts customer calls.
  General. Serves all types of libraries west of the Mississippi: particularly in Oregon, Washington, Alaska, and Idaho. U.S., foreign. 50,000 titles. Periodicals, irregular, and less than annual serials. Will make an effort to order hard to locate titles. CATALOGS: *Periodical Guide*, annual catalog of some 50 titles. COMMENTS: Librarian reports that this "is an agency formed by handicapped persons. We have had excellent service from them."
RATINGS (One library, Pacific Coast):
  Excellent: 1 medium-to large-sized school system

Capitol Documents Service. *See* Broadbent, Marv and Capital Document Service.

Central News Co. 111 E. Voris St., Akron, Ohio 44311. Ms. Betty J. McMasters.
  General. Serves school, public, and university and college libraries. U.S. 2,250 titles. Periodicals, newspapers, annuals, paperbacks. Will not make an effort to order hard to locate titles. CATALOGS: Uses the Moore-Cottrell catalog. CHARGES: Agent adds a flat service charge to cost price of all titles; average service charge not stated. Agent will bid. CLAIMS: Send claims to agent. Agent acknowledges claims. COMMENTS: Agent supplies some forms.
RATINGS (One library):
  Good: Medium- to large-sized school system

*China Books and Periodicals. 2929 24 St., San Francisco, Calif. 94110. (415) 282-2994. Henry J. Noges.
  Special. "We represent Guozi Shudian of Peking and Zunhasaba of Hanoi— both exporting agencies for Chinese and Vietnamese magazines." Serves some

1,500 libraries of all types. People's Republic of China; North Vietnam. 14 titles. Periodicals. Usually makes no effort to order hard to locate titles. CATALOGS: *Annual Catalog.*

Cox, W. T. Subscription Agency. Rt. 6, 411 Marcia Dr. Goldsboro, N.C. 27530
General. Primarily serves school and public libraries in the southern states. U.S. 3,000 titles. Periodicals. Will make an effort to order hard to locate titles. CATALOGS: *Magazine Check-Off Order,* semiannual.
RATINGS (One library, South):
Excellent: 1 large school system

Crowley, The Magazine Man. 330 E. 204 St., Bronx, N.Y. 10467.
RATINGS (Two libraries, Midwest, Pacific Coast):
Good: 1 small public
Fair: 1 small university

Darr, Dale C., Subscription Agency. Centralia, Kans. 66415. Dale C. Darr.
General, serving primarily smaller school and public libraries. U.S. 2,500 titles. Periodicals. Will make an effort to order hard to locate titles. CATALOGS: *Magazine Subscription Guide for School Officials & Librarians,* annual, about June 1. CHARGES: Agency charges the library a flat service charge on all titles at cost price. Amount of charge not given. No service charge if few no-discount titles included in a large order. CLAIMS: Send claims to agent. "Will take care of complaints." COMMENTS: Agent supplies some forms. "I have been dealing with schools and libraries since 1937, mostly in Kansas, but am interested in business elsewhere. I can handle orders up to $2,500.

DeBoer, D. 188 High St., Nutley, N.J. 07110.
Special. Little and scholarly university magazines. Primarily U.S. About 65 titles. Periodicals. CATALOGS: Mail-order brochures. COMMENTS: DeBoer has been in operation for the past 35 years, and is the leading agency for distinguished little and literary titles, many of which are not normally handled by large agents. See the June 1973 number of *More* for a short article on this most famous of all little-literary magazine agents.
RATINGS: No official rating, but librarians who have used the DeBoer service, have nothing but praise for it.

DeLong Subscription Agency, Inc. 308 North 4 St., Lafayette, Ind. 47902. (317) 742-6491.
General. Serves primarily school and public libraries. U.S. 1,500 titles. Periodicals and newspapers. Will make an effort to order hard to locate titles; searches for o.p. titles. CATALOGS: *Educational Magazine Guide,* annual. CHARGES: Agency charges the library a flat service charge on all titles on cost price. Service charge is usually 1 to 2 percent above cost of title. Agent adds service charge for titles where it receives no discount and passes on discount to library for titles where it receives such a discount. Agent will bid. CLAIMS: Send claims to agent. Agent acknowledges claims. COMMENTS: Agent supplies some forms.
RATINGS (One library, South):
Good: 1 small public

Demco Educational Corp. Box 1488, Madison, Wis. 53701. *See* Alesco.

Dexter Magazine Subscriptions. 1020 N. Second St., Phoenix, Ariz. 85004. (602) 275-3693. Accepts customer calls.
  General. Serves all types of libraries. U.S., foreign. Periodicals, newspapers, annuals, irregular and less than annual serials, proceedings and transactions (domestic and international), monographic series, government documents, works in parts. 30,000 titles. Will make an effort to order hard to locate titles. CATALOGS: Issued occasionally, but no titles or description given.
  RATINGS (One library, Southwest):
    Excellent: 1 small public

Dial-A-Magazine Library Service. 30 Washington Sq., Worcester, Mass. 01604. (617) 757-3876. Accepts customer calls. John Kerbel, Pres.
  General. Serves all types of libraries throughout the United States, with particular emphasis on school libraries. U.S. Periodicals, newspapers. Will make an effort to order hard to locate titles; searches for o.p. titles. CATALOGS: *Magazine Subscription Trade Price List,* annual. *Check-Off-Price-List,* biennial select list for schools and small libraries. CHARGES: Agency charges the library a flat service charge on all titles at cost price, but adds 5 percent service charge for titles where agent receives no discount and passes on discount to library for titles where it receives a discount. Charges 1.5 percent per month on past-due accounts after 60 days from billing date. Agent will bid. CLAIMS: Send claims to agent. Agent acknowledges claims. COMMENTS: Agent supplies all forms.
  RATINGS (Four libraries, Midwest and New England; ratings of three libraries were for Magazine Supply House, a subsidiary of Dial-A-Magazine.)
    Excellent: 2 small- to medium-sized school system
    Good: 2 small- to medium-sized school system

Dolphin Service. P.O. Box 8927, Washington, D.C. 20003. K. Z. Furness.
  General. Serves public, university, and special libraries. U.S., foreign. Periodicals, newspapers, annuals, irregular and less than annual serials, proceedings and transactions (domestic and international), monographic series, government documents, works in parts. Will not make an effort to locate hard to locate titles. CATALOGS: *Foreign Catalogue for Newspapers and Periodicals,* annual. CHARGES: Flat service charge on cost of titles. Agent will not bid. CLAIMS: Send claims to agent. Agent acknowledges claims. COMMENTS: Agent supplies claims forms.

Ebs Book Service. 290 Broadway, Lynbrook, N.Y. 11563. Mrs. Watts.
  Although sometimes listed in directories as a subscription agency, Ebs Book Service supplies only books.

*Ebsco Subscription Services. 1 Avenue N. at 13 St., Birmingham, Ala. 53203. (205) 323-6351. Accepts customer calls. J. T. Stephens, Pres.
  General. Serves all types of libraries. U.S. foreign serials available through trade channels. 70,000 plus titles. "Researchers add about 1,000 titles a month." Periodicals, newspapers, annuals, continuations, irregular and less than annual serials, proceedings and transactions (domestic and international),

monographic series, book series, government documents, works in parts, international congresses. "Considers research and identification of hard to locate titles a very important part of its services." CATALOGS: *Librarian's Handbook: A Guide to Periodicals/Serials,* annual of over 1,000 pages. *Periodicals for Elementary and Secondary School Libraries,* annual of some 2,000 titles. *500 Selected Periodicals for the Medical Library,* annual. All free to libraries (*Librarian's Handbook* is sold to noncustomers at $8).

Educational Subscription Service. 3308 So. Cedar, Suite No. 11, Lansing, Mich. 48910. Marjorie Audubon.

General. A publisher's agent serving individuals in schools, universities, and colleges, as well as libraries. U.S. 60 titles. Periodicals and newspapers. Will not make an effort to locate hard to locate titles. CATALOGS: Rate cards and advertising brochures for 60 popular titles. CHARGES: Straight discount of 25 to 50 percent. Agent will not bid. CLAIMS: Send claims to agent. Agent does not acknowledge claims. COMMENTS: The advertising of the titles handled by this firm is evident on almost any academic or school campus. Most promise considerable reductions on popular magazines. Agent is actually a publisher's salesman, i.e., works directly with the publishers of magazines such as *Time, Newsweek, Reader's Digest.* Agent accepts orders from libraries. Approximately 300 library customers. Sends invoices; allows up to 90 days to pay. Does not automatically renew subscriptions.

Ellsworth Magazine Service. 332 S. Michigan Ave., Chicago Ill. 60604. (312) 939-3390/939-2665. Accepts customer calls. Gladys Uline.

General. Serves all types of libraries in the Midwest. U.S., foreign. "All titles accepted by agencies." Periodicals, newspapers, annuals, irregular and less than annual serials, proceedings and transactions, monographic series. Will make an effort to order hard to locate titles. CATALOGS: *Ellsworth Magazine Service,* annual some 40-page catalog. COMMENTS: Agent supplies a number of forms, including claims forms. "We feel that our simple adjustment forms are responsible for the prompt and satisfactory response we have received from publishers on claims."

RATINGS (Five libraries, Midwest):
   Excellent: (3) 1 medium-sized school system, 2 small college
   Good to excellent: 1 anonymous (about 5,000 titles)
   Good: 1 medium-sized public

Empire Circulation Co. 2933 N. 52 St., Lincoln, Nebr. 68504.

Engineers Book Service. 290 Broadway, Lynbrook, N.Y. 11563.
   COMMENTS: One library reports that "the agent will collate, and will also try for foreign publications, but we have not tested these services."

Evergreen Library Service. 6709 S.E. Division, Portland, Oreg. 97206.
RATINGS (One library, Pacific Coast):
   Fair: 1 medium-sized college

Faculty Periodicals Service. *See* Synergetic Marketing Corp. Faculty is a division of Synergetic, and often sells popular journals to individuals only, i.e., faculty members.

Farnsworth, Craig. 9 Rolling Brook Dr., Elnora, N.Y. 12065. Craig Farnsworth.

General. Serves school and academic libraries in 14 northern New York counties. 25,000 titles. Periodicals, newspapers, annuals, irregular and less than annual serials. Will make an effort to locate hard to locate titles. CATALOGS: Uses *Moore-Cottrell Trade Price List* overstamped with the name "Farnsworth," biennial. CHARGES: No service charge. Agent will bid. CLAIMS: Send all claims to agent. Agent acknowledges claims. COMMENTS: Supplies all forms.
RATINGS (One library, Northeast):
Excellent: 1 large school system

*F. W. Faxon Company, Inc. 15 Southeast Park, Westwood, Mass. 02090. (617) 329-3350. Accepts customer calls. Frank F. Clasquin, VP.

General. Serves 12,000 libraries of all types. U.S. and foreign serials available through trade channels. 50,000 plus titles. Periodicals, newspapers, annuals, irregular and less than annual serials, proceedings and transactions (domestic and international), monographic series, works in parts, international congresses. Will make an effort to order hard to locate titles. CATALOGS: *Faxon Librarians' Guide to Periodicals,* annual, free to libraries; lists over 50,000 American and foreign periodicals. *Bulletin of Bibliography and Magazine Notes,* quarterly, $10. *Serials Updating Service Quarterly,* $7; Details on slow publication titles, last issue or volume published, merger, discontinued titles, changes in name, revised publication schedules, etc.

*Fennell, Reginald F., Subscription Service. 508 W. Michigan Ave., Jackson, Mich. 49201. (517) 782-3132. Accepts customer calls. D. Fennell.

General. Serves all types of libraries. U.S. and foreign. "Thousands of titles." Periodicals, newspapers, and "complete service on all publications." Will make an effort to order hard to locate titles. CATALOGS: *Magazine Subscription Trade Price List,* annual. CHARGES: Not explained. Agent will bid: "We need a list, in duplicate, of your order with the titles arranged alphabetically. We will price the list, return one copy to you for review or acceptance." CLAIMS: Send claims to agent. Agent acknowledges claims. "We send you a copy of the claim, and the publisher's reply, if he returns it to us." COMMENTS: "Our agency is one of the oldest in the country. We have been active for more than 60 years."

Four Continent Book Corp. 156 Fifth Ave., New York, N.Y. 10010. (212) 242-4500.

Special. Official Soviet book agency in the U.S.; serves U.S. libraries with materials from the U.S.S.R. U.S.S.R. All publications of Mezhdunarodnaia Kniga, the state book distributor in the U.S.S.R. Periodicals, limited number of serials, and government documents. Limited search for hard to locate titles. CATALOGS: Short annual list of more popular periodicals.
RATINGS (Four libraries):
Excellent: 1 special
Good: (2) 1 large university, 1 medium-sized college
Fair: 1 large university

Franklin Square Agency. *See* Ebsco Subscription Services.

*French & European Publications, Inc. Rockefeller Center Promenade, 610 Fifth Avenue, New York, N.Y. 10020. (212) 247-7475. Emanuel Molho, VP.

General. Serves all types of libraries. Provides serials from France, Spain, and Latin America. Over 45,000 French and Spanish titles (i.e., books and serials); actual number of periodicals not known. Periodicals, newspapers, annuals. Will make an effort to order hard to locate titles. CATALOGS: *French Books*, some 500 pages. *Spanish Books*, some 576 pages. *Afro Writers*. Frequency of catalogs not stated.

Genevieve's. 2502 N. 53 St., Milwaukee, Wis. 53210. (414) 442-2640. Accepts customer calls. Genevieve Mentel.

General. Serves all types of libraries. U.S., and foreign. Will make an effort to order hard to locate titles.

Goldberger, Herman, Agency. 253 Summer St., Boston Mass. 02210. (617) 426-2686. F. T. Conlan.

Although sometimes listed in directories as a subscription agent, Herman Goldberger does not deal with libraries. "We have not been engaged with library orders since July 1967."

Grand Rapids Subscription Service. 2230 Edgewood, S.E., Grand Rapids, Mich. 49506.

RATINGS (Two libraries, Midwest):
 Good: 1 small- to medium-sized school
 Fair: 1 small- to medium-sized school

Haagens, Gerard E. 26 Pondfield Road W., Bronxville, N.Y. 10708. Gerard E. Haagens.

Since the beginning of 1974 subscription services have been restricted to the customers who also order books. "We found to handle subscriptions only unprofitable with the correspondence about non-arrival claims and the like. Books which are on a subscription basis (i.e., standing orders for serials) are still taken care of by us."

Hayward, Don. P.O. Box 212, Portsmouth, V. 23705. (804) 487-0491. Accepts customer calls. Don Hayward.

General. Primarily serves school and public libraries in Virginia. Also Specializes in military and Veteran Administration publications. U.S. 25,000 titles. Periodicals, newspapers. Will make an effort to order hard to locate titles. CATALOGS: Annual.

RATINGS (One library, South):
 Good: 1 medium- to large-sized school system

Hearst Magazines, Inc. 250 W. 55 St., New York, N.Y. 10019. (212) 262-8300. (Has various field agents, e.g., Periodical Publishers Service Bureau, Inc., and International Magazine Service.)

RATINGS (One library, Mid-Atlantic):
 Good: 1 special

Heron, Colin M. 6786 Highway No. 9, Felton, Calif. 95018. (408) 335-4494. Accepts customer calls. Colin M. Heron.

General. Primarily school libraries, and limited number of other libraries in Santa Cruz County, California, vicinity. U.S., foreign. 4,000 titles. Periodicals and "a few" newspapers and annuals. Does not usually make an effort to order hard to locate titles. CATALOGS: "I do not print my own lists. I use lists printed as general retail lists for me by a large catalog agency. Distributed twice a year." COMMENTS: "I'm age 67, and I do not have the time or the energy to expand my business beyond the continuing volume I've previously built up over 26 years as an independent contractor."

*Instructor Subscription Agency, a Department of Instructor Publications, Inc. Instructor Park, Dansville, N.Y. 14437. (716) 987-2221. L. I. Portnow, Mgr.

General. Serves all types of libraries, but primarily school and public. U.S., "many foreign." 10,000 titles. Periodicals, "some" newspapers, annuals, irregular and less than annual serials, proceedings and transactions. Will make an effort to order hard to locate titles. CATALOGS: *Librarians Periodical Catalog*, annual.

RATINGS (One library, Midwest):
Fair: 1 small public

International University Booksellers, Inc. 101 Fifth Ave., New York, N.Y. 10003. (212) 691-5252. Does not accept customer calls. Max J. Holmes.

Special. Serves university, college, and special libraries throughout the U.S. Back issues an important part of service. U.S., foreign. Periodicals, annuals, irregular and less than annual serials, proceedings and transactions (domestic and international), monographic series, government documents. Will make an effort to order hard to locate titles; searches o.p. titles. CATALOGS: "We publish catalogs of general and subject matter," e.g., *Environmental Sciences: Periodicals, Reference Works.* CHARGES: Agent will bid. CLAIMS: Send claims to agent. Agent acknowledges claims. COMMENTS: Agency does not supply forms. Major supplier of back issues (originals, reprints, microforms). Has offices in London and Munich.

Iredeco, Inc. P.O. Box 3146, Stamford, Conn. 06905.

Japan Publications Trading Co. (USA), Inc. 1255 Howard St., San Francisco, Calif. 94103. (415) 431-3394. Central P.O. Box, 722, Tokyo, Japan.

Special. Supplies libraries in all parts of the world. Japan and other Far Eastern countries. Periodicals, annuals, irregular and less than annual serials, proceedings and transactions (domestic and international), monographic series, government documents, newspapers. Makes an effort to obtain hard to locate titles; searches for o.p. titles. CATALOGS: Occasional lists. CHARGES: Agent will bid. CLAIMS: Send claims to agent. Agent will acknowledge.

RATINGS (Five libraries):
Excellent: 1 university
Good: 4 large university

Johnson, Walter J. Inc. 355 Chestnut St., Norwood, N.J. 07648. (201) 767-1303. Accepts customer calls. Sotir Nikola, Mgr.

General. Serves public, academic, and special libraries. U.S., foreign. Back issues and reprints of periodicals, annuals, irregular and less than annual serials, proceedings and transactions (domestic and foreign), monographic series. Will make an effort to order hard to locate titles. CATALOGS: *Periodical Catalogue of Sets and Files*, annual. CHARGES: Agent adds 15 percent service charge to price of titles on which it receives no discounts, but passes on discount to library for titles on which it receives an adequate discount. Agent will bid. COMMENTS: Has stock of over 75,000 noncurrent periodicals; quotes on single issues; supplies "serial reprints whenever available."

Kamkin, Victor Inc. 12224 Parklawn Dr., Rockville, Md. 20852. (301) 881-5973.

Although located in America, agent is primarily concerned with periodicals, newspapers and other types of serials from the U.S.S.R. Issues a catalog.
RATINGS (One library, Mid-Atlantic):
Excellent: 1 large college

Kraus Periodicals Co. Rt. 100, Milwood, N.Y. 10546. (914) 762-2200. Herbert W. Gstalder, Mgr.

Reprint and back-issues dealer. Primarily serves university and college libraries. U.S., foreign. Provides primarily reprints, but some back-issues sets and microforms of periodicals, annuals, irregular and less than annual serials, proceedings and transactions (domestic and international), monographic series, government documents. CATALOGS: *General Reprint Catalog*, biannual. Various subject catalogs.

Ludwig, Fred Periodica. 3801 E. Kleindale Rd., Tucson, Ariz. 85716. (602) 326-2513. Accepts customer calls. Fred Ludwig.

Back-issues dealer. Serves all types of libraries. U.S., foreign. 30,000 titles. Periodicals, irregular and less than annual serials, monographic series. Will make an effort to order hard to locate titles. CATALOGS: Eight sales lists a year.

McGraw-Hill Export Subscription Agency. McGraw-Hill Publications Co., P.O. Box 416, Hightstown, N.J. 08520. (609) 448-1700. F. W. Gerhardt, Mgr.

Special. Sells subscriptions of American serials to overseas booksellers and subscription agencies. Europe and Canada (in special circumstances). 2,000 plus titles. Periodicals, irregular and less than annual serials, government documents. Will make an effort to order hard to locate titles. CATALOGS: *McGraw-Hill Export Subscription Catalog*, annual. Free in bulk quantities to booksellers, which may send copies to libraries. CHARGES: Agency charges the bookseller a flat service charge on cost price of all titles. $2 service charge for each title not listed in the catalog. Agent does not bid. CLAIMS: "We will acknowledge claims by booksellers and subscription agents where the publisher has given a reply. Changes of address are not acknowledged." COMMENTS: The agent supplies some forms. "We do not deal direct with libraries as is the custom in the United States and Canada. We deal with booksellers and subscription agents in each country with whom the librarian customarily places their order."

*McGregor Magazine Agency. Mount Morris, Ill. 61054. (815) 734-4183.

General. Serves all types of libraries. U.S., foreign. "Handles subscriptions to all magazines, both American and foreign, that can be handled by an agency." Periodicals. Will make an effort to order hard to locate titles. CATALOGS:

214 Guide to Magazine and Serial Agents

Librarian's Reference Catalog, annual; lists about 6,000 titles. *Periodicals Bulletin,* three times a year; lists new titles, discontinuations, and interim rate changes. All free to customers; others, $3.

Magazine Subscription Service. 38-33 Clearview Expressway, Bayside, N.Y. 11361. (212) 229-1705. Does not accept customer calls. Merton and Dorothy Jefts.

General. Serves all types of libraries. Acts as a "retail subscription agent for those interested in additional income." (See Comments.) U.S., some foreign. 2,000 titles. Periodicals, newspapers from large metropolitan cities. Will make an effort to order hard to locate titles. CATALOGS: *Magazine Guide,* annual some 40-page guide. CHARGES: Agent adds 5 percent service charge to price of titles for which it receives no discount and passes on discount to library for titles for which it receives such a discount. Agent will bid. CLAIMS: Send claims to agent. Agent does not acknowledge claims unless requested by library. "All claims are handled with the publishers and if service is to be delayed institution is notified." COMMENTS: Agent supplies some forms. Agent offers a commission to libraries that agree to sell subscriptions for it to library users.

Magazine Supply House, Inc. *See* Dial-a-Magazine Library Service. Magazine Supply House, a subsidiary of Dial-a-Magazine, is a publishers' subscription agency.

Majors Scientific Books, Inc. 8911 Directors Row, Dallas, Tex. 75247. (214) 631-1470. Telex: 73-0200. Accepts customer calls. Flonnie Freeman.

Special. Medical and allied fields. "We will only serve medical and dental school libraries; hospital medical libraries; and others that can list their items primarily allied to medicine such as pharmaceutical libraries." As of 1975, offers an approval plan. U.S., foreign. Periodicals, newspapers, annuals, irregular and less than annual serials, proceedings and transactions (domestic and foreign), monographic series, government documents, works in parts. Will make an effort to order hard to locate titles. CATALOGS: *Select List of Books and Journals for the Small Medical Library* by Dr. Al Brandon, a reprint of list that appears periodically in the *Medical Library Bulletin.*

Manzer, Harold. 2366 Parkview Pl., Baldwin, N.Y. 11510. (916) BA 3-4692. Accepts customer calls. Harold Manzer.

COMMENTS: "I expect to retire this year [late 1973 reply]. I've handled most publications, some foreign. Not an agency but an independent agent. Prefer to order direct rather than through agency. Not a big agency. A very personal one. I've enjoyed my work."
RATINGS (One library, Mid-Atlantic):
Excellent: 1 medium-sized public

Margins Readers Service. 2912 N. Hackett, Milwaukee, Wis. 53211. Does not accept calls. Tom Montag.

Special. Little magazines, "but only as listed in my magazine, *Margins,* i.e., the Reader Service section." Serves all types of libraries. U.S., some foreign. See Comments. Little magazines, annuals, some irregular and less than annual serials. Will make an effort to order hard to locate titles. CATALOGS: "Margins Readers Service Listing," a regular department in the magazine *Margins*. COMMENTS: "Aim to provide small press books and little magazines (on a per issue basis—standing orders accepted). Our intent is to make many of these hard to locate little magazines and small press titles easily and centrally accessible. Titles being carried are listed in each issue of *Margins*, which appears six times a year."

*Maxwell International Subscription Agency, purchased by Moore-Cottrell, a division of Maxwell Scientific International, Inc., Fairview Park, Elmsford, N.Y. 10523. (914) 592-9141. Accepts customer calls. A. J. Fornal, Asst. to the Pres.

General. Serves all types of libraries. U.S., foreign. 50,000 plus titles. Particularly strong in pure and applied sciences. Periodicals, newspapers, irregular and less than annual serials, proceedings and transactions (domestic and foreign), monographic series, government documents, works in parts. Will make an effort to order hard to locate titles. CATALOGS: *Subscription Rates*, annual listing of more popular titles. Note: Agent began distribution of first part of proposed eight-part catalog, *The Catalogue of Research Journals*, in July 1974, containing periodicals in all languages in science, technology, medicine, and the humanities. Also gives total information on current and o.p. periodicals from place of publication to availability of microform. Charge for the catalog undetermined. Interested librarians should write the agent for details.

Mayfair Agency. *See* Ebsco Subscription Services. Mayfair was merged with Franklin Square, which, in turn, was merged with Ebsco.

Mid South Magazine Agency. P.O. Box 4585, Jackson, Miss. 39216. (601) 366-2654. Accepts customer calls. P. J. Gosskopf.

General. Serves school libraries and some public libraries. U.S. 10,000 plus titles. Periodicals. Will make an effort to order hard to locate titles. CATALOGS: "We list only 150 to 160 titles which are most frequently used by school libraries. Publish small one page price list which can be used as an order form."
RATINGS (Two libraries, Southeast):
Good: 1 anonymous (up to 199 titles)
Fair: 1 small school system

*Moore-Cottrell Subscription Agencies. North Cohocton, N.Y. 14869. (716) 534-5221. Accepts customer calls. S. L. Smith, Office Mgr.

General. Serves all types of libraries. U.S. and foreign serials available through trade channels. 50,000 plus titles. Periodicals, newspapers, annuals, irregular and less than annual serials, proceedings and transactions (domestic and international), monographic series, government documents, works in parts. Will make an effort to order hard to locate titles. CATALOGS: *Librarians Guide*, annual; lists some 4,000 most commonly ordered titles. *News-Grams*, annual; provides data on title changes, etc. *Catalog*, annual, complete list of titles. COMMENTS: Moore-Cottrell is part of a conglomerate consisting of Perfect Film (the parent company) and by Cadence Industries and the Perfect Sub-

216 Guide to Magazine and Serial Agents

scription Company. As of mid-1974, Maxwell Subscription Agency was purchased by the group (the other Maxwell companies continue their independent existence).

National Organization Service, Inc. 401 Shops Bldg., 8 and Walnut, Des Moines, Iowa 50309. (515) 244-3032. Accepts customer calls. Robert Dunn.

General. Serves school, public, and special libraries. Does not serve academic libraries. U.S., foreign. 20,000 titles. Periodicals, irregular and less than annual serials, monographic series. "Some" proceedings and transactions and government documents. Will make an effort to order hard to locate titles; searches for o.p. titles. CHARGES: "On all school library orders we offer [an appropriate] discount on total order." Agent will bid. CLAIMS: Send claims to agent. Agent acknowledges claims. COMMENTS: Agent supplies some forms.

New England Book Service. Charlotte, Vt. 05445. (802) 425-2461. Accepts customer calls. M. L. Coleman.

General. Primarily serves university, college, and special libraries, but will serve other types as well. U.S., foreign. "All" titles. Periodicals, newspapers, annuals, irregular and less than annual serials, proceedings and transactions (domestic and international), monographic series, government documents, works in parts. Will make an effort to order hard to locate titles.

Neighborhood Periodical Club, Inc. 330 Dixie Terminal Bldg., Fourth and Walnut St., Cincinnati, Ohio 45202. (Also under the following names: QM Readers' Service, Premium Readers' Service, Neighborhood Readers' Service, and North American Readers' Service.)

Field agent "specializing in direct sales of the more popular, widely circulated, general interest and hobby-type magazines for the family." U.S. 125 titles. Periodicals. CATALOGS: *Neighborhood's Catalog of Available Publications*, an annotated listing with single-copy price and publication dates of titles. Separate price lists available to local agents.

Noble, C. E., Agency. Rolling Prairie, Ind. 46371. (219) 362-8079. H. N. Francis.

General. Serves all types of libraries. U.S., some foreign. "Practically all" titles. Periodicals, newspapers, irregular and less than annual serials, proceedings and transactions, government documents. Will make an effort to order hard to locate titles. CHARGES: "Figure our cost and add small profit percentage. If there are sufficient number of general discount titles, publishers rates usually more than cover the cost to the library." Agent will bid. CLAIMS: Send claims to agent. Agent will acknowledge claims, "if circumstances warrant." COMMENTS: Some forms available. Will accept multiple-year subscriptions.

Norton News Agency. P.O. Box 696, Dubuque, Iowa 52001. (319) 556-8300. Accepts customer calls. James L. Norton.

General. Serves all types of libraries, but particularly school libraries. U.S. "Unlimited." Periodicals, newspapers, annuals. Will not make an effort to order hard to locate titles; does not search for o.p. titles. CHARGES: Agency charges a flat service charge on the cost price of titles, usually 10 to 15 percent

of the cost of the title. Agent will bid. CLAIMS: Send claims to agent. Agent acknowledges claims. COMMENTS: Agent supplies some forms.
RATING (One library, Midwest):
Good: 1 school system

Olympic Periodical Agency. 909 S. 28 St., Tacoma, Wash. 98409. (206) 272-4021. Accepts customer calls. Tom Rogers, Owner.
General. Serves school and academic libraries. U.S., select foreign. 5,000 titles. Periodicals, newspapers, annuals, irregular and less than annual serials, proceedings and transactions, monographic series, government documents. Will make an effort to order hard to locate titles. CLAIMS: Send all claims to agent. Agent acknowledges claims. COMMENTS: Agent supplies all forms: Has been a bookseller for twenty years. It began selling periodicals in early 1970s.
RATINGS (Three libraries, Pacific Coast):
Excellent: 1 medium-sized college
Good: (2) 1 medium-sized college, 1 large university

Peck, Walter, Magazine Agency. 3331 Bank of Galesburg Bldg., Galesburg, Ill. 61401. W. D. Cameron.
General. Serves some 100 libraries of all types. U.S. 5,000 titles. Periodicals, proceedings and transactions, monographic series. Will make an effort to order hard to locate titles.
RATINGS (Two libraries, Midwest):
Good: 1 small college, 1 small- to medium-sized public

Perfect Subscription Co. *See* Moore-Cottrell Subscription Agencies.

Periodical Sales. 1st Ave. N at 13 St., Birmingham, Ala. 35023. *See* Ebsco Subscription Services. A division of Ebsco, the firm claims to be "the oldest field selling magazine subscription agency in the world." Does not sell to libraries.

Phiebig, Albert, Inc. Box 352, White Plains, N.Y. 10602. (914) WH 8-0138. Albert Phiebig.
Special. Primarily o.p. book dealer but also handles some back sets. Serves all types of libraries with foreign books and periodicals. Foreign. "Any" title. Periodicals, annuals, irregular and less than annual serials, proceedings and transactions (domestic and international), monographic series, government documents, works in parts. Will make an effort to order hard to locate titles; searches for o.p. titles ("promises single issues only on firm order"). CATALOGS: "All foreign national bibliographies, publishers' catalogues and rate sheets."
CHARGES: Agent charges a flat service fee on top of publisher's list price.
CLAIMS: Send claims to agent. Agent acknowledges claims. COMMENTS: Agent supplies some forms. Agent specializes in irregular and less than annual serials and proceedings and transactions, and "building special collections." Agent has particular interest in rare books.

*Popular Subscription Service. P.O. Box 1566, Terre Haute, Ind. 47808. (812) 466-1258. Accepts customer calls.
General. Serves all types of libraries. U.S., foreign. "We process subscriptions to any and all titles published throughout the world." 50,000 titles. Periodicals,

newspapers, annuals, irregular and less than annual serials, proceedings and transactions (domestic and international), monographic series, government documents, works in parts. Will make an effort to order hard to locate titles. CATALOGS: *Directory of Periodicals Listings,* Annual; list the approximately 4,000 titles most frequently ordered by schools and libraries; gives current price and frequency of publication.

Prebound Periodicals. *See* American Magazine Services.

Prince, E. A., & Son. 1312 E. River St., Anderson, S. C. 29621.
RATINGS (One library, South):
  Good: 1 small public

Publishers Clearing House. 382 Channel Dr., Port Washington, N.Y. 11050. Robert H. Treller, Mgr.

Claims to be the largest field agent for publishers, but does not service library accounts. However, has vast network of salespersons who sometimes call on libraries. Not recommended.

Publishers Continental Sales Corp. 2601 E. Michigan Blvd., Michigan City, Ind. 46360. Watts-1-348-8552. Ms. Ruth Holmes, Office Mgr.

General. Source of titles for field agents (see Comments). U.S. Approximately 50 popular titles. Periodicals, books. Agent will not make an effort to order hard to locate titles. CATALOGS: Issue price cards. CLAIMS: Send claims to agent. Agent acknowledges claims. COMMENTS: "This company is a clearing house for magazines and books. Hundreds of independent contractors clear their orders thru this office. These contractors work on a door-to-door basis, and plan their own itinerary. The prices on our price cards are subject to change from month to month, depending on the publisher of magazine or books. If we are contacted directly in this office, the cost to libraries is the amount noted in mail-in-balance column on price cards." Most titles at 50% discount on retail price.

Publix Circulation Service, Inc. 9219 New Benton Hwy., Little Rock, Ark. 72209.

Railsback, Leigh M. 1276 N. Lake Ave., Pasadena, Calif. 91104. (213) 798-7851. Accepts customer calls "within reason." L. M. Railsback.

General. Serves all types of libraries, primarily in Southern California. 70,000 titles. Periodicals, newspapers, annuals, irregular and less than annual serials, government publications. Will make an effort to order hard to locate materials "within our capabilities." CATALOGS: *Magazine Subscription Trade Price List,* annual. CHARGES: Service charges varies according to profit on the list. Sometimes a discount is possible. Agent will bid, but "again within our capabilities. We will not extend to sacrifice services." CLAIMS: Send claims to agent. Agent will only acknowledge claim when a reply is received from the publisher. COMMENTS: Agent supplies order and claim forms. "We have enjoyed a very fine reputation for our services since 1930. We also service nearly 14,000 retail customers in their periodical needs. Our main goal is to give the finest service possible. We will not try to take on more than we can handle properly and efficiently and promptly."

RATINGS (Two libraries, Pacific Coast):
Excellent: 1 small public
Fair: 1 medium-sized junior college

Rayner Agency. 338 Elm St., Elgin, Ill. 60120. (312) 695-2264. Accepts customer calls. Richard W. Rayner, Jr.

General. Serves all types of libraries. U.S., foreign. 50,000 titles. Periodicals, newspapers, annuals, irregular and less than annual serials, government documents. "We will attempt to provide all printed materials and will make an effort to find any publisher." Will make an effort to order hard to locate titles. CATALOGS: *Trade Price List,* annual subject catalog; *School Librarians Price Book,* annual; *School Title Rate Sheets,* semiannual. COMMENTS: "We offer automatic renewal service, one source for ordering back issues of periodicals lost or damaged, and a single invoice [listing all periodicals]."
RATINGS (Four libraries, Midwest):
Good: (2) 1 medium-sized college, 1 small public
Fair: 1 medium-sized college
Poor: 1 small- to medium-sized school system

*Read-More Publications, Inc. 140 Cedar St., New York, N.Y. 10006. (212) 349-5540. Mel Mason, V.P.

Special. Serves university and college and special libraries. U.S. scientific and most foreign serials. 20,000 plus titles in medicine, pharmacy, chemistry, physics and biomedica. "But can order other subject material." Periodicals, newspapers, annuals, irregular and less than annual serials, proceedings and transactions (domestic and international), monographic series, government documents. Will make an effort to order hard to locate titles. CATALOGS: "We issue printouts of all titles presently handled by our computer . . . . We can obtain orders to journals upon request, even if not on our printout. The printouts are issued free upon request."
RATINGS (Eight libraries, Mid-Atlantic, Midwest):
Good: (6) 3 small- to medium-sized special, 1 small public, 1 medium-sized university, 1 large university
Fair: 1 large special

Research Services Corp. 5280 Trail Lake Dr., P.O. Drawer 16549, Fort Worth, Tex. 76133. (817) 292-4270. Accepts customer calls. O. A. Battista.

Special. Serves special libraries with medical and scientific books and periodicals. U.S., foreign. "Unlimited." Periodicals, newspapers, annuals, irregular and less than annual serials, proceedings and transactions (domestic and international), monographic series, government documents, works in parts. Will make an effort to order hard to locate titles; searches for o.p. titles. CATALOGS: None, but "on request we get catalogs." CHARGES: Service charge is usually 5 to 10 percent above cost of titles. Agent adds service charge for titles where he receives no discount and passes on discount to library for titles where discount received. Note: "No service fee for clients who order all their books and periodicals from us." Agent will bid. CLAIMS: Send claims to agent. Agent acknowledges claims. "Every claim is made and a copy sent to client."

220 Guide to Magazine and Serial Agents

COMMENTS: Agent supplies some forms.
RATINGS (Three libraries, Midwest):
  Good: 2 medium-sized special
  Poor: 1 medium-sized special

Seaboard Subscription Agency, Inc. P.O. Box 1482, Allentown, Pa. 18105. (215) 435-8174. Accepts customer calls. Leonard J. Heckenberger, Pres.

General and special (scientific, technical, medical). Serves all types of libraries (500 school, 75 public, 30 university and college). Also serves 200 medical and research and development libraries. U.S., foreign. 40,000 titles. Periodicals, newspapers, annuals, irregular and less than annual serials, proceedings and transactions, monographic series, government documents. Will make an effort to order hard to locate titles. CATALOGS: *General Trade Price List,* annual; *Secondary School and Public Library List,* annual; *Medical List,* annual. The latter two list titles alphabetically and by subject.
RATINGS (Three libraries, New England and South):
  Poor: 1 medium-sized junior college, 1 small special, 1 small public

Slack, Charles. 6900 Grove Rd., Thorofare, N.J. 08086.
RATINGS (One library, Mid-Atlantic):
  Fair: 1 medium-sized junior college

Smith's, Don, National Geographic Magazines. 3930 Ranking St., Louisville, Ky. 40214. Don Smith.

Special. Serves all types of libraries with out-of-print *National Geographic* magazines. Only handles the one magazine and will search for o.p. issues. Sends free price list and offers schools and libraries a 10 to 20 percent discount. Issue two titles in this area: *Collect National Geographic Magazines for Fun and Profit* ($5) and *Circular,* evaluating collections ($2). Also purchases early back issues.

Smith's Subscription Service. Rt. 4, Box 70, Bemidji, Minn. 56601. (218) 751-4327. Accepts customer calls. Don Smith.

General. Serves all types of libraries, primarily within Minnesota. U.S., foreign. 6,000 titles. Periodicals, newspapers, annuals, irregular and less than annual serials, proceedings and transactions (domestic and international), government documents. Will make an effort to order hard to locate titles.
RATINGS (One library, Midwest):
  Fair: 1 small public

Solle's Inc. 304 WCCO Radio Bldg., Minneapolis, Minn. 55402. (612) 338-7519. Does not accept calls.

General. Primarily serves school and public libraries. U.S., some foreign. Periodicals, some newspapers. Will make an effort to order hard to locate titles.
CATALOGS: Moore-Cottrell's "with our name printed on outside."
RATINGS (Two libraries, Midwest):
  Good: 1 small school system
  Poor: 1 small public

Southwest Business Publications Co. 12633 Memorial Dr., Suite 33, Houston, Tex. 77024. (713) 467-3373. Accepts customer calls. H. A. Kissman.

General. Serves 3,000 school libraries, 300 military libraries, 10 public libraries, and 15 special libraries. U.S. 40,000 titles. Periodicals, newspapers, annuals, irregular and less than annual serials, proceedings and transactions. Will make an effort to order hard to locate titles. CATALOGS: *Trade Price List*, annual listing of the "more popular titles."
RATINGS (Two libraries, Midwest):
  Good: 1 small- to medium-sized special
  Poor: 1 small- to medium-sized school system

Squire Magazine Agency. 6009 Pinewood Rd., Oakland, Calif. 94611. (415) 547-2479. Accepts customer calls. Ben B. Squire.

General. Serves all types of libraries, primarily in the far western states, but "we do not refuse orders from other parts of the United States." U.S., foreign. 35,000 titles. Periodicals, newspapers, annuals (where subscription possible), irregular and less than annual serials, proceedings and transactions, monographic series, government serials. Will make an effort to order hard to locate titles. CATALOGS: Typewritten catalogs, semiannual, which list periodicals commonly subscribed to by schools. Retail catalogs, annual general listing. "We follow closely the format used by most catalog agencies for their confidential trade price lists." COMMENTS: "We don't advertise any more, except in a very minor way.... We don't like to enter competitive bids any more, even though our prices are competitive, because we don't pretend to meet the prices of agencies so hungry for business that they'll bid at close to their costs. Our business, for the most part, consists of library and school accounts which we've had for years and years—to the point where we are given orders without having to quote on them, since our accounts *know* we will do our best for them pricewise and servicewise. We've never lost one because of bad service."
RATINGS (Eight libraries, Pacific Coast):
  Excellent: (5) 4 small public, 1 small school system
  Good to Excellent: 1 small public
  Good: 1 small public
  Fair: 1 large public

Stacey. *See* Bro-Dart, Inc.

*Stechert-Macmillan, Inc. 866 Third Ave., New York, N.Y. 10022. (212) 935-4262. Accepts customer calls. Eleanor P. Vreeland, V.P.

General. Serves all types of libraries. U.S., foreign. 40,000 plus titles. Periodicals, newspapers, annuals, irregular and less than annual serials, proceedings and transactions (domestic and international), monographic series, government documents, works in parts. Will make an effort to order hard to locate titles. CATALOGS: *Stechert-Macmillan News*, quarterly report on periodical title changes, mergers, splits, and cessations. *Stechert-Macmillan Serial News*, monthly reports on 3 x 5 index cards, giving advance announcements of new serial titles throughout the world and expected publication dates of forthcoming editions of annuals and new volumes of existing series.

Student Subscription Service. 301 E. Ohio St., Chicago, Ill. 60611.

A field agency for Time Inc., selling *Money, Fortune, Sports Illustrated*, and *Time* at reduced rates to students and teachers.

222 Guide to Magazine and Serial Agents

Synergetic Marketing Corp. 10629 Bay Pines Blvd., St. Petersburg, Fla. 33708.
RATINGS (One library, South):
  Good: 1 junior college

Tricon Imports. P.O. Box 524, Murray Hill Station, New York, N.Y. 10016. (212) 243-2453.
  Special. Handles limited list of Cuban periodicals and newspapers. Cuba. 6 to 10 titles. Periodicals, newspapers, books. CATALOGS: Brochures. CHARGES: Publisher's net price, with different prices for private institutions, tax-supported institutions, and individuals.

*****Turner Subscription Agency, Inc.** 235 Park Ave. S. New York, N.Y. 10003. (212) 254-4454. Accepts customer calls. Malcolm D. Severance, Pres.
  General. Serves all types of libraries. U.S., foreign. 50,000 plus titles. Periodicals, newspapers, annuals, irregular and less than annual serials, proceedings and transactions (domestic and international), monographic series, government documents, works in parts. Will make an effort to order hard to locate titles. CATALOGS: *Magazine Catalog for Librarians,* annual list of titles most frequently ordered; *Periodical Exposition Display Catalog,* irregular list of some 1,500 titles displayed by agent at national and state library conferences.

*****Universal Periodical Services.** 2500 Rackard Rd., Ann Arbor, Mich. 48104. (313) 971-3702. An affiliate of Ebsco as of July 1975.
  General. Serves all types of libraries. U.S., foreign. 50,000 plus titles. Periodicals and various other serials. Will make an effort to order hard to locate titles. CATALOGS: *Reference Source for Frequently Ordered Periodicals,* annual listing of some 10,000 titles.

Universal Subscriptions. 1541 Kings Highway, Shreveport, La. 71103.

Vulcan Service. 1 Ave. N. at 13 St., Birmingham, Ala. 35203. (205) 879-0641. *See* Ebsco Subscription Services. A division of Ebsco, this is a field service unit that "promotes and sells magazine subscriptions through resident agents, both part time and full time." Does not sell to libraries.

Wallace, Dan, Publisher's Representative. 5234 E. Polk St., Phoenix, Ariz. 85008. Dan Wallace.
  General. Serves school and academic libraries. 3,000 to 4,000 titles. U.S., foreign. Periodicals, newspapers. Will make an effort to order hard to locate titles. CATALOGS: None; "send out brochures, etc." CHARGES: Agent gives a discount on pro rata basis on those publications where he receives a discount from the publisher. No service fee. CLAIMS: Send claims to agent. Agent acknowledges claims. COMMENTS: Agent supplies some forms.

Watson, W. R. 1181 Euclid Ave., Berkeley, Calif. 94708. (415) 524-6156. Accepts customer calls. Ms. W. R. Watson.
  General. Serves all types of libraries. U.S. 50,000 titles. Periodicals. Will make an effort to order hard to locate titles. CATALOGS: *Magazine Trade Price List,* annual (for agents). *Price Lists,* going with current changes "as often as needed" (for agents).

West Coast Organization Plan. P.O. Box 5366, San Bernardino, Calif. 92408.
RATINGS (Eight libraries, Pacific Coast):
Excellent: (3) 1 medium-sized college, 2 small public
Good: (5) 2 small public, 1 small- to medium-sized school system, 2 anonymous (1-199 titles each)

West Magazine Service. Box 3262 Ridgeway Sta., Stamford, Conn. 06905.

World Readers Service, Inc. 248 Sisson Ave., Hartford, Conn. 06105. (203) 233-8205.

Yerger, Don, Subscriptions and Book Service. 2200 N. Scottsdale Rd., Scottsdale Plaza, Scottsdale, Ariz. 85257.
RATINGS (Four libraries, Southwest and Rocky Mountain):
Excellent: 1 small public
Good: (2) 1 medium-sized junior college, 1 small public
Fair: 1 small public

Zeitlin Periodicals Co., Inc. 817 South La Brea, Los Angeles, Calif. 90036. (213) 933-7175. Accepts customer calls. Stanley L. Zeitlin.
  Back-issues and reprint dealer. Serves all types of libraries. U.S., foreign. 5,000 titles. Periodicals, irregular and less than annual serials, proceedings and transactions (domestic and international), monographic series, government documents. Will make an effort to order hard to locate titles. CATALOGS: *General Catalog,* annual list of available sets and titles. CHARGES: Charges standard prices for back-issues periodicals and government publications. Usually allows discount on reprints from any supplier, domestic or foreign. Agent will bid. COMMENTS: Specialists in back-issues and reprint periodicals, many of which are o.p. and hard to find. Carry in stock millions of issues and thousands of sets.

CANADIAN AGENTS

Central Readers Service. 67 Yonge St., Suite 628, Toronto, Ont. M5E 1J8. (416) 366-1082. Accepts customer calls. J. Sherwood.
  General. Primarily serves Canadian school and public libraries. Canada, U.S., foreign. 2,000 titles. Periodicals, newspapers, annuals, irregular and less than annual serials, proceedings and transactions (domestic and international), monographic series, government documents, works in parts. Will make an effort to order hard to locate titles. CATALOGS: None; "rates supplied on request."

Ebsco Subscription Services, Ltd. 6 Thorncliffe Park Dr., Toronto, Ont. M4H 1H3. (416) 421-9000. Canadian branch of Ebsco.

Educational Magazine Service. R.R. 2, Haliburton, Ont. (705) 457-1463. Accepts customer calls. Roy Neville.
  General. Primarily serves schools, university and college libraries, including "teachers and students." Canada, U.S., foreign. 3,000 titles. Periodicals, newspapers, annuals, irregular and less than annual serials, proceedings and transactions, government documents. Will make an effort to order hard to locate titles. CATALOGS: *Price List,* annual "summary of contents of chief periodicals."

Hood's, Dora, Book Room, Ltd. 34 Ross St., Toronto 20b, Ont. (416) 925-3219. G. Hannon, Subscription Clerk.

General. Serves all types of libraries in U.S. and Canada. Canada only. Periodicals, newspapers, annuals, irregular and less than annual serials, proceedings and transactions (domestic and international), monographic series, government documents, works in parts. Will make an effort to order hard to locate titles; searches o.p. titles. CATALOGS: *Catalogue of Canadiana,* issued three times a year. CHARGES: There is a $3 placement charge on new continuation orders. On annual renewal of serials, there is a 30 percent agency charge. Intermittent publications in series are supplied at retail except when discount is insufficient to allow agent a 30 percent gross profit. Agent will not bid. CLAIMS: Send claims to agent. Agent acknowledges claims. "We keep complete records on all subscriptions for our customers and follow up all claims promptly."
COMMENTS: Agent does not supply forms. "Payment is made well in advance on subscriptions to ensure that there is uninterrupted service for our customers. We then bill annually at the beginning of the year for all renewals, listing order number, title in alphabetical order, and price. Because of our specialized knowledge of library requirements, we try to be meticulous in informing libraries of changes in name of periodicals, publishing frequency and rates. Annually, at renewal time, we check both the serials and intermittent publications to ascertain what has been published in previous years and what the latest issue has been and inform the library if any difficulties have arisen or seem likely to arise."
RATINGS (One library):
Good: 1 large university

Periodica International Subscription Agency. 7045 av. du Parc, Montreal, 303, Que. (514) 274-5468. Accepts customer calls, "but not for order or claim requests." B. Baril.

General. Serves all types of libraries, but primarily school, public, college in Canada and the U.S. Canada, U.S., and foreign, but primarily French language publications from Canada, France, and other French-speaking nations. 2,000 titles. Periodicals, newspapers, and some other serials. Does not usually make an effort to locate hard to locate titles. CATALOGS: *Selective Catalog of French Publications,* annual subject listing of some 1,000 most sought-after titles.

Troyka Ltd. 799 College St., Toronto, Ont. M6G 1C7. (416) 535-6693. Mr. Nazerec.

Special. Serves all types of libraries in U.S. and Canada with Russian language periodicals and books. Soviet Republics. Periodicals, newspapers, annuals, irregular and less than annual serials, proceedings and transactions (domestic and international), monographic series, government documents, works in parts, international congresses. Will make an effort to order hard to locate titles; searches for o.p. titles. CATALOGS: *Periodicals of the USSR,* annual. CHARGES: Charges for retail prices. Agent will not bid. CLAIMS: Send claims to agent. Agent acknowledges claims. COMMENTS: Agent supplies all forms. Agent will supply microfilm and photocopies of o.p. periodicals.

RATINGS (One library):
Good: 1 large university

Western Canada Subscription Agencies, Ltd. 101 Confederation Bldg., 10355 Jasper Ave., Edmonton, Ala. T57 1Y6. (403) 422-8535. Accepts customer calls. E. Carlson.

General. Serves all types of libraries in western Canada. Canada, U.S., foreign. 3,000 titles. Periodicals, proceedings and transactions. Will make an effort to order hard to locate titles. CATALOGS: *Price Lists,* every three months.

INTERNATIONAL AGENTS

Allen, Edward G., & Son, Ltd. 10–14 Grape St., Shaftesbury Ave., London WC2H 8DZ, Eng. 01-836-3287. R. B. Skidmore, Asst. Secy.

General. Serves all types of libraries worldwide. All British, "and some from European countries if requested." Periodicals, newspapers, annuals, irregular and less than annual serials, proceedings and transactions (domestic and international), monographic series, government documents, works in parts. Will make an effort to order hard to locate titles. COMMENTS: "Our subscription department is able to handle continuing subscriptions for almost any journal or society. These are automatically renewed yearly and billed to the client once a year for their convenience. A 15 percent service charge is made, and for this we handle from this office all claims and queries."
RATINGS (One library):
Excellent: 1 small public

Almqvist & Wiksell Periodical Co. 26 Gamla Brogatan, P.O. Box 63, S. 101 20 Stockholm 1, Sweden. F. Davids Thomsen, Managing Dir.

General. Serves all types of libraries; strong emphasis on Swedish scientific materials. Scandinavia, other European countries. 30,000 titles. Periodicals, newspapers, annuals, irregular and less than annual serials, proceedings and transactions (domestic and international), monographic series, government documents, works in parts. Will make an effort to order hard to locate titles. CATALOGS: Subject catalog in all academic fields. Catalogs list journals from the whole world. NOTE: Mr. Thomsen claims the agency "is by far the biggest within its field. It is fully computerized and to my knowledge it works to the complete satisfaction of our customers." The agency is publisher for a number of Swedish universities, the Royal Swedish Academy of Science, and other learned societies.

Angus & Robertson Subscription Div. GPO Box 3904, Sydney, N.S.W. 2001, Australia. M. H. Haslam.

General. Serves all types of libraries. Australia, United Kingdom, Southeast Asia. 10,000 titles. Periodicals, newspapers, annuals, irregular and less than annual serials, proceedings and transactions. Will make an effort to order hard to locate titles. CATALOGS: "In the process of publishing [mid-1974] own catalog of publications available." CHARGES: All charges depend on the cost of subscription and discount by publishers. Agent will bid. CLAIMS: Send claims to agent. Agent acknowledges claims. Duplicate copy of publisher's acknowl-

edgment sent to client for use when delivery still not made. COMMENTS: Agent supplies all forms. Computerized periodical accession cards (7½ x 5½) provided free to all libraries upon request. Card is automatically replaced whenever a change occurs in title, address, etc. Preaddressed envelopes provided for return of all renewal authorizations and claims.
RATINGS (Two libraries):
Fair to Good: 2 large university

Aux Amateurs De Livres. *See* Blancheteau, Marcel.

Barbazan, Julian. Calle de los Libreros 4, Madrid, Spain.
General. Serves all types of libraries worldwide. Spain. Periodicals, some serials.
RATINGS (One library):
Excellent: 1 large public

*****Blackwell's Periodicals.** Box 40, Hythe Bridge St., Oxford, OXI 2EU, England. Oxford 44944. Telex: 83118. J. B. Merriman, Dir., Periodicals Div.
General. Serves some 12,000 libraries of all types worldwide. Great Britain and most foreign serials available through trade channels. 25,000 plus titles. Periodicals, newspapers, annual, irregular and less than annual serials, proceedings and transactions (domestic and international), monographic series, government documents, works in parts. Will make an effort to order titles hard to locate. CATALOGS: *Blackwell's Back Issues Catalogue Annual*, includes new and secondhand items, reprints; *Blackwell's Periodicals Subscription Catalogue*, annual.

*****Blancheteau, Marcel (Aux Amateurs de Livres).** 62, av. de Suffren, Paris XV, France. 783-18-38/ 566-60-91. M. N. Blancheteau.
General. Primarily serves university and college and some school and public libraries. All French-speaking countries. Periodicals, newspapers, annuals, irregular and less than annual serials, proceedings and transactions (domestic and international), monographic series, government documents. Will make an effort to locate hard to locate titles. CATALOGS: *French Book Selection,* a monthly select list at the university level.
RATINGS (Two libraries):
Excellent: 1 large college
Good: 1 large college

British Book Center. *See* Domestic Agents.

Broadbent, Marv. *See* Domestic Agents.

*****Brockhaus, F. A.** Rapplenstrasse 20, Stuttgart, Federal Republic of Germany. 29-5551.
General. Primarily serves university and college and special libraries worldwide. All German, Austrian, and Swiss serials available through trade channels. Periodicals, newspapers, annuals, irregular and less than annual serials, proceedings and transactions (domestic and international), monographic series, government documents, works in parts. Also books. Will make an effort to order titles hard to locate. CATALOGS: Publisher's catalogs on request.

Subscription Agents Directory   227

Cambiero, Fernando Garcia. Ave. del Mayo 560, Buenos Aires, Argentina.
Serves Central and Latin America.
RATINGS (One library):
 Fair: 1 university

Cambray, R., and Co. Private Ltd. Kent House P33, Mission Row Extension, Calcutta, 13, India. 23-6149.
 Special. Serves all types of libraries world-wide. Indian literary, legal, and scientific periodicals, "both rare and current." India, Singapore, Malaya, Hong Kong, Ceylon, Bangladesh. Periodicals, newspapers, annuals, proceedings and transactions, monographic series, government documents. Will make an effort to order hard to locate titles; will search for o.p. titles. CATALOGS: *Texts and Serials,* biennial. CHARGES: Agent charges a flat service charge on cost price of titles. CLAIMS: Send claims to agent.
RATINGS (One library):
 Fair: 1 large university

Casalini Libri. Via Leopardi 4, 50121, Florence, Italy.
RATINGS (One library):
 Good: 1 large college

Chiao Liu Publication Service. 38 Moody Rd., 8th Floor, Kowloon, Hong Kong. 3-662009. K. S. Loh, Mgr.
 General. Serves all types of libraries worldwide, particularly university and government libraries with Chinese and Asian materials. Both Chinas, Japan, North and South Korea, North Vietnam, Southeast Asia, etc. 2,900 titles. Periodicals, newspapers, annuals, irregular and less than annual serials, proceedings and transactions (domestic and international), monographic series, government documents, works in parts. Will make an effort to order hard to locate titles; searches for o.p. titles. CATALOGS: *Special List,* intermittently, of new titles. *Book News,* bimonthly. CHARGES: A service charge of HK $12 (U.S. $2.40) will be added to any single order of less than HK $50 (U.S. $10) from individuals. Libraries are exempt from such charges. Agent will not bid. CLAIMS: Send claims to agent. Agent will acknowledge claims. COMMENTS: Agent supplies some forms and offers blanket order plan. "Special enquiries on book purchases, subscription to periodicals and newspapers are welcome. We are not book sellers, like many other agencies. We run a specialized service catering to the needs of libraries. Our firm has been established for 20 years and among our customers: Library of Congress, Harvard, Yale, Michigan, University of Washington, various California campuses...."
RATINGS (One library):
 Good: 1 large university

China Books and Periodicals. *See* Domestic Agents.

***Chinese Materials and Research Aids Service Center, Inc.** P.O. Box 22048, Taipei, 100, Taiwan.
 General. Serves libraries of all types. Taiwan and Hong Kong. 1,070 periodicals and newspapers. Periodicals, newspapers, annuals, irregular and less than

annual serials, proceedings and transactions (domestic and international), monographic series, government documents. Will make an effort to order hard to locate titles. CATALOGS: *An Annotated Guide to Taiwan Periodical Literature*, issued about every three to four years. Catalog gives Chinese, romanized, and translated titles; date of first issue, frequency, availability of back issues, yearly subscription rate, short description of content.

*Collet's Holdings, Ltd. Dennington Estate, Wellingborough, Northants, England.

General. Primarily serves university and college and special libraries worldwide. Great Britain, United Kingdom, Western Europe, Socialist countries (U.S.S.R., China, North Vietnam). 10,000 plus titles. Periodicals, newspapers, annuals, irregular and less than annual serials, proceedings and transactions (domestic and international), monographic series, government documents, works in parts. Will make an effort to locate hard to locate titles. CATALOGS: *Periodicals— Scientific, Technical & Others*, annual, broken down into 85 subject categories. RATINGS (One library):

Excellent: 1 medium-sized university

*Collins Book Depot Pty Ltd. 86 Borke St., Melbourne, 3000, Australia. 662-2711. Cables: Colbook. M. G. Zifcak, Managing Dir.

General. Serves all types of libraries worldwide. Australia. All Australian titles. Periodicals, newspapers, annuals, irregular and less than annual serials, proceedings and transactions, monographic series, government serials. Will make an effort to order hard to locate titles. CATALOGS: *Current Australian Serials*, irregular, published by the National Library of Australia, but available through agent.

Danesh, Ltd. 357 Saadi Ave., Tehran, Iran. 315427.

General. Serves all types of libraries worldwide. Iran. Periodicals, newspapers, annuals, irregular and less than annual serials, proceedings and transactions, monographic series, government documents, works in parts. Will make an effort to order hard to locate titles. CATALOGS: A quarterly list of titles. Includes title, place of publication, and price in local currency. CHARGES: 10 percent on publishers price, plus postage. OTHER SERVICES: Supplies back issues, o.p. items, microforms, reprints. Does binding and consolidates orders.

Dawson, William & Sons, Ltd. Cannon House, Folkestone, Kent, CT 19 5EE, England. Folkestone 57421. Telex: 96392. D. A. Drewer, Asst. Managing Dir.

General. Serves all types of libraries. All countries. 30,000 titles. Periodicals, newspapers, annual, irregular and less than annual serials, proceedings and transactions (domestic and international), monographic series, government documents, works in parts. Will make an effort to order hard to locate titles; searches for o.p. titles. CATALOGS: *Guide to the Press of the World*, annual selection of worldwide subscription rates. CHARGES: Agent adds 10 percent service charge for titles for which it receives no discount and gives discount to library when occasion warrants. CLAIMS: Send all claims to agent. Agent only acknowledges claims upon request. COMMENTS: Agent supplies all forms. "Continuity is

ensured because we inform you when subscriptions are due for renewal and, to make re-ordering easier, we will line-up your order so that there is one common expiration date, wherever possible, resulting in one invoice for your complete annual order."
RATINGS (Six libraries):
  Good: 5 university of various sizes
  Fair: 1 large university

*Dawson-France S. A, a subsidiary of William Dawson and Sons, Ltd., London. B.P. 40 Palaiseau 911121, France. 909-01-22. Telex: 60394. J. Vidal, Mgr.

General. Serves all types of libraries worldwide. France and most foreign serials. 100,000 plus titles. Periodicals, newspapers, annuals, irregular and less than annual serials, proceedings and transactions (domestic and international), monographic series, government documents, works in parts. Will make an effort to order hard to locate titles. CATALOGS: *Guide Pratique des Journaux et Periodiques Francais et Etrangers*, annual of some 6,000 titles.
RATINGS (Three libraries):
  Excellent: 1 large university
  Good: 1 large university
  Fair: 1 medium- to large-sized university

European Book Center. P.O. Box 4, 1700 Fribourg, 2 Bourg, Switzerland.
RATINGS (One library):
  Excellent: 1 university

Flammarion, Les Librairies. 4, r. Casimir-Delavigne, 75006 Paris, France.
RATINGS (One library):
  Fair: 1 college

Four Continent Book Corp. *See* Domestic Agents.

French & European Publications, Inc. *See* Domestic Agents.

Hachette, Département des Universités Étrangères. 58 r. Jean Bleuzen F. 92170 Vanves, France. 645 21-62. Ms. Edwards: periodicals, newspapers, annuals; Mr. Camblong: other serials.

General. Serves all types of libraries with all French titles. France and all French language titles. "All French titles." Periodicals, newspapers, annuals, irregular and less than annual serials, proceedings and transactions (domestic and international), monographic series, government documents, works in parts. Will make an effort to order hard to locate titles; searches for o.p. titles, "if we have in stock." CATALOGS: *Subscription Tariff*, annual. ("We are planning a tariff adapted more closely to the librarian's needs.") CHARGES: Service charge is usually 4 percent above cost of titles. Agent will bid. CLAIMS: Send claims to agent. Agent will acknowledge claims. COMMENTS: Agent supplies renewal and claim forms.
RATINGS (Three libraries):
  Good: 2 large university
  Fair: 1 large university

Harding's (George) Bookshop Subscription Dept. 106 Great Russell St., London WC1, England. London 636-2293.

General. Serves all types of libraries, but primarily university and college, with English serials. Great Britain. Periodicals, newspapers, annuals, irregular and less than annual serials, proceedings and transactions, monographic series, government documents. Will make an effort to order hard to locate titles; searches for o.p. titles. CHARGES: Service charge is usually 10 percent above cost of titles. CLAIMS: Send claims to the publisher. Agent acknowledges claims.
RATINGS (One library):
Excellent: 1 large college

*Harrassowitz, Otto. Taunusstrasse 5, 6200 Wiesbaden, Federal Republic of Germany. (0 61 21) 52 10 46. Knut Dorn, Mgr.

General. Primarily serves university and college and special libraries worldwide. Continental Europe. Specialty: German language areas. 35,000 plus titles. Periodicals, newspapers, annuals, irregular and less than annual serials, proceedings and transactions (domestic and international), monographic series, government documents, works in parts. Will make an effort to order hard to locate titles. CATALOGS: *German Book Digest;* bimonthly, information on new publications from the German language area. Special compilations of reprints, periodicals, and yearbooks.

Heffer, W. & Sons, Ltd. 20 Trinity St., Cambridge CB2 3NG, England.
RATINGS (One library):
Good: 1 large college

*Hill, R. & Son, Ltd. P.O. Box 147, 20 Burlington St., Crows Nest, N.S.W. Australia. 43-6658/ 43-91541. W. K. Stone, Managing Dir.

General. Serves all types of libraries worldwide. Australia, New Zealand and elsewhere on demand. 20,000 titles. Periodicals, newspapers, annuals, irregular and less than annual serials, proceedings and transactions (domestic and international), monographic series, government documents, works in parts. Will make an effort to order hard to locate titles.
RATINGS (One library):
Excellent: 1 large university

Indian Publications Trading Co. A/7, Nizamuddin East, New Delhi, 13, India.
RATINGS (One library):
Fair: 1 university

Insula Libreria de Ciencias y Letras. Benito Butierrez, 28, Madrid, Spain. Merche del Amo.

General. Serves all types of libraries with Spanish serials. Spain, Europe, and worldwide. Periodicals, newspapers, annuals, irregular and less than annual serials, proceedings and transactions, monographic series, government documents, works in parts. Will make an effort to order hard to locate titles. CHARGES: Service charge of 10 percent on titles for which the agent receives no discount.

CLAIMS: Send claims to agent. Agent acknowledges claims when reply is received from publisher.
RATINGS (One library):
  Good: 1 large university

International Bookhouse Private, Ltd. 9 Ash Lane, Mahatma Gandhi Rd., Bombay, 1, India.
RATINGS (One library):
  Poor: 1 large college

Inter-Prensa S.R.L. Florida 229, Buenos Aires, Argentina.
  General. Serves all types of libraries worldwide. Latin America. "No limit." Periodicals, newspapers, annuals, irregular and less than annual serials. Will make an effort to order hard to locate titles.

Japan Publications Trading Co. *See* Domestic Agents.

Kamkin, Victor. *See* Domestic Agents.

Kubon und Sagner. P.O. Box 68, 8 Munich 34, Federal Republic of Germany.
  General. Primarily serves academic libraries worldwide. Albania, Bulgaria, Czechoslovakia, Hungary, Poland, Rumania, U.S.S.R., Yugoslavia. Periodicals, newspapers, annuals, proceedings and transactions, government documents. Will make an effort to order hard to locate titles.
RATINGS (Two libraries):
  Fair: 2 large university

Lang, Herbert & Co., Ltd. Munzgraben 2, Bern, Switzerland. Telex: 33' 173 1booc ch. Charles Lang.
  General. Serves all types of libraries worldwide with European titles. Particular emphasis on scientific and technical materials. Switzerland and other European countries. Periodicals, newspapers, annuals, irregular and less than annual serials, proceedings and transactions (domestic and international), monographic series, government documents, works in parts. Will make an effort to order hard to locate titles; will search o.p. titles. CATALOGS: "Catalogues of our own publications, catalogues of other European publishers." CHARGES: Agent adds 30 percent service charge for titles where receives no discount and passes on discount to library for titles where receives such a discount. "Special arrangements are provided for regular customers." Agent will bid. CLAIMS: Send claims to agent. Agent acknowledges claims. COMMENTS: Agent supplies all forms. Has blanket order arrangement, and supplies microforms and Zerox for o.p. books. Claims to be "greatest scientific publisher in Switzerland with over 200 new books in the field per year." Handles 15,000 continuation orders. "We sell new books from all over Europe at the original publisher's price according to national bibliographies *postpaid.* Special charges only for air-cargo. For a fast service please order through Telex. We work closely together with Stiftung fur Hochschul und Forschungsdokumentation, Munzgraben 2, Berne, and can provide information about scientific books in preparation in Germany, Switzerland and Austria. Special computer-bulletin in preparation."

RATINGS (One library):
   Good: 1 large university

Librairie Saint Albert le Grande. r. du Temple, 1, 1700 Fribourg, Switzerland.
RATINGS (One library):
   Good: 1 university

Librart, S.R.L. Casilla Correo Central 5047, Buenos Aires, Argentina. Erica Wartensleben.
Special. Provides Argentine scientific periodicals to all types of libraries worldwide. Argentina. "All Argentine publishers." Periodicals, newspapers, annuals irregular and less than annual serials, proceedings and transactions, monographic series, government documents, works in parts. Will make an effort to order hard to locate titles. CATALOGS: *News and Notes About Argentina Scientific Publications,* weekly, in English. *Analytical Indexes (Cumulative) of Argentine Scientific Periodicals.* Catalogues of Argentine scientific periodicals. All free. Catalogs "contain general indexes, abstracts in English, title indexes, author indexes, title page information, translation of Spanish titles into English."

Library Service Association. 47, r. Barrault, 75013, Paris, France. M. T. Picard and J. M. Sene.
General. Serves university and college and special libraries. French language, worldwide. Periodicals, newspapers, annuals, irregular and less than annual serials, proceedings and transactions (domestic and international), monographic series, government documents, works in parts. Will make an effort to order hard to locate titles. CHARGES: The agent charges the library a 25 percent service charge on cost price of all titles. Agent will not bid. CLAIMS: Send claims to agent. Agent acknowledges claims. COMMENTS: All correspondence, billing, claims adjustments, reports in English and by airmail.
RATINGS (One library):
   Good: 1 university

Les Livres Étrangers, Inc. 10, r. Armand-Moisant, Paris, 15e, France. Telex. (1) 734-2727. Accepts customer calls. B. & G. Delorme.
Special. Serves all types of libraries with Soviet serials. U.S.S.R. and others where Slavic languages are used. 7,000 titles. Periodicals and newspapers, (U.S.S.R. titles only, and only those allowed for export), annuals, irregular and less than annual serials, proceedings and transactions (U.S.S.R. titles only, and only those allowed for export), monographic series, government documents (U.S.S.R. titles only, and only those allowed for export). Agent will check only own stock for hard to locate titles, and o.p. materials. CATALOGS: *Dealer's List of Acquisitions,* quarterly. *Periodicals from the U.S.S.R.,* annual. *Prepublication Catalogue of Academy of Sciences of USSR,* annual. *Prepublication. Catalogue: Novye Knigi SSSR,* weekly, $5.40 per year. CHARGES: Publisher's price. Postage charged for books only. Agent will not bid.
RATINGS (One library):
   Fair: 1 university

MACH (Material Academicos de Consulta Hispanoamericana). Apartado Postal 45-659, Mexico 1, D.F.
RATINGS (One library):
  Good: 1 university: "The firm is approximately five years old. We find they give good service on material published in Mexico."

Maruzan Co., Ltd. P.O. Box 605, Tokyo, Japan.
General. Serves all types of libraries worldwide. Japan, other Asian countries. All titles published in Japan that are available through normal trade channels. Periodicals, newspapers, irregular and less than annual serials, government documents. Will make an effort to order hard to locate titles.
RATINGS (One library):
  Good: 1 large university

Marzocco, Liberia, formerly Beltrami. Via Martelli 22/R, 50129 Florence, Italy.
RATINGS (One library):
  Fair: 1 university

Mass, Rubin, Publisher. P.O. Box 990, Jerusalem, Israel. 32565.
General. Serves all types of libraries worldwide, emphasizes on Hebraica and Judaica libraries. Periodicals and books published in Israel. Periodicals, newspapers, annuals, proceedings and transactions, government documents. Will make an effort to order hard to locate titles. CATALOGS: Catalogs of own publications; monthly list of recent publications from Israel.

Messaggerie Italiane. Settore Esportazione, Via Lomazzo 52, Milan, Italy.
General. Serves all types of libraries worldwide. Italy and other European countries. Periodicals, annuals, irregular and less than annual serials, selected government documents. Will make an effort to locate hard to locate titles.
RATINGS (One library):
  Fair: 1 large university

Munksgaards Boghandel. 6 Nooregade, DK 1165, Copenhagen K, Denmark. J. Vagn Jensen, Export Mgr.
General. Serves all types of libraries, primarily university and college, with Scandinavian journals and books. Scandinavia. Periodicals, newspapers, annuals, irregular and less than annual serials, proceedings and transactions (domestic and international), monographic series, government documents, works in parts. Will make an effort to order hard to locate titles; searches o.p. books. CATALOGS: *Munksgaard Messenger,* annotated list of books issued biennially in English. CHARGES: Agent charges retail price. No discount to libraries. Agent will bid. CLAIMS: Send claims to agent. Agent does not acknowledge first claim but does for second or third claim. COMMENTS: Agent publishes about 40 international journals. Has til-forbid system for periodicals. Sends annual invoice. Supplies continuations. Has blanket-order plan.
RATINGS (One library):
  Excellent: 1 large university

234 Guide to Magazine and Serial Agents

Nigerian Book Suppliers, Ltd. 54/56, Bankole St., P.O. Box 3879, Lagos, Nigeria.
RATINGS (One library):
   Excellent: 1 university

*Nijhoff, Martinius, B.V. Lange Voorhout 9-11, The Hague, Netherlands. 070-469-460.
   General. Serves public, university, and special libraries worldwide. The world except U.S. 50,000. Periodicals, newspapers, annual, irregular and less than annual serials, proceedings and transactions (domestic and international), monographic series, government documents, works in parts. Will make an effort to order hard to locate titles; searches for o.p. titles. CATALOGS: *Recent and Forthcoming Publications,* a subject list issued two to three times a month of monographs and serials. Subject lists and catalogues of retrospective and o.p. materials. About 10 catalogs and 15 lists a year. *Martinius Nijhoff Catalogue,* Nijhoff's own publications, irregular. CHARGES: Service charge is usually 0 to 20 percent on periodicals. For other serials it amounts to approximately 0 to 5 percent. The size of the service charge depends on the size of discount received from the publisher and costs of postage, tax, packing, and insurance. Agent will not bid. CLAIMS: Send claims to agent. Agent does not acknowledge claims unless a particular problem arises. COMMENTS: Agent supplies some forms. Has bibliographical information service. Supplies quotations on current serials and in-print backfiles. Correspondence in English, French, and German. Collects and ships periodicals that tend to give problems rather than having them send direct by publisher.

Perkins Oriental Books. P.O. Box 24, Nakagyo Post Office, Kyoto, Japan.
   General. Serves all types of libraries worldwide. Japan, Formosa, Korea, Phillipines, Hong Kong, Singapore. 2,000 titles. Periodicals, newspapers, annuals, irregular and less than annual serials, proceedings and transactions (domestic and international), monographic series, government documents. Will make an effort to order hard to locate titles.

Presses Universitaire de France. 12 r. Jean de Beauvais, 75 Paris V, France.
RATINGS (One library):
   Poor: 1 university

Ruch, Export and Import Enterprise. 23 Vronia St., Warsaw 1, Poland.
   General. Serves all types of libraries, particularly university and special. Poland. Periodicals, newspapers, annuals, irregular and less than annual serials, proceedings and transactions, monographic series, government documents. Will make an effort to order hard to locate titles.
RATINGS (One library):
   Fair: 1 large university

Saabrach, W. E. Follestrasse 2 (Saarbach-Haus), P.O. Box 1510, Cologne, Germany Democratic Republic.
RATINGS (One library):
   Fair: 1 university

Sansoni, Licosa: Liberia Commissionaria S.P.A. Via Lamarmora 45, Florence, Italy. 57-97-51-23. Mirko Zanello.

General. Serves all types of libraries worldwide with Italian publications. Italy. "Indefinite number." Periodicals, newspapers, annuals, irregular and less than annual serials, proceedings and transactions, monographic series, government documents (those from the Istituto Poligrafico dello Stato), works in parts. Will make an effort to order hard to locate titles; searches for o.p. titles. CATALOGS: *Periodical Esteri* and *Periodical Italiani,* both annual. CHARGES: Agent adds 10 percent service charge to titles when it receives no discount and passes on discount to library for titles when it receives a discount. CLAIMS: Send all claims to agent. Agent acknowledges claims.
RATINGS (One library):
 Poor: 1 large university

Seeber, Liberia Internationale. Via Tornabuoni 70 r 50123, Florence, Italy.

General. Serves all types of libraries worldwide. Italy. Periodicals, newspapers, annuals, irregular and less than annual serials, proceedings and transactions (domestic and international), monographic series, government documents, works in parts, international congresses. Will make an effort to order hard to locate titles. CHARGES: Charges at list price. Agent will not bid. CLAIMS: Send all claims to agent. Agent acknowledges claims. COMMENTS: Agent supplies all forms.
RATINGS (One library):
 Good: 1 large public

Sirovic Bookshop. P.O. Box 615, Cairo, Egypt, United Arab Republic. 42591.

A bookstore. "We are not a subscription agency, but an export-agent which supplies all kinds of books, also newspapers and magazines." United Arab Republic. Periodicals and newspapers. OTHER SERVICES: Back-issues and o.p. service. All types of books in Arabic, English, and French.

Stechert-Macmillan. *See* Domestic Agents.

*Stevens, B. F. & Brown, Ltd. Ardon House, Mill Lane, Godalming, Surrey, England. Godalming 4391/3. A. S. Smith.

General. Serves all types of libraries worldwide. Great Britain, Australia, New Zealand. Periodicals, newspapers, annuals, irregular and less than annual serials, proceedings and transactions (domestic and international), monographic series, government documents, works in parts. Will make an effort to order hard to locate titles. CATALOGS: *Stevens & Brown Subject Guide to Serials, S&B List of Periodicals, S&B Subject Guide to Books.*

*Swets & Zeitlinger B.V. Subscription Service. Heereweg 347b, Lisse, Netherlands. 02521-19113. North American office: L. Burkels, Box 517, Berwyn, Pa. 19312. (215) 644-4944. W. Luijendijk.

General. Serves some 5,000 libraries of all types worldwide. Most foreign serials available through trade channels. 50,000 plus titles. Periodicals, newspapers, annuals, irregular and less than annual serials, proceedings and transactions (domestic and international), monographic series, government documents, works in parts. Will make an effort to order hard to locate titles. CATALOGS: *S.S.S. Catalog*, biennial. *Swets Info*, bimonthly furnishing information on current periodicals and other serials.

Touzot, Jean. 11, r. de Varenne, Paris 7e, France.

General. Serves all types of libraries worldwide. French language, notably France, Switzerland, Belgium, and French-language countries in Africa. Periodicals, annuals, irregular and less than annual serials, "some" government documents. Will make an effort to order hard to locate titles.
RATINGS (One library):
  Good: 1 university

Wilson, Hubert, Ltd. 161 Borough High St., London SE1, England. W. K. Trueman, Managing Dir.

General. Serves all types of libraries worldwide. United Kingdom, Europe, and elsewhere. Periodicals, newspapers, annuals, irregular and less than annual serials, proceedings and transactions (domestic and international), monographic series, government documents, works in parts. Will make an effort to order hard to locate titles. CHARGES: We add a service charge where we receive no discount. Percentages by negotiation. Agent will not bid. CLAIMS: Send claims to agent. Agent acknowledges claims.
RATINGS (Three libraries):
  Excellent: (2) 1 large university, 1 small- to medium-sized college
  Good: 1 small- to medium-sized college

GEOGRAPHIC INDEX

This index has three parts: domestic agents, selected Canadian agents, and selected international agents. Arrangement in each section is by address of the home office, not necessarily by areas served.

Domestic Agents

Large agents with divisions and branches are indicated in parentheses. See agent's main entry for central address.

Alabama
Ebsco

Arizona
Dexter
Ludwig
Yerger
Wallace

Arkansas
Publix

California
Bro-Dart
China Books
(Ebsco)
Heron

Japan
(Maxwell)
Railsback
Squire
Watson
West Coast
Zeitlin

Colorado
American Collegiate
Book Home
(Ebsco)

Connecticut
Bliss
Iredeco

Subscription Agents Directory 237

West
World
District of Columbia
Associates, C. W.
Bernan
Burke
Dolphin
Florida
Faculty
Synergetic
(Universal)
Georgia
Austin
(Universal)
Illinois
(Ebsco)
McGregor
Peck
Rayner
Student
(Universal)
Indiana
Black
Book Stable
DeLong
Noble
Popular
Publishers Continental
Iowa
National
Norton
Kansas
American Magazine
Darr
Kentucky
Smith's
Louisiana
Universal Subscriptions
Maryland
Broadbent
Kamkin
Massachusetts
Dial-a-Magazine

(Ebsco)
Faxon
Goldberger
(Universal)
Michigan
Educational
Fennell
Grand Rapids
Universal
Minnesota
Aquinas
(Ebsco)
Smith's
Solle's
Mississippi
Mid-South
Missouri
Alban
Nebraska
Empire
New Jersey
Alesco
Baker & Taylor
DeBoer
(Ebsco)
Johnson
McGraw-Hill
Perfect
(Universal)
New York
Abrahams
Adco
Ancorp
Barbers
Boley
Bookmart
British Book
Campus
Crowley
Ebs
Engineers
Farnsworth
Four Continent
French & European

Haagens
Hearst
Instructor
International
Kraus
Magazine Subscription
Manzer
Maxwell
Moore-Cottrell
Phiebig
Publisher's Clearing
Read-More
Stechert-Macmillan
Tricon
Turner

North Carolina
Cox

Ohio
Bartley
Central News
Neighborhood

Oregon
Abel
Adler
Candelighters
Evergreen

Pennsylvania
Seaboard

Rhode Island
American Literary

South Carolina
Prince

Tennessee
Alspaugh

Texas
(Ebsco)
Majors
Research
Southwest
(Universal)

Utah
By's

Vermont
New England

Virginia
(Ebsco)
Hayward

Washington
Olympic

Wisconsin
Demco
Genevieve's
Margins

Canadian Agents

Alberta
Western

Ontario
Central
Educational
Hood's
Troyka

Quebec
Periodica

International Agents

Argentina
Cambiero
Inter-Prensa
Librart

Australia
Collins
Hill

China
Chiao
Chinese Materials

Denmark
Munksgaards

Egypt
Sirovic

England
Allen
Blackwell's
Collet's
Dawson
Hardings
Heffer
Stevens
Wilson

France
Blancheteau
Dawson-France
Flammarion
Hachette
Library Service
Les Livres
Presses
Touzot

Germany
Brockhaus
Harrassowitz
Kubon
Saabrach

India
Cambray
Indian
International

Iran
Danesh

Israel
Mass

Italy
Casalini
Marzocco
Messaggerie
Sansoni
Seeber

Japan
Maruzan
Perkins

Mexico
MACH

Netherlands
Martinius Nijhoff
Swets & Zeitlinger

Nigeria
Nigerian Book

Poland
Ruch

Sweden
Almqvist & Wiksell

Switzerland
European
Lang
Librairie